Developing Creativity in Higher Education

UNIVERSITY COLLEGE
WINCHESTER

Our ability to imagine and then invent new worlds for ourselves is one of our greatest assets and the origin of all human achievement, yet the importance of creativity in learning and achievement is largely unrecognised in a higher education world that places more value on critical and rational thinking. It is a vision of a higher education world in which students' creativity is valued alongside more traditional forms of academic achievement that provides the driving force for this book.

Developing Creativity in Higher Education has grown out of the Imaginative Curriculum network-based collaborative learning project. It is the first book to systematically address the issue of creativity in higher education. It features:

- an analysis of the problem of creativity in higher education and rich perspectives on the meanings of creativity in different teaching and subject contexts;
- illustrative examples of teaching and assessment strategies, augmented by web-based curriculum guides and aids to encourage teachers to examine their own understandings of creativity in order to help students to develop their own creativity;
- practical advice on how to foster creativity at an individual and an institutional level.

Developing Creativity in Higher Education will appeal to teachers, educational developers and institutional managers who want to enrich the higher education experiences of their students and enable them to develop more of their creative potential.

Norman Jackson is Director of the University of Surrey Centre for Excellence in Professional Training and Education (SCEPTrE) and Professor of Higher Education. **Martin Oliver** is a Senior Lecturer at the London Knowledge Lab, Institute of Education, London. **Malcolm Shaw** is Professor of Educational Development at Leeds Metropolitan University. **James Wisdom** is a higher education consultant, Co-Chair of the Staff and Educational Development Association and a visiting Professor at Middlesex University.

Developing Creativity in Higher Education

An imaginative curriculum

Edited by
Norman Jackson, Martin Oliver,
Malcolm Shaw and James Wisdom

Routledge
Taylor & Francis Group

LONDON AND NEW YORK

First published 2006
by Routledge
2 Park Square, Milton Park, Abingdon, Oxon OX14 4RN

Simultaneously published in the USA and Canada
by Routledge
270 Madison Ave, New York, NY 10016

Routledge is an imprint of the Taylor & Francis Group, an informa business

© 2006 Norman Jackson, Martin Oliver, Malcolm Shaw and James
Wisdom selection and editorial matter; individual chapters the contributors

Typeset in Times by Wearset Ltd, Boldon, Tyne and Wear
Printed and bound in Great Britain by Antony Rowe Ltd, Chippenham, Wiltshire

British Library Cataloguing in Publication Data
A catalogue record for this book is available from the British Library

Library of Congress Cataloging in Publication Data
Developing creativity in higher education : an imaginative curriculum /
[edited by] Norman Jackson ... [et al.].
    p. cm.
  Includes bibliographical references and index.
1. Creative thinking.   2. Education, Higher.   I. Jackson, Norman,
1950–

LB1062.D495 2006
378.1'99–dc22

                                                    2005030864

ISBN10: 0-415-36533-3 (hbk)
ISBN10: 0-415-36532-5 (pbk)

ISBN13: 978-0-415-36533-8 (hbk)
ISBN13: 978-0-415-36532-1 (pbk)

Contents

List of figures   vii
List of tables   viii
List of appendices   ix
List of contributors   x
Acknowledgements   xv
Abbreviations   xvii

Foreword: developing creativity   xviii
MIHALY CSIKSZENTMIHALYI

1 **Imagining a different world**   1
NORMAN JACKSON

2 **Public policy, innovation and the need for creativity** 10
RICHARD SMITH-BINGHAM

3 **Creativity in schools**   19
ANNA CRAFT

4 **Interfering with the interference: an emergent perspective
   on creativity in higher education**   29
PAUL TOSEY

5 **Students' experiences of creativity**   43
MARTIN OLIVER, BHARAT SHAH,
CHRIS McGOLDRICK AND MARGARET EDWARDS

6 **Creativity and curricula in higher education: academics'
   perspectives**   59
MARGARET EDWARDS, CHRIS McGOLDRICK AND
MARTIN OLIVER

 7 **Facilitating creativity in higher education: a brief account of National Teaching Fellows' views** 74
   MARILYN FRYER

 8 **Developing subject perspectives on creativity in higher education** 89
   NORMAN JACKSON AND MALCOLM SHAW

 9 **Views from the chalk face: lecturers' and students' perspectives on the development of creativity in art and design** 109
   RUTH DINEEN

10 **Developing students' creativity: searching for an appropriate pedagogy** 118
   NORMAN JACKSON AND CHRISTINE SINCLAIR

11 **Enhancing students' creativity through creative-thinking techniques** 142
   CAROLINE BAILLIE

12 **How should I assess creativity?** 156
   JOHN COWAN

13 **Evaluating creativity through consensual assessment** 173
   TOM BALCHIN

14 **Developing higher education teachers to teach creatively** 183
   JAMES WISDOM

15 **Making sense of creativity in higher education** 197
   NORMAN JACKSON

   References 216
   Index 231

Figures

4.1	'Agreement and certainty' matrix	34
8.1	Representations of creative processes in disciplinary problem working contexts	106
10.1	The complex interactions and interdependencies between teacher, learner and task	129
10.2	Model of a teaching and learning system designed to help students develop their creative potential	131
11.1	The medicine wheel	148
12.1	From alignment to integration	160
13.1	Spread of scores from individual scorers of one of the products	180
13.2	Spread of scores from consensual scorers of the product	180
15.1	Representation of a creativity system	202
15.2	Representation of a higher education teaching and learning system that has been established to promote students' creativity	204
15.3	Representation of creativity in the problem working process that relates to teaching	212
15.4	A constellation of interconnected practices, cultures and conditions that are more likely to promote creativity in the higher education environment	213

Tables

4.1	Command and control versus emergent organisations	41
7.1	Aspects of creativity with which the NTFs identify	78
7.2	Constraints on NTFs teaching	85
8.1	Frequency of references made in subject benchmark statements to the 18 possible indicators of creativity identified in the evaluation tool	92
10.1	The reasoning underlying our strategy for the development of students' creativity	120
10.2	Steps in creativity, knowledge, understanding and skill acquisition	122
10.3	Summary of expert–novice differences in any domain	123

Appendices

8.1   Example of the analytical tool used to evaluate subject benchmark statements for indications of support for creativity in students' learning   107

10.1   The reasoning underlying our strategy for the development of students' creativity in higher education   133

10.2   Ideas and resources to help teachers develop their own strategies to develop students' creativities   138

12.1   Conversations in an evolving debate   168

12.2   Sources of descriptions and evaluations of the practices that underlie the plan for assessing students' creativity   171

Contributors

Caroline Baillie is the Dupont Canada Chair of Engineering Education Research and Development at Queens University, Kingston, Ontario. Her role is to enhance the learning experience of engineering students across the faculty whilst maintaining her research and teaching interests in materials science and engineering. Her research is currently focused on how engineering can be transformed to be socially just in its endeavours and practices, and to develop educational strategies to facilitate the learning of future engineers to this end. She has explored the use of different creative-thinking approaches, ranging from systematic (such as TRIZ) to very esoteric (such as abstract representation using finger painting) with a wide variety of groups, including designers, engineers, head teachers, researchers, scientists, unemployed women and actors.

Tom Balchin is a Research Fellow at the Brunel Able Children's Education Centre (BACE) at Brunel University. He conducts research in the field of design and technology education, specifically to find ways to reward creativity. He has recently produced creativity-assessment tools suitable for teachers and students to analyse creative effort and produce appropriate feedback. A former school teacher, he completed his doctorate at Goldsmiths College in 2005, gaining sponsorship by being chosen for the posts of research officer for a LEGO/NESTA collaboration to investigate creativity in Systems and Control, and the national DfEE/QCA Innovating Assessment Project team. His main research interests are aspects of creativity theory, gifted children selection procedures and technology curriculum provision in secondary schools.

John Cowan retired from full-time employment in 1997, at which time Sir John Daniel as the Open University's VC, told the degree ceremony that John was 'someone with a passion, which some might describe as an obsession, with student learning'. Not a bad tribute for someone whose academic career has been, and still is, characterised by a constant search for innovative ways of enhancing the learning experiences of his own students. In the context of this volume, his contribution comes from being one of the original signatories to the Education for Capability Manifesto, who has worked for 40 years, gaining a number of awards in the process, to develop problem-solving and creativity in learner-directed situations; and who was one of the early exponents of self-assessed undergraduate learning in Engineering Design.

Anna Craft is Senior Lecturer in Education at The Open University and Visiting Scholar at Harvard University. She co-ordinates the British Educational Research Association Special Interest Group, Creativity in Education. As well as collaborating with researchers, she works with policy-makers and practitioners to develop creativity in education, both in England and abroad, and recently co-founded the journal Thinking Skills and Creativity. She is currently leading projects on Possibility Thinking and Progression in Creative Learning (each with Pamela Burnard and Teresa Grainger). Her books include *Can You Teach Creativity?* (Education Now, 1997), *Creativity Across the Primary Curriculum: Framing and Developing Practice* (RoutledgeFalmer, 1998), *Creativity and Early Years Education: a Lifewide Foundation* (Continuum, 2002) and *Creativity in Schools: Tensions and Dilemmas* (Routledge, 2005). She is co-editor of *Creativity in Education* (Continuum, 2001).

Mihaly Csikszentmihalyi is one of the world's leading authorities on creativity as a socially and culturally constructed phenomenon. His life's work has been to study what makes people truly happy. Drawing upon years of systematic research, he invented the concept of 'flow' as a metaphorical description of the rare mental state associated with feelings of optimal satisfaction and fulfillment. His book, *Flow: the Psychology of Optimal Experience* (1990), has been translated into 15 languages. His analysis of the internal and external conditions giving rise to 'flow' show that it is almost always linked to circumstances of high challenge when personal skills are used to the utmost. He is currently the C.S. and D.J. Davidson Professor of Psychology at the Peter F. Drucker Graduate School of Management at Claremont Graduate University and Director of the Quality of Life Research Center, and also Emeritus Professor of Human Development at the University of Chicago, where he chaired the department of psychology.

Ruth Dineen is a Course Director for a graphic communication degree at the University of Wales Institute, Cardiff, and Visiting Professor at Sichuan Institute of Fine Arts, Chongquin, China. She is the project director for a comparative study into the promotion of learner creativity in the contexts of UK and China and the Welsh co-ordinator for the Imaginative Curriculum network.

Margaret Edwards is Director of the School of Social Science, Liverpool John Moores University, and previously led the Sociology Department there. Her research interests include: management and organisational issues in higher education, university curricula, work–life balance and combining work with family life.

Marilyn Fryer is founder/director of The Creativity Centre Ltd and co-founder of The Creativity Centre Educational Trust. She is a chartered psychologist and qualified teacher. Formerly a reader in psychology at Leeds Metropolitan University, Marilyn has 20 years' experience of devising and delivering creativity development programmes at undergraduate and post-graduate levels. She specialises in creativity research and consultancy for national and international organisations, including government bodies. She has published and presented in the USA, Europe and Asia. She is author of the book *Creative Teaching and Learning* and editor of the internationally-authored book, *Creativity and Cultural Diversity*. She has written numerous book chapters, reports and articles in the academic and popular press.

Norman Jackson began his professional career as a 'hard rock' geologist, holding teaching, research and industrial posts in the UK and Saudi Arabia. Although education is now his chosen field of endeavour, he still explores it as a geologist might – using his eyes and his imagination! After completing a stint as Her Majesty's Inspector for geoscience education, he forsook the world of geology in 1993 for higher education, working for a number of national bodies in policy, research and development. In 2000 he joined the newly formed Learning and Teaching Support Network (LTSN) as a senior advisor and transferred to the Higher Education Academy when it formed in 2004. In December 2005 he became Director for the University of Surrey Centre for Excellence in Professional Training and Education (SCEPTrE). In January 2001 he initiated the Imaginative Curriculum project – an emergent programme of research and development work formed around the idea of creativity in higher education, the fruits of which are synthesised in this book. Norman is a Visiting Professor of Higher Education at the University of Hertfordshire. His research interests and publications embrace change and evaluation in higher education and how people, organisations and systems learn. This book and the Imaginative Curriculum network are a testament to his strong commitment to network-based collaborative learning in order to promote large scale cultural change.

Chris McGoldrick teaches Geography and works within Base Line Research and Survey, a consultancy unit set up within the School of Social Science at Liverpool John Moores University. Recent research includes employability in HE, other aspects of university curricula, and issues affecting disadvantaged older people.

Martin Oliver is a senior lecturer at the London Knowledge Lab, which is part of the Institute of Education, and is an editor of *ALT-J*, the journal of research in learning technology. His research is focused on higher education, addressing topics such as technology, change, academic development and creativity in higher education, completing two commissioned studies for the Imaginative Curriculum project. With an interest in the social construction of knowledge, these studies were an opportunity to see what academics and students made of the idea of 'creativity'; his personal position is that the idea remains (and should remain) usefully ambiguous, but that if it is a quality that employers value, we should help students become fluent in using that ambiguity to their own advantage.

Bharat Shah was involved in the Imaginative Curriculum project as a contracted researcher while a research assistant at University College London University. He now works in student support for City University.

Malcolm Shaw is Professor of Educational Development at Leeds Metropolitan University and was, until his recent retirement, responsible for supporting generic aspects of curriculum development across the university and the development and delivery of the induction course for new lecturers – a post-graduate programme that embraces many of the principles and strategies that are suggested within this book as facilitating creativity and creative approaches. He was a founder member of the small team that started the Imaginative Curriculum project and is currently retained by Leeds Met to carry out educational development project work overseas, primarily in sub-Saharan Africa.

Christine Sinclair has a background in philosophy, education and (temporarily) mechanical engineering. She became an engineering student to find out more about students' experience of higher education, and discovered that students frequently have to behave creatively to cope with new practices that are strange and sometimes alienating. This natural tendency in students can be positively and usefully exploited, while making the environment more conducive. As a lecturer in the Centre for Academic Practice and Learning Enhancement at the University of Strathclyde in Glasgow, Christine works with staff and students, and values approaches that recognise the joy of learning for both. She is the Scottish co-ordinator for the Imaginative Curriculum network.

Richard Smith-Bingham is Head of Policy and Research at the National Endowment for Science Technology and the Arts. He is responsible for strategic planning, internal policy development, research, corporate evaluation, intelligence-gathering, and policy and public affairs work. Prior to this he taught in higher education, set up a clean water project in El Salvador, did a short spell in TV, and worked on strategic planning, policy and research for the Heritage Lottery Fund. NESTA, which operates as a catalyst for creativity and innovation in the UK by investing in the development of talented individuals, innovative start-up businesses, and new ways of teaching and learning, has been collaborating with the Imaginative Curriculum Network since 2004.

Paul Tosey is a senior lecturer in the School of Management, University of Surrey, where he is programme leader for the MSc Change Agent Skills and Strategies, an advanced programme for consultants and HR professionals. He is Director of a HEFCE FDTL5 Project on Enquiry-based Learning. In 2004/5 he received the University of Surrey's Learning & Teaching Award. His research interests include systemic thinking, transformative learning and neuro-linguistic programming.

James Wisdom is a higher education consultant, specialising in educational development. He is Co-Chair of the Staff and Educational Development

Association and the Editor for SEDA Series published through Routledge-Falmer, a Visiting Professor of Educational Development at Middlesex University and a consultant with the Oxford Centre for Staff and Learning Development. He has held educational development posts at Kingston University and London Guildhall University, where he was Head of Educational and Staff Development. His most recent publication (with Ranald Macdonald) is *Academic and Educational Development: Research, Evaluation and Changing Practice in Higher Education*, Kogan Page.

Acknowledgements

This book has been co-created by many people. Many of the chapters were grown from conversations with academics or students, were captured in transcripts, working papers or notes of meetings and then reworked through further conversation with peers. We would like to thank everyone who contributed to the peer review process: Christine Sinclair, John Cowan, Russ Law, Michael Pittilo, Fred Buining, Richard Seel, John Biggs, Lewis Elton, Ron Barnett and Victor Borden. The book would have been very different without their critical and constructive contributions.

In the sort of emergent and socially constructive knowledge-building process we are engaged in, it is sometimes very difficult to associate an idea with an individual, a conversation or event. Throughout the Imaginative Curriculum project, people have been very generous with their ideas and opinions in order that we might all advance our understanding. This book is dedicated to every academic, student, staff and educational developer, manager and researcher who contributed to our project; without your contributions this book would not have been possible. We would particularly like to pay tribute to the members of the Imaginative Curriculum network who have participated in email conversations and network events, or who have provided personal accounts of their teaching, and the 94 National Teaching Fellows, 100+ academics and 100+ students who contributed to our five research studies.

The project would not have been possible without the financial support provided by the Learning and Teaching Support Network Generic Centre (January 2001–May 2004) and the Higher Education Academy, which replaced the LTSN (May 2004–present). We also acknowledge the financial assistance and encouragement provided by the National Endowment for Science Technology and the Arts (NESTA). Support for network meetings was also provided by the Centre for Academic Practice at the University of Strathclyde and the Centre for the Enhancement of Learning and Teaching at the University of Hertfordshire.

Professor Mihaly Csikszentmihalyi has inspired many people with his thinking and writing on creativity, and influenced our approach to exploring the idea of creativity in higher education. Thank you for adding your voice to those of the other contributors.

In keeping with the idea that creativity is a socially constructed phenomenon we must also recognise that it is a socially supported phenomenon and acknowledge the enormous contribution made by our families to giving us the time and space to turn our imaginations into reality. You thought we were mad but thank you, Taraneh, Navid, Yalda, Neda, Ben, Jodie, Gemma, Kathy, Elizabeth, Daniel, Jenny, Jasmine and Jake for putting up with us.

Finally, we would like to acknowledge the creative contributions of the Routledge team especially Kirsty Smy and Helen Pritt, and Hannah Dolan and colleagues from Wearset Publishing Services, in shaping our book.

Abbreviations

CACE	Central Advisory Council for Education (England)
CETL	Centres of Excellence for Teaching and Learning
CPD	Continuing professional development
DCMS	Department for Culture, Media and Sport
DFEE	Department for Education and Employment
DFES	Department for Education and Skills
DTI	Department of Trade and Industry
HEFCE	Higher Education Funding Council England
ILTHE	Institute of Learning and Teaching in Higher Education
LTSN	Learning and Teaching Support Network
NACCCE	National Advisory Committee on Creative and Cultural Education
NCSL	National College for School Leadership
NESTA	National Endowment for Science Technology and the Arts
OFSTED	Office for Standards in Education
SEDA	Staff and Educational Development Association
QCA	Qualifications and Curriculum Authority
QAA	Quality Assurance Agency

Foreword

Developing creativity

Mihaly Csikszentmihalyi

Doctoral students drop out of universities before graduation not because they cannot pass exams or get good grades in courses, but because they cannot come up with an original idea for a dissertation. They are bright and know an enormous amount, but all their academic careers they have learned how to answer questions, solve problems set for them by others. Now that it is their turn to come up with a question worth answering, all too many of them are at a loss.

One hears the same story in industry and the business world, in civil service and scientific research. Technical knowledge and expertise might abound, but originality and innovation are scarce. Yet the way our species has been developing, creativity has become increasingly important. In the Renaissance creativity might have been a luxury for the few, but by now it is a necessity for all.

There are several reasons for this, some that are in conflict with each other. The first is the undeniable increase in the rate of change, mainly spearheaded by technology but also involving lifestyles, beliefs and knowledge. Today's technical marvel is obsolete tomorrow; the diet so many swear by today turns out to be unhealthy after all; the scientific specialty one has trained in for many years no longer provides a stable career. Great nations collapse, wealthy corporations dissolve in bankruptcy. It takes creativity not to be blinded by the trappings of stability, to recognize the coming changes, anticipate their consequences and thus perhaps lead them in a desirable direction.

A second trend is the rapid globalization of economic and social systems. Ideally, this would lead to a better distribution of labor and of resources; a better integration of beliefs, values, and knowledge. At the same time, globalization involves a great deal of what Schumpeter called 'creative destruction' – without a certainty that the destruction will actually result in a creative outcome. It will take a good dose of creativity to avoid the result that the division between rich and poor will not replicate on a global scale the former division between capitalists and proletariat; that the valued traditions of less powerful cultures will not be lost, but integrated with the Western patterns so as to enrich the future instead of impoverishing it.

Another emerging trend is the specialization of knowledge, leading to new forms of fragmentation based on knowledge rather than tradition. A great number of breakthroughs in science of the past century have come at the interface of disciplines: between physics and chemistry, between chemistry and biology. As each discipline keeps becoming deeper and more complex, it is easy to lose sight of those neighboring branches of knowledge that might help transform one's own.

Any society, any institution that does not take these realities into account is unlikely to be successful, or even to survive in the coming years. On the other hand, individuals who see the opportunities in this new scenario are going to be in a better position to add value to their communities, and prosper in the process. But this requires the ability to recognize the emerging realities, to understand their implications, and to formulate responses that harness the energy of evolution to build products, ideas, and connections that add value to life. And that requires creativity.

How is education preparing young people for this creative task? So far, not very well. The culture-lag between what is needed in the present and what the schools offer has always existed; now it threatens to grow ever larger. Schools teach how to answer, not to question. They teach isolated disciplines that, as the years pass, become more and more difficult to integrate. Reference to the present, let alone to the future, is lacking in most school curricula which are dominated – understandably, perhaps – by a concern with transmitting past knowledge. Yet the past is no longer as good a guide to the future as it once had been. Young people have to learn how to relate and apply past ways of knowing to a constantly changing kaleidoscope of ideas and events. And that requires learning to be creative.

The present volume, edited by Norman Jackson and colleagues, is thus very timely. To my knowledge, this is the first volume addressing the role of creativity in higher education. It is a difficult but essential project. Difficult for several reasons, some more easily avoidable than others. The most obvious danger is that of reducing creativity to a facile routine of exercises in 'thinking outside the box.' These days the popular view of a creative person is someone who spins off original ideas left and right, a person one would like to hang out with at a cocktail party so as to be amused by a constant stream of witty apperceptions.

But if one is to go by the evidence of the creative individuals of the past, creativity requires a focused, almost obsessive concern for a clearly delimited problematic area. Neither Isaac Newton nor Leonardo da Vinci would have been great hits at a party. Neither Johann Sebastian Bach nor Dante Alighieri were known for their witty repartee or fluid imagination – except in their own work. There are occasional exceptions: Benjamin Franklin was more like the current conception of what a creative person should be like, as apparently he *was* the life of the party at the French court during his residence there. But within their domain of interest, all creative individuals love the task that engages their whole energy. They all echo the words of Paolo Uccello, the Florentine who was one of the first to learn how to use perspective in painting, who according to his wife used to walk up and down the bedchamber all night, shaking his head and muttering: 'Ah, what a beautiful thing is this perspective!'

So if one wishes to inject creativity in the educational system, the first step might be to help students find out what they truly love, and help them to immerse themselves in the domain – be it poetry or physics, engineering or dance. If young people become involved with what they enjoy, the foundations for creativity will be in place. Vittorino da Feltre, who at the turn of the 1400s started one of the first liberal arts colleges in Europe, well understood the relationship between enjoyment and creative learning. He called his school *La Gioiosa* – The Joyful Place – and many of his students ended up among the leading thinkers of the next generation.

But how can the joy of learning be instilled in modern universities? There are several approaches one can take: First, making sure that teachers are selected in part because they model the joy of learning themselves, and are able to spark it in students; second, that the curriculum takes into account the students' desire for joyful learning; third, that the pedagogy is focused on awakening the imagination and engagement of students; and finally that the institution rewards and facilitates the love of learning among faculty and students alike.

But even this is just a first step, a setting of the stage, so to speak. When students are eager to immerse themselves in learning because it is a rewarding, enjoyable task, the basic prerequisites for creativity are met. What next? That is where the readings of this volume come in. They present a variety of perspectives on the stimulation of creativity, on how to support and nurture it. Taken together, they provide a much needed cornerstone for the systematic introduction of creativity into higher education.

Claremont, December 2005

1 Imagining a different world

Norman Jackson

Imagination is the beginning of creation.

(George Bernard Shaw)

Imagine a different world of higher education

Our ability to imagine and then invent new worlds for ourselves is one of our greatest human assets and the origin of all human achievement. It is the vision of a higher education world in which students' creativity is valued alongside more traditional forms of academic achievement that provides the driving force for this book and energises the Imaginative Curriculum network:[1] a loose association of people campaigning for greater consideration of the role of creativity in higher education. Underlying this project are the assumptions that: helping people to be creative is a good thing; that people tend to be more satisfied if they are able to be creative; and that individually and collectively we need to be creative to continually adapt and invent in an ever-changing and increasingly complex world. But, more than anything else, we are campaigning for creativity because we believe that students' experiences of higher education and their future lives will be enriched if teachers help them recognise, experience and develop more of their potential. Pragmatically, we believe that students will become more effective learners and, ultimately, successful people if they can recognise and harness their own creative abilities and combine them with more traditional academic abilities.

This book is part of a strategy to encourage higher education to think more deeply about its responsibilities and practices for nurturing students' creativity and to provide practical help and advice to teachers who want to develop their curricula and teach in ways that are more likely to foster students' creativity. Our strategy reflects Michael Fullan's (2003: 23) wise advice for accomplishing complex change:

- Start with the notion of moral purpose, key problems, desirable directions, but don't lock in.
- Create communities of interaction around these ideas.
- Ensure that quality information infuses interaction and related deliberations.

- Look for and extract promising patterns, i.e. consolidate gains and build on them.

The book draws together the results of many of these interactions to 'extract promising patterns'. Our objective is not to provide definitive scientific definitions of what creativity in higher education means. Rather, it is to open up the many rich and diverse conceptions of what creativity means to individuals and groups of people and how it is enacted in different teaching and learning contexts. Our hope is that readers will find things that resonate with their world and be inspired to see their own practices in a new light. In doing so we are seeking to give substance to the *voices* of higher education teachers in their individual practice settings. In producing this book our objectives are to:

- show why higher education should be helping to develop the creative potential of students and advance understanding about the role of creativity in higher education.
- stimulate interest/curiosity in creativity in higher education beyond the disciplinary fields that have traditionally embraced the idea.
- provide practical advice and aids to encourage more teachers to examine their own understandings of creativity in their disciplinary and curriculum contexts and develop their practice in ways that will enable students to experience and develop their own creativity.

The formulation of a problem is far more often essential than its solution, which may be merely a matter of mathematical or experimental skill. To raise new questions, new possibilities, to regard old problems from a new angle requires creative imagination and marks real advances in science.

(Albert Einstein)

Finding the problem

Finding and working with problems is core to the academic creative enterprise and when we began to explore the question of, 'what does creativity mean in higher education?' Anderson's Law came into force with a vengeance.

I have yet to see any problem, however complicated, which, when you looked at it in the right way, did not become still more complicated.

(Anderson's Law)

The 'right way of looking' entailed exploring the issue of creativity through multiple perspectives, engaging with the lived experiences of teachers and students and using the research literature on creativity to try to make sense of the patterns that emerged. I like to think that the imaginative curriculum project has helped to create the conditions for the emergence of sense-making in this complex perceptual and practice world (see Tosey, Chapter 4, for an elaboration of the concept of emergence). Inevitably, the approach is leading to a deeper appreciation of the complexity underlying our problem, some of the dimensions of which are examined below.

Problems are things or states that someone thinks are worthy of attention or investigation. They might be visualised from two very different perspectives. The first sees a problem as an issue that needs to be resolved or rectified, the second that there is an opportunity for something different. The problem called 'creativity in higher education' contains both of these perspectives but is much more about the latter than the former.

Finding a problem requires someone to be looking for it – people who will own and care enough about the problem to do something about it. In our network-building activities through the Imaginative Curriculum project we have encountered many individuals – teachers, staff and educational developers, managers, educational consultants/advisers, and researchers who care enough about a problem called 'creativity in higher education' to commit their time, energy and minds to trying to understand and work with it. The Imaginative Curriculum network was invented to provide a social structure to enable people who cared about creativity in higher education to connect, communicate and collaborate by pooling their knowledge and resources to develop a deeper understanding of the problem and how it might be addressed and to co-create new opportunities for students' and teachers' creativity.

The ill-defined problem we are engaging with is associated with a question like, 'how can we improve the higher education experiences and the future lives of students by giving greater attention to the role of creativity in their learning?' Or, if you are a teacher you might prefer, 'how can I be a part of the educational experience of students fostering creativity in pursuit of our shared goals?' Such a representation locates our problem in the ultimate moral purpose of education – 'making a difference to students' lives' (Fullan, 2003: 18) and provides us with our inspiration and motivation.

Our problem is not chronic, in the sense that the vast majority of teachers believe there is an issue to be addressed. It is more of a sense of dissatisfaction with a higher education world that seems, at best, to take creativity for granted, rather than a world that celebrates the contribution creativity makes to academic achievement and personal well-being.

Our intellectual curiosity is aroused by questions like, 'what does creativity mean to a teacher of history or engineering?' Our response has been to engage higher education teachers in conversation about creativity, in the belief that it is only through conversation that meanings can be shared and new understandings co-created. Our current perceptions of the problem are outlined below.

First, our problem is not that creativity is absent, but that it is omnipresent. That it is taken for granted and subsumed within analytic ways of thinking that dominate the academic intellectual territory. Paradoxically, the core enterprise of research – the production of new knowledge – is generally seen as an objective systematic activity rather than a creative activity that combines, in imaginative ways, objective and more intuitive forms of thinking. The most critical argument for higher education to take creativity in students' learning more seriously is that creativity lies at the heart of learning and performing in any subject-based context and the highest levels of both are often the most creative acts of all. Our problem then becomes one of co-creating this understanding within different disciplinary academic communities.

Second, although teaching and designing courses are widely seen as sites for creativity, teachers' creativity and creative processes are largely implicit and are rarely publicly acknowledged and celebrated. Teachers are reluctant to recognise and reveal their own creative thinking and actions in the many facets of their practice. In the UK, the introduction of National Teaching Fellows[2] and institutional teaching fellowships which evidence and publicly reward individual teachers' commitments to teaching and innovation, and the establishment in England of over 70 Centres for Excellence in Teaching and Learning,[3] which reward innovative and effective teaching teams, departments and institutions, is beginning to change this situation. We have a long way to go, though, before the unique creative contributions of every teacher are valued and recognised.

Third, although students are expected to be creative, creativity is rarely an explicit objective of the learning and assessment process (except for a small number of disciplines in the performing and graphic arts). Creativity is inhibited by predictive outcome-based course designs, which set out what students will be expected to have learned with no room for unanticipated or student-determined outcomes. Assessment tasks and assessment criteria which limit the possibilities of students' responses are also significant inhibitors of students' and teachers' creativity.

Fourth, for teachers whose motivation derives primarily from their passion for the subject, creativity only has meaning when it is directly associated with the practices and forms of intellectual engagement in their discipline. Many teachers find it hard to translate the generic language and processes of creativity into their subject-specific contexts. Conversely, many higher education teachers have limited knowledge of creative approaches to teaching, even within their discipline. Most higher education teachers are unfamiliar with the body of research into creativity and how creative-thinking techniques can be used to facilitate problem working. So the problem becomes one of growing awareness and understanding of the meanings of creativity in the discipline and of persuading teachers that teaching for creativity is no more or less than good teaching to achieve particular outcomes in disciplinary learning.

Fifth, while many higher education teachers recognise the intrinsic moral value of promoting students' creativity, they baulk at what they perceive as the additional work necessary to successfully implement more creative approaches. Furthermore, any conversation about creativity raises many organisational barriers and factors that inhibit or stifle attempts to nurture creativity. Paradoxically, for some teachers these barriers are themselves catalysts for creativity.

It is hard to imagine a more difficult set of conditions to work with, and academics recognise that they will not make much headway with changing these conditions unless they can influence the behaviours of the organisations in which they work. It is not enough for teachers to overcome such organisational barriers through their own ingenuity and persistence; ultimately, organisational systems and cultures themselves have to be changed. Such changes have to be led through sympathetic, inspiring and energetic leaders. The problem of creativity in higher education is also one of leadership at many different levels. Our message to higher education leaders and managers is to seize the opportunity for leading higher education into the sort of world we are imagining.

In exploring the nature of the problem, it has been posited as teachers doing something for students to foster their creativity. But what if we were to turn this around and see it as a problem of teachers doing it for themselves in order to satisfy unfulfilled needs? For example, to work in different ways with students, to develop different sorts of relationships and engage in different sorts of conversations to achieve different sorts of outcomes that they felt were missing or under-represented in the curriculum. There is evidence in many of the conversations we have had with teachers that these sorts of values and beliefs are an important source of inspiration and motivation for engaging in discussion about creativity in higher education. So perhaps our problem is also about satisfying value-based personal and professional needs in a higher education system that increasingly seems to ignore such things.

What sort of problem is it?

Apart from the obvious – a blooming big, complex and fuzzy one – our problem is a systems problem involving the thinking, relationships and actions of many participants and contexts. Checkland (1999) described two very different ways of viewing a system. The first perspective is an engineered system in which the entities, their relationships and the way they function can be defined, designed and predicted with accuracy. He used the term 'hard system' to characterise the thinking that is applied to the analysis, definition and understanding of the functioning of such systems. A hard-systems approach to problem solving attempts to define, analyse and resolve problems within a conceptual framework that relies on and seeks to create a highly ordered real world.

But, in socially constructed systems, such as that in which our problem is embedded, the very nature and complexity of human thinking, action and relationships defies such a rational and logical approach to the definition of the system and its behaviour. Checkland used the term 'soft system' to describe this type of situation. A 'soft systems' view of the world accepts confusion, diversity and complexity and uses this as a resource and a source of inspiration to orchestrate enquiry and grow new learning. Soft systems theory does not see all new perspectives as problems to be solved. Rather, it sees different perspectives as routes that can be taken to open up and examine possibilities.

Checkland (1999: 154) identified two different types of problem that systems thinking might be used to resolve. Structured problems are those that can be explicitly defined in a form that implies a theory might be developed to enable them to be resolved. These are amenable to hard systems thinking. Unstructured problems manifest themselves in a feeling of unease but they cannot be explicitly stated without appearing to oversimplify the situation. These are more amenable to soft-systems thinking.

Solving problems that can be defined in hard systems terms, through proven techniques, strategies and theories is a feature of many disciplinary learning contexts, but the problems associated with teaching and learning, including the problem of how we can improve the conditions for creativity in higher education, requires a soft systems approach. The Imaginative Curriculum project has, through its growing network of interest, created a social system for learning about what creativity means and how students' creativity is enabled in many different higher education contexts. Through this process, we are harnessing our collective imaginations and intellect to find ways of changing higher education to make it a more creative place.

> We will either find a way, or make one.
>
> Hannibal

Why are we working on this problem now?

We believe that this is a challenging problem that needs to be explored now. UK higher education is in a process of inventing, or co-creating, a different system. The process involves all the agents (people, organisations, networks and other collaborative associations) continually interacting and influencing each other in ways that cannot be conceived or explained in detail, but from which new forms of organisation, new relationships and patterns of behaviour emerge. Everything we see in higher education we have created, our imagination and creativity is there for all to see, yet rarely do we acknowledge its presence or effects. This is the great paradox of a society in transformation, and addressing this deficit is a central purpose of this book.

Higher education is a place where we try to understand the world in all its rich complexity and glorious detail, but it is also a place where we prepare students for a lifetime of working with their own complex issues and problems. An important theme developed throughout this book is that to grapple with complex problems requires complex learning and thinking that draws on all of our mental and emotional capacities and capabilities. Ron Barnett (2000) sums it up well when he proposes that higher education is faced with preparing students for a supercomplex world: a world in which individuals have to continually reconstitute themselves through their lives. These ideas are reflected in the sorts of personal qualities, abilities and capacities that employers seek when they recruit graduates. Here is concise synthesis of the sorts of things employers want in their graduate recruits:

> research over a quarter of a decade finds a broad consensus about the attributes that employers expect to find in graduate recruits. They should exhibit the following: imagination/creativity; adaptability/flexibility; willingness to learn; independent working/autonomy; working in a team; ability to manage others; ability to work under pressure; good oral communication; communication in writing for varied purposes/audiences; numeracy; attention to detail; time management; assumption of responsibility and for making decisions; planning, coordinating and organizing ability.
>
> (Pedagogy for Employability Group, 2004: 5)

Higher education is full of intelligent, creative people and the professional act of teaching, with the significant autonomy attached to this role, provides fertile conditions for people to be creative in order to promote students' learning. But many teachers do not take advantage of this opportunity. All too often they prefer to replicate well-tried methods and designs rather than experiment with more imaginative but riskier, perhaps less comfortable, ways of doing things. The constant pressure for greater efficiency and cost effectiveness, increasing levels of personal accountability, quality assurance and peer review systems that favour conservatism, and resistance in colleagues to anything that involves doing things differently, are just a few of the things that can inhibit our individual and collective creativity. In fact, when we get down to thinking about it, the organisational and professional worlds we inhabit are full of conditions, beliefs, attitudes and practices that constrain our ability to be creative. We can't escape the problem! Yet in spite of these seemingly unfavourable conditions, many higher education teachers invent new strategies, designs and materials to make a difference to the lives of their students every day of their working lives.

The book

We are exploring the idea of creativity in higher education from four different but inter-related standpoints: contextual, perceptual, practical and conceptual. The first three themes create the organisational framework for the book while the fourth runs throughout.

The book begins by examining the contemporary social, educational and organisational contexts within which our discussion of creativity in higher education is located. Richard Smith-Bingham provides a policy perspective on creativity and the key role of education in promoting a more creative society; a theme which is continued in Anna Craft's excellent synthesis of the policies and work being done on creativity in schools. Paul Tosey sets us off on our exploration of creativity in higher education by examining universities as complex adaptive systems through which creativity emerges through every-day social interaction and conversation. Paul locates creativity in universities in terms of a change paradigm and concludes that, 'The spaces for emergence in HE currently seem ill-matched to the issue of change that appear most urgent to address'.

The stepping-stone to advancing teaching and learning practices is to develop and elaborate our understanding of creativity. The second part of the book synthesises the results of a number of research studies that have been undertaken within the Imaginative Curriculum project. Martin Oliver, Chris McGoldrick and Margaret Edwards describe studies in two universities aimed at understanding creativity from the teachers' and the students' perspectives. Marilyn Fryer describes the results of a survey of views on creativity conducted within the community of English National Teaching Fellows, and Norman Jackson and Malcolm Shaw develop a subject perspective on creativity based on the views of academics in four disciplinary communities. The quintet of studies is completed with Ruth Dineen's account which combines teachers' and students' views in the field of Art and Design, a field that actually does value and celebrate creativity. An important conclusion from these studies is that academics appear to share beliefs on the main features of creativity in the higher education teaching and learning contexts, although how these beliefs become operationalised varies enormously across the disciplines.

The final section of the book turns to the practicalities of designing programmes and learning environments, teaching and assessments that develop students' creativity and enable them to experience being creative. Chapters in this part of the book are supported by the Curriculum Guides and other resources that can be found on the Imaginative Curriculum website. On the site, Norman Jackson and Christine Sinclair describe their search for an appropriate pedagogy and provide a map of resources to underpin a strategy to aid students' creative development. The theme is developed further by Caroline Baillie, who describes some of the techniques that might be used to stimulate creative thinking and draws out the learning gained from an experiment to develop the facilitation skills of higher education teachers. Assessing creativity is the most contentious, contested and poorly understood aspect of creativity in higher education, and John Cowan tackles the issue in his own highly individualistic style, providing us with novelty that may perhaps influence the domain. His strategy for integrating the construction of meanings, formulating and evaluating standards by students and tutors points us in a direction that could spark a much-needed assessment revolution! Tom Balchin fans the flames of revolution with research-based insights into the idea of consensual assessment.

In the penultimate chapter, James Wisdom considers how we might give more support and encouragement to developing creative teachers and valuing the contribution of creativity to the higher education teaching and learning process. In the final chapter, I try to draw together some of the themes that have emerged, outline a systems perspective on teaching environments to support students' creativity and elaborate some principles for the design of teaching and learning environments to promote students' creative development in higher education.

Finding our creative voices

So far we have avoided trying to define creativity, but definitions contain ideas that can inspire and it seems appropriate to introduce one here. I particularly like the one proposed by Dellas and Gaier (1970), which suggests that personal creativity is the ability to use imagination, insight and intellect, as well as feeling and emotion, in order to move an idea from its present state to an alternate, previously unexplored state. The idea of 'moving an idea from one state to another' captures my imagination and seems to me to lie at the heart of our intellectual and practical enterprise. But movement requires decisions to be made and energy, imagination and skill to turn an abstract idea into concrete reality. Covey (2004) provides us with another inspiring view of creativity as something that we have the freedom to choose to do, or not to do:

Between stimulus and response there is a space.
In the space lies our freedom and power to choose our response.
In those choices lie our growth and our happiness.

Covey (2004: 4)

The act of creation or re-creation is the purposeful process of exploration. Russ Law (2005) has coined the term 'explorativity' to embody the state of mind and being that enables us to overcome feelings of inertia and helplessness, and of opening the way to a more rewarding existence, by the development of attitudes, approaches and practices that harness the potential that each of us has in our own way. To overcome inertia we need to be inspired: our imaginations need to be fired and our curiosity aroused. I encountered such a moment when, browsing in a newsagents on Liverpool Lime Street Station, I came across Stephen Covey's book, *The 8th Habit: From Effectiveness to Greatness*. My curiosity aroused, I thumbed through the book to find his eighth habit: something that he called 'voice' – 'the unique personal significance we all possess – the voice of hope, intelligence, resilience and the limitless human potential to effect positive change'. I read and was captivated by the idea that:

> voice lies at the nexus of **talent** (your natural gifts and strengths – [including creative talents]); **passion** (those things that naturally energize, excite, motivate you); **need** (including what the world needs enough to pay you for [and the needs you identify and feel a need to fulfill]); and **conscience** (that still, small voice within that assures you of what is right and that prompts you to actually do it).
>
> (Covey, 2004: 5, with my additions)

This set of ideas and meanings connects in a profound way the idea of self-identity with the abilities, attitudes, motivations and purposes so necessary for creativity within an ethical framework that guides personal decisions and actions. This representation of voice seemed to me to embody the essence of what underlies and gives expression to our unique personal significance – our creativity. It ultimately defines our individual identities as people, be it as students, teachers, managers, administrators or members of support staff, and underlies the core moral purpose of education. This book is about trying to give expression to the individual and collective voices that make up our world of higher education.

Notes

1 The Imaginative Curriculum project was launched in January 2001. Information about the project, the activities of the network and the resources produced can be found at: www.heacademy/creativity.htm.
2 Information about the National Teaching Fellowship scheme can be found at: www.ntfs.ac.uk/.
3 Information about the Centres for Excellence in Teaching and Learning (CETL) can be found at: www.hefce.ac.uk/learning/TInits/cetl/.

2 Public policy, innovation and the need for creativity

Richard Smith-Bingham

Introduction

As I write, in July 2005, there is a renewed burst of interest by policy-makers in creativity. To give a few examples, Paul Roberts has just begun to review creativity in English schools; the Cultural Commission in Scotland has recently produced a sizeable and far-reaching report on Scotland's creative needs; the new Creative Industries Minister in England, James Purnell, has outlined his vision for the creative industries; George Cox is reviewing how small and medium-sized enterprises can make better use of 'creative specialists'. These projects, covering different spheres of endeavour, form a good starting point for why creativity is considered a valuable attribute for society, and how, within a policy-making community increasingly focused on delivery, the 'c'-word is of interest. This chapter also considers some of the questions or difficulties that policy-makers have with making creativity a policy priority, briefly surveys the strategies for creativity adopted by NESTA (the UK's National Endowment for Science, Technology and the Arts), and touches on the implications of the creativity agenda for higher education.

The need for creativity

There are economic, social and cultural arguments as to why creativity should be a prized asset. 'Creativity is becoming a key resource for individuals and societies. [It] will enable us to make the most of new opportunities, and to find the most productive responses to challenges as well as threats' (Jupp *et al.*, 2001: 6). In other words, creativity is a means of envisaging solutions and ways forward, of thriving in a 'supercomplex' environment (Barnett, 2000) with numerous different needs.

The context is the pressing dominance of the innovation agenda, which has achieved global resonance.[1] 'For the past 25 years we have optimised our organisations for efficiency and quality. Over the next quarter century, we must optimise our entire society for innovation' (Council on Competitiveness, 2004: 5). So begins the *Innovate America* report, and much the same sentiment is manifest in the European Council's desire (expressed through the Lisbon agenda and in the national strategies underpinning it) to build a dynamic, competitive, knowledge-based economy in the European Union. In economic terms, the innovation agenda is driven by a number of factors relating to competitiveness, including trade liberalisation and a rapid fall in communication and transport costs; developments in technology and scientific understanding; and the speed at which consumer tastes and demands are changing (DTI, 2003: 4). As a result, the future prosperity of developed and developing countries will increasingly depend on their capacity to innovate, to develop ideas into new products and services, to develop new technologies and new forms of production, to introduce products and services to new markets, and as they do so quite probably engaging with consumers or beneficiaries in new ways.

But the innovation agenda extends beyond the field of business, and applies to the ability of governments, organisations and society at large to make greater headway against engrained problems: meeting the key environmental challenges of the future, raising levels of health across the planet, and enhancing educational opportunities and learning potential (DTI, 2003; IBM, 2005). The role of creativity rests on its potential to provide insight, make new connections, identify potential solutions and communicate them. In this context, creativity is manifest in organisational models and services as well as products; science and technology as well as the arts; healthcare and democracy as well as cultural achievement; communication and community-building as well as product generation.

But before being able to articulate the role of creativity, what type is required and who the actors might be, in this broad conceptualisation of innovation, one must have a clearer sense as to the nature of the innovation process, and the position of creativity within it. The traditional linear or waterfall conception of innovation (the amount of basic research determines the number of innovations and therefore productivity) has been criticised for quite some time (e.g. Pavitt, 1984; 2001). In a fast-changing world, the ability of ideas to create social and/or economic value, whether they emerge from public, private or third sector enterprises, needs a creative dynamic between knowledge-creation, entrepreneurialism and consumers/beneficiaries. Without new knowledge there will be no products or services to offer, and possibly no effective platforms through which to deliver them; without entrepreneurialism it is not possible to take advantage of the potential or benefit within new knowledge and to take that to market; without take-up by the market, be that social or economic in conception, there will merely be novelty.

However, notwithstanding variances from sector to sector, the initiation and achievement of innovation can be driven by the consumer, the production line and the marketing department (and their equivalents), as well as the laboratory. It is rarely achieved solely by a lone actor, but is more often achieved, and thrives, through dynamic interactions, operating through multiple feedback loops, between individuals, teams and organisations with different forms of knowledge, skill-sets, and operational capacities that enable the cross-fertilisation of ideas and the realisation of new opportunities (Florida, 2002; Sitra, 2005). As a result, innovation, and the creativity that underpins it, is not just about radical, disruptive and paradigm-shifting outcomes; it is also about incremental and cumulative forms of innovation that rely on the enhancement of existing products and practice. In this way, the creativity that underpins the creation of value comes from understanding a particular domain, and an ability to feed off the traditions it is challenging whilst at the same time mindful of its likely reception and its capacity to change that domain or establish a new one (Csikszentmihalyi, 1997).

The breadth, pervasiveness and urgency of the innovation agenda, the fluidity of the process and the multiple means of engagement have considerable implications for the workforce of the future, the focus of its endeavours, and the skills and attributes it might need. A knowledge-based economy needs workers and enterprises that are highly adaptable, that can respond more effectively to changes in technologies or product markets (Kok, 2003). Significant investment in human capital is essential: work must be a real option for all, and the stock of well-educated and well-skilled workers, who would have to update their skills regularly in order to be able to respond effectively to change and enhance their employability, needs to be enhanced. 'Shifts in the nature of business organisations and the growing importance of knowledge-based work ... favour non-routine cognitive skills, such as abstract reasoning, problem-solving, communication and collaboration' (Karoly and Panis, 2004: xiv). Employees are essential to innovation, and diversity is a source of competitive advantage; organisations that prosper will be those that are pro-actively geared for constant change and innovation, by virtue of their openness to opportunity, flexible structures, and investment in employee skills (EU Presidency Conference, 2004; Work Foundation, 2005).

Challenges for policy-makers

The terms 'creativity' and 'innovation' are broad-based and cut across public policy. Those at the vanguard of the agenda have turned towards broad definitions of innovation, and advocate a coherent 'third-generation' agenda which 'place[s] innovation at the heart of each policy area' (Lengrand, 2002: 11), rather than as an adjunct to each area, or as a separate agenda. Often, however, in its manifestation as policy, innovation is more narrowly considered and is not strongly aligned with creativity. In UK policy discourse, creativity is largely associated with culture (especially the arts), business (with respect to the creative industries) and education (as part of a drive for deep learning and personal development that is more than achievement in tests).[2] Innovation, with its stronger connotations of delivery and value, is used most often in an investment and business context in relation to research and development, particularly with respect to deriving commercial and economic value from new knowledge in science and technology, and often also to deriving efficiency savings from various types of public service reform. Thus, across Whitehall, devolved governments and the regional development agencies, there exists a range of innovation funds, groups, networks and hubs.

James Purnell has recently said that the Government is interested in four areas of creativity: the ability of the education system to turn out a large supply of creative people; the UK's ability to turn innovative ideas into successful companies; the implications of the need for organisational diversity on government policy; the need for the UK to work with other creative industries across the world and not to try to close its borders to outside innovation.[3] While these areas will no doubt be unpacked further in the light of ongoing work, it is arguable that, as yet, the attributes of creativity and innovation are not sufficiently internalised and integrated by policy-makers and delivery agents, and that interventions and initiatives that support or embrace them manifest themselves in ways that do not represent a truly joined-up 'innovation system'.

This issue is perhaps clearest at the point where creativity relates to innovation. For, while the UK is making great efforts with respect to increasing UK spending on research and development activity, largely by strengthening the publicly funded science base, it is arguably not sufficiently supporting or recognising innovation in manufacturing that is not R&D or patent-based, in service industries and in the creative industries. The assumption that major investments in scientific research is the solution to innovation is challenged (Salter *et al.*, 2000), particularly given the moderate track record of university spin-out companies, and it has been argued that greater policy thinking with respect to innovation should go into nurturing talent and entrepreneurialism rather than investing in research (Allott, 2005). It is important to balance the data relating to R&D expenditure (at 1.9 per cent of GDP admittedly low in comparison with competitor nations, particularly in terms of business expenditure) and shortcomings around patent filing, with the weak culture of entrepreneurship in the UK, and data that suggests that UK small and medium-sized enterprises are less likely to grow into world beaters than those from other countries (Strategy Unit, 2005).

One therefore looks to contexts and environments that can bring forth the type of individuals who can help to generate a dynamic enterprising society, both the genius innovator, whose 'universal creativity' leads to recognisable social benefit through achievements that have properly cumulative, or even transformative, value (Swede, 1993; Csikszentmihalyi, 1997) and those whose 'personal creativity' is a straightforward survival skill based more around 'possibility thinking' (Craft, 2000), leading to enhanced developmental capacity and well-being for that person and their immediate networks, and contributing by largely untracked paths to the general good.

But whether one is seeking to nurture a creative elite, who can achieve breakthroughs and realise demonstrable product-outcomes, or, under more 'democratic' conceptions of creativity (NACCCE, 1999), simply insightful lateral thinkers, the question is what policy should do to promote, support and identify talent and enable it to thrive, to make the aspiration of creativity a reality. Creativity tends to emerge most strongly from environments that encourage it, interactions that spark it off, people that nurture it, situations that reward it, although that is not to say that it cannot defiantly emerge from environments that appear to do exactly the opposite. But it cannot be straightforwardly taught or directed; it is not a simple skills issue, despite the plethora of seminars and short courses available. The arguments around management are similar: on the one hand management is antithetical and destructive to creativity; on the other, structure creates focus and purpose. The dynamic of creative activity operates within this space, oscillating between empowerment and critique, abstraction and practical realisation, time for reflection and pressure for delivery.

At the very least this requires approaches to 'teaching' and 'management' that are highly sophisticated, at times hands-off, and at times resource-intensive. It requires trusting the experts, not having over-rigid funding stipulations, and not expecting results on every occasion. Writers and artists often work in bursts of creativity, and, as Max Perutz wrote, thinking of the 'apparent idleness' of Watson and Crick, 'they sometimes achieved most when they seemed to be working least'; 'creativity in science, as in the arts, cannot be organized. It arises spontaneously from individual talent. Well-run laboratories can foster it, but hierarchical organization, inflexible bureaucratic rules, and mountains of futile paperwork can kill it' (Perutz, 2003; see also DCMS, 2001b: 3). Policy-makers are more comfortable in situations when needs can be assessed, policies developed, resources applied, activities monitored, results observed. But initiatives designed to nurture creativity do not release their value along such mechanical lines and, often, as in the education sector, have requirements that conflict or compete with norms of operation and 'standards' of performance and behaviour. As a result, they often appear bolted on to mainstream activities rather than being properly integrated.

In crude terms, creativity is often unpredictable, unmanageable and unquantifiable. The high-level policy rhetoric that creativity is the answer to key problems, a panacea, leads to questions around how creative approaches and support for creativity can be validated, accounted for and economically justified over any sensible timescale. In terms of investment, there is discomfort with acknowledging the creative process, accepting that failures are inevitable and necessary, and that returns are often difficult to articulate. When success comes, the tendency is to show the outcome as being an effective and efficient use of money by criteria external to the initiative, rather than to celebrate the creativity or innovation. The cultural sector best exemplifies these issues. Against a backdrop of problems around claiming the intrinsic value of culture in a postmodern world that has questioned and relativised traditional cultural values, there is on the one hand a sense of frustration that 'we lack convincing language and political arguments for how culture lies at the heart of a healthy society' (Jowell, 2004: 8), but on the other complaints about the 'skittishness on the part of government, which sometimes sees culture and creativity *only* in the instrumental terms of what it can do for the economy, for learning or for health' (Frayling, 2005: 27; see also Holden, 2004). The value of creativity cannot easily be demonstrated, and therefore justified as an end in itself, within an audit culture, where clear measures of achievement, in terms of quantifiable short-term outputs and standards, are considered benchmarks of success. Indeed, the skewing of programmes to deliver against such measures, in particular where the goals, social and economic, are not central to the core field of endeavour, risks both undermining the core purpose of such enterprises and diminishing their potential to have deeper impact in the long term.

National Endowment for Science, Technology and the Arts

The putative creativity agenda should not be entirely subsumed into other agendas; nonetheless, it is important to recognise the breadth of its value, particularly with respect to the demands of a knowledge-based economy. One initiative focused on creativity that is a partial response to some of the issues identified above is the UK's National Endowment for Science, Technology and the Arts (NESTA). NESTA was established on the basis that a number of highly creative and talented individuals were not finding support from existing funders and investors, and the UK needed a more dynamic and risk-taking national culture in order to encourage ground-breaking endeavour and fuel the knowledge-based economy. Prior to its inception in 1999, there was a sense that the UK was weak at turning its wealth of ideas into reality. With a remit to 'support and promote talent, innovation and creativity in the fields of science, technology and the arts' (National Lottery Act, 1998 ch. 22, para. 17.1), NESTA has focused on helping individuals who have demonstrated outstanding talent and originality to take time out from their current occupations and explore new creative territory; helping individuals and small teams to commercialise their ideas; and piloting innovative methods of creative learning.

In its first six years NESTA has had three overarching goals. The first is to have invested in individuals and teams that have become successes and high achievers on the back of NESTA's catalytic support. The second is to have had a positive impact on culture, society and the economy in the UK through the products, services, technologies and techniques whose development NESTA has supported. The third is for its learning and models for supporting talent, innovation and creativity to have advanced thinking and practice in terms of funding and investment in these areas.

NESTA has a pluralistic view of creativity (and innovation), and its investment strategy is responsive to the different aspects of its agenda. In other words, it has worked with creativity in a developmental context, offering three- to five-year awards to talented individuals for their self-directed personal development; in a commercial context, investing in very early stage business ideas (taking a stake in the companies); and an educational context, supporting action research projects that seek to improve engagement with the learning process and new forms of pedagogy. Aside from supporting the experiments of others within the framework of its programmes, NESTA has also explored particular models of support for creativity. It has set up residential 'labs' for talented 10–15 year-olds, and project-based partnerships for 16–21 year olds, enabling them to express and enhance their creativity, both individually and in small teams. It has instituted an Academy that has helped art and design graduates to set up businesses around their ideas, through a combination of inspirational and instructive sessions, presenting business needs and processes in a way that chimes with creative mindsets. It has gathered together representatives of diverse groups (including teachers, software designers, educational researchers and the games industry) to develop and test prototypes for projects that might bring about more imaginative uses of ICT in education.[4]

Investing in people and projects at an early stage involves a high degree of risk. This can refer to the identification of appropriate projects for support, as their potential, in terms of quality, commerciality and sustainability is often unknown and difficult to ascertain. It can refer to NESTA's management of its investments, given the unanticipated routes and unexpected developments a project might have. And it can also refer to the sustainability of the career, project or business after NESTA's funding period. NESTA's overarching principle is to embrace risk, rather than to shy away from it, but to do so with both eyes open. It uses experts in the fields in question to identify talented individuals, and assess the innovative quality and feasibility of investment proposals. It provides high levels of non-financial assistance (e.g. mentors, specialist advice and training, and introductions to potential [business] partners and further funders) to those it has funded. This assistance, which is tailored to the needs of individual projects, treads a fine line between empowerment and monitoring, but has to be sensitive to the unexpected and with an eye on the ultimate goal. Projects rarely suffer from a lack of creativity, but sometimes need reminding of what constitutes achievement and success. First-time entrepreneurs, for example, often need to be guided to focus on markets and revenues, and not simply on the product, in order to ensure business viability. NESTA expects those it has invested in to factor in the need for considering career development, raising further finance, or other means of achieving sustainability, from an early stage.

NESTA has taken on projects that anticipate both social and commercial outcomes, so long as there are clear criteria for operational decision-making when different objectives conflict. NESTA's business model has accepted that a number of its investments will fail or make little headway, some will have been solidly worthwhile and a few will be runaway successes. NESTA has learnt how to manage a diverse portfolio of projects, and is in the process of codifying its learning about operating in different fields. So far relatively few projects have reached the end of their funding period, but NESTA is examining, through a variety of evaluation mechanisms, the effectiveness of its approaches and models.

Implications for higher education

The best management strategy is to create institutional cultures in which the best young people are free to express their creativity and set their own agendas, not being entrained in hierarchies of deference to their seniors, no matter how distinguished these might be. I also believe that such cultures are most easily maintained on university campuses, thoroughly infested as they are by the irreverent young.

(May, 2002)

Creativity needs to be nurtured from an early age and given opportunities to flourish that accord with an individual's stage of development. Time spent in higher education is the culmination of formal education for many young people, a pivotal moment, encouraging them to engage in intellectual practice with both greater rigour and greater freedom than any time previously, and quite possibly any time in the future. At the same time, universities are repositories of research and knowledge that have enormous innovation potential, and are key agents in the innovation agenda, in a variety of ways (DTI, 2003; Lambert, 2003). And they can interconnect with ideas from across the world, with industry and with local and regional agenda. They therefore need to make the most of this confluence of people and ideas and have in place broad-based policies with respect to innovation, mindful not simply of the short-term potential of spin-out companies, but of the long-term investment in the creative talent that makes them the crucible of learning that they are. This applies equally to staff and students, and relates to the cultivation of forward-thinking, entrepreneurial and networked mindsets that thrive on the application of discipline and imagination in relation to subjects of investigation.

The cultivation of creativity in the context of critical practice is essential for the furtherance of the knowledge-based economy, and for redressing the innovation weaknesses that the UK has in comparison with some of its competitors. It is therefore important to ask what more could be done with knowledge-transfer activities to enhance creative thinking, and how higher education can build on schemes and structures, such as the National Teaching Fellowships and the Centres for Excellence in Teaching and Learning, to encourage a greater appreciation and development of student creativity by teachers and course designers. In addition one should consider what more can be done to encourage the cross-fertilisation of ideas between university departments and to promote entrepreneurialism in the informal or unstructured aspects of the higher education experience.

In this setting, the Imaginative Curriculum project is an important organic initiative, codifying what creativity means with respect to teaching and learning in different subjects, and establishing the best mechanisms for engagement, but the time is ripe for a larger and more holistic debate around creativity in higher education, drawing on practice in other domains and from higher education systems abroad, and covering individual achievement, idea realisation and organisational dynamics, in order to ensure we have graduates and institutions that can respond to the needs and drivers of the twenty-first century. As Michael Fullan has written:

> Policy makers will have to design policy levers which give them less control than they would like . . . in exchange for the potential of higher yield innovation and commitment on the ground.
>
> (Michael Fullan, 2003: 26)

Notes

1 The *Innovate America* report's definition of innovation is as good as any in this context: 'the intersection between invention and insight, leading to the creation of social and economic value' (Council on Competitiveness, 2004: 6).

2 The creative industries include advertising, architecture, design, designer fashion, film, interactive leisure software, music, the performing arts, publishing, radio and television (DCMS, 2001a).
3 Oral answer in response to questions following a speech to welcome the Work Foundation report on creativity in the BBC (*The Tipping Point: How Much is Broadcast Creativity at Risk?*), 28 July 2005.
4 Further information on all these initiatives can be found on the NESTA websites, www.nesta.org.uk and www.nestafuturelab.org.

3 Creativity in schools

Anna Craft

Introduction

Surviving and thriving in the twenty-first century require a sort of 'personal effectiveness' in coping well with unknown territory and in recognising and making choices. This has been called creativity in everyday life, or life-wide creativity (Craft, 2002); life-wide resourcefulness in charting a course of action by seeing opportunities as well as overcoming obstacles. This may occur in personal and social matters or in undertaking an activity in a disciplinary or professional area. It is 'know-how' (Ryle, 1949), concerned with the skills involved in manoeuvring and operating with concepts, ideas and the physical and social world – including the skills of social interaction and engagement.

It involves some knowledge. It goes beyond 'doing it differently', 'finding alternatives' or 'producing novelty', for it involves having some grasp of the domain and thus of how the ideas relate to existing ones. It does not necessarily result in a product-outcome but always involves a process. It involves the use of imagination, intelligence, self-creation and self-expression.

For educators, it means fostering resourcefulness and encouraging learners to consider and implement alternative possibilities. And as a backdrop to that task for educators, the last 20 or so years has seen a global revolution so that, in many places, creativity has moved from the fringes of education, and/or from the arts, to being seen as a core aspect of educating. Creativity is no longer seen as an optional extra. The kind of creativity being valued is a generative approach to ongoing problem-identification and problem-solving, rather than a kit-bag of pre-ordained tools for life. The reasons for this resurrection of interest emerge from a coalescence of political, economic and social change.

Why creativity in education?

The globalisation of economic activity has brought with it increased competitiveness for markets, driving the need for nation states to raise the levels of educational achievement of their potential labour forces (Jeffrey and Craft, 2001). Changes in our economy mean an increased proportion of small businesses, or organisations, employing less than five people and with a turnover of less than £500,000 (Carter *et al.*, 2004). Employment in any one organisation is not for life. We have shifted our core business from manufacturing to a situation where 'knowledge is the primary source of economic productivity' (Seltzer and Bentley, 1999: 9).

Education has a dynamic relationship with this shifting world of employment and the wider economy. Accordingly, what is considered significant in terms of educational achievement is changing. For it is no longer sufficient to have merely excellence in depth and grasp of knowledge. Creativity is critical to surviving and thriving. It is creativity that enables a person to identify appropriate problems, and to solve them. It is creativity that identifies possibilities and opportunities that may not have been noticed by others. And, it is argued, creativity forms the backbone of the economy based on knowledge (Robinson, 2001).

In the wider social environment, certitudes are in many ways on the decrease. Roles and relationships in family and community structures, unchanging for centuries, are shifting fast; a young person growing up in the twenty-first century has a much more active role than perhaps ever before, in making sense of their experiences and making choices about their own life (Craft, 2001).

Alongside all this, information and communication technology plays an increasing role, both offering potential for creativity but also demanding it, in the ways that we represent and engage with the physical and social world, demanding simultaneous operation with multiple and co-existent sets of possibilities by aligning virtual and physical space in the co-occupation of time.

Our conceptualisations, too, of creativity, how to investigate and foster it, are changing. The notion of creativity as 'universalised', that is, the perspective that everybody is capable of being creative given the right environment, is now commonplace (Jeffrey and Craft, 2001).

History of policy for creativity in schools

We can describe what has happened in schools' education policy and practice as regards creativity, at least in England, as occurring in three waves.

The 'first wave' of creativity in education was perhaps in the 1960s, codified by Plowden (CACE, 1967) but drawing on a long line of child-centred policy, philosophy and practice. The second wave occurred nearly ten years after the introduction of the National Curriculum, in the late 1990s. And the third is just beginning.

First-wave thinking and developments

The first wave, stemming from the ideas codified in the Plowden Report (CACE), left a legacy of child-centred, activity-based learning, which required a facilitative pedagogy that gave a central role to learners' interests and aimed to nurture learner engagement. This wave had far-reaching effects on pedagogy, altering the ways in which classrooms were set out and resourced, as well as how teachers grouped children for learning activities, and the quality interactions between adults and children such that adults understood the crucial role of active listening. It was, however, critiqued at many levels, and in terms of creativity, it could be argued that during this period, play became over-conflated with creativity, and creativity was both seen as strongly affiliated to the arts (and thus not to other curriculum areas) and yet the role of knowledge in creative engagement, even in the arts, was played down. The child-centred framing offered by the first wave has proved to endure; however, this early conception of creativity in education has gradually shape-shifted into a new form, via a period of what could be described as suffocation in the early years of the implementation of the National Curriculum.

Second-wave thinking and developments

The second wave has been the most significant to date. During the late 1990s, after some 20 years of creativity being out of fashion, due to the swing away from child-centred practices espoused by Plowden and previous theorists, there was a resurgence of interest in psychology and education research, accompanying policy shifts to include creativity in the curriculum of school children. Three major curriculum-based initiatives occurred:

* the commissioning of the National Advisory Committee on Creative and Cultural Education reporting at the end of the 1990s (NACCCE, 1999).
* the Qualifications and Curriculum Authority (QCA) and Department for Education and Employment (DfEE) identified 'creative thinking skills' as a key skill in the National Curriculum (DfEE/QCA 1999a, 1999b)
* the inclusion of 'Creative Development' as one of the Early Learning Goals for early years children (DfEE/QCA, 2000).

All kinds of other policy initiatives have flowed from these major developments in the second wave. These include:

* Excellence in Cities, a scheme replacing Education Action Zones and designed to raise achievement, particularly in the inner-city, the first phase of which was launched in 1999. Initially targeted at secondary schools and then introduced to primary schools too, this programme was widely believed to have led to higher attainment in both GCSEs and vocational equivalents, for pupils whose schools were in the scheme. The programme had six main strands:

    - In-school learning mentors.
    - Learning support units for difficult pupils.
    - Programmes to stretch the most able 5 per cent to 10 per cent of pupils.
    - City learning centres to promote school and community learning through state-of-the-art technology.
    - Encouraging schools to become beacons and specialists.
    - Action zones, where a cluster of schools work together.

Excellence in Cities included some schools and action zones focusing specifically on creativity (OFSTED, 2004; DfES 2005a).

- DfES Best Practice Research Scholarships and Professional Bursaries for teachers were funded for several years at the end of the 1990s and the start of the 2000s, to encourage teachers' creativity and thinking, disseminated through Teachernet on the DfES website (DfES 2005b). From 2004, the theme was continued through the Creativity Action Research Awards offered by Creative Partnerships and DfES (Creative Partnerships, 2004).
- OFSTED took a perspective on creativity through two reports published in August 2003: *Expecting the Unexpected* (OFSTED, 2003a) and *Raising Achievement Through the Arts* (OFSTED, 2003b).
- DfES published the document, *Excellence and Improvement*, for primary schools, in May 2003 (DfES, 2003), exhorting primary schools to take creative and innovative approaches to the curriculum and to place creativity high on their agendas.
- DfES established the Innovation Unit as a sub-unit of the Department, with the brief to foster and nurture creative and innovative approaches to teaching and learning.
- DfES also funded a number of research, development and CPD initiatives including a series of creative citizenship conferences throughout 2004; also a research programme which explored the application into education of Synectics, a business model for creativity (Synectics Education Initiative, Esmee Fairbairn Foundation and DfES, 2004).
- The Arts Council and DCMS were integrally bound into the delivery of Creative Partnerships and associated activities (Creative Partnerships, 2005).
- A creativity strand was established within the DTI from the end of the 1990s (DTI, 2005).
- QCA developed creativity CPD materials for Foundation Stage through to KS3, and made these available to teachers from Spring 2005 (QCA, 2005a, 2005b).
- The National College for School Leadership developed the notion of Creative Leadership for fostering creativity in pupils (NCSL, 2005).
- The introduction of the 'personalized learning' agenda (DfES, 2004a, 2004b, 2004c).

The work of the QCA in this second wave is particularly significant as a landmark, offering an attempt to both describe and promote creativity in schools. In the year 2000, the QCA initiated a creativity curriculum project, *Creativity*; *Find it! Promote it!* It hoped to exemplify creativity across the curriculum and the products of this work are being disseminated from autumn 2005. At the heart of the QCA's findings, drawing on development and research, is a creativity framework. This provides early years and school settings with both a lens and strategies, for finding and promoting creativity. Specifically, the QCA (QCA, 2005a, 2005b) suggest that creativity involves pupils in:

- questioning and challenging.
- making connections, seeing relationships.

- envisaging what might be.
- exploring ideas, keeping options open.
- reflecting critically on ideas, actions, outcomes.

There are many other aspects to it, including suggestions for pedagogical strategies and ways in which whole schools might develop their creativity, but perhaps a part of the story yet waiting to be told is the making explicit of the underlying *model* of learning, within practices that aim to nurture creativity.

Third-wave thinking and developments

We are now moving from a second to a third wave, which moves beyond seeing creativity as universalised, to characterising it as *everyday* – seeing creativity as necessary for all, at a critical period for our species and our planet. The students in our schools will help to shape the world in which they grow up and in which we grow old. Their ability to find solutions to the problems they inherit from us, and to grow beyond the restrictions we have placed upon our own world view will – more than in any other generation – define the future of our species and our planet. But the third wave *also problematises* creativity and does not shy away from some of the tensions and dilemmas encapsulated in fostering it. The discourse, then, which surrounds creativity in education is shifting to include dissidence and critique (Craft, 2003, 2005; Claxton, 2005; Gardner, 2005a, 2005b)

Conceptions of creativity

A common perspective found in second-to-third-wave work in creativity – including that which focuses on creative partnerships of a variety of kinds – is the assumption that creativity is situated in a social and cultural context. A situated perspective emphasises the practical, social, intellectual and values-based practices and approaches involved in creative activities.

A situated perspective sees 'creative learning' as an apprenticeship into these, with a central role being given to the expert adult offering induction to the relative novice. Aspects of apprenticeship include:

- *Modelling expertise and approaches*. This seems, perhaps unsurprisingly, to be particularly powerful when the adults taking a lead role in stimulating young people to work creatively are creative practitioners in their own fields, and can therefore offer novices ways into their own artistic practices. This model of teaching and learning could be seen as quite different to that of the traditional classroom teacher in a school.
- *Authenticity of activity/task*. Unsurprisingly, we know that the greater the genuine cultural authenticity of activities for the adult expert, the more likely the authenticity of opportunities for pupils to engage, transforming the relationship with the adult expert. The result is much more effective

integration of knowing that with knowing how, and higher chances of learners finding personal relevance and meaning in them (Murphy *et al.*, 2004).

- *Locus of control.* We know from work in the last 15 years by Woods and Jeffrey (Woods 1990, 1993, 1995, 2002; Woods and Jeffrey, 1996; Jeffrey, 2001a, 2001b, 2003a; Jeffrey and Woods, 2003) and in a ten-country pan-European study (Jeffrey 2003b, 2004), the importance of the locus of control resting in the hands of the young person. And the *quality of interactions* between adults and pupils determines, in large part, the decision-making authority.
- *Genuine risk-taking.* If the locus of control resides with the pupils, this can facilitate greater and more authentic risk-taking than might otherwise have been undertaken. Recent work (Craft *et al.*, 2004) suggests that it is significant that the role and expertise of the catalyst and mentors for these processes are distinct from the roles and processes generally found in schools. There could be implications here for the ways in which schools can genuinely foster children's creativity.

When the apprenticeship is led, then, by creative practitioners, it involves engaging young people in coming to understand the artist's own ways of working as a set of practices, as well as the opportunity to see work created as a part of the leader's own artistic or commercial practices.

The model of creative learning as apprenticeship emphasises the intention for young people to take ownership of ideas, processes, directions, and to engage with motivation in their own creative journey. But an apprenticeship is finite. Ultimately the novice becomes a newly fledged expert, letting go of the edges, standing alone without the scaffolding, making their own map. Creative practitioners who are particularly skilled are sensitive to when it is appropriate to encourage young people to move to the edge of, and then beyond, the scaffolding, as documented by Griffiths and Woolf (2004).

The relationship between individual and collective work

There are two other issues touched on but perhaps not yet adequately explored by the QCA framework in this particular incarnation. The first concerns the relationship between individual and collective work. This relationship, raised as an issue by Amabile (1983, 1988, 1995, 1997), and which others have continued to research (Craft, 1997; John-Steiner, 2000; Miell and Littleton, 2004; Sonnenburg, 2004; Wegerif, 2004), is still not well understood.

One aspect of the individual/collective negotiation is negotiating the balance between the creative needs of the individual and the collective creative needs of a group. Nourishment and support for the individual must be set in the wider context of others. Seeing how ideas 'land' is a part of this, and therefore so is evaluative feedback, in written, dramatic, symbol-based and other forms. Feedback is not one way; it is important for the creator to be able to negotiate meaning and possible implications with evaluators. This interactive feedback, which serves both to express and deepen disciplinary understanding and to strengthen creative engagement, is what the researchers at Harvard's Project Zero call a 'performance of understanding' (Blythe, 1999). It is an aspect of their Teaching for Understanding framework, in which precise understanding goals are taught through generative topics and assessed and developed through performances of understanding (Blythe and associates, 1998; Perkins, 1999).

In the classroom, generative, thoughtful creativity, then, takes account of the frameworks that it challenges, and emerges through conversation or interaction, and the consideration of potential impacts that new ideas may have. Ritchart (2002), also at Project Zero, describes the creative disposition as involving open-mindedness and curiosity. By harnessing these and other thinking dispositions in the classroom, we enable learners to apply their understandings and to generate their own ideas.

But this is an area we still need to know a great deal more about. For example, what are the interactions between wider culture, individual and collective creativity (Craft, 2005)? What sorts of engagement might we document and detect between the unconscious, the spiritual and the wider ecology of existence on earth (Bohm and Peat, 1989).

Developing creativity – with a caution

It may not be fruitful to consider creativity as something that can be seen as being 'triggered' in any direct or simple way; as with all social science, it is very hard to be sure of cause–effect relationships. But we do have some working hypotheses implied in some key terms: teaching for creativity, creative teaching and creative learning.

Creative teaching focuses on the practitioner. Studies (Woods and Jeffrey, 1996; Jeffrey and Woods 2003) suggest that practitioners feel creative when they control and take ownership of their practice, are innovative and ensure that learning is relevant to learners. The creative practitioner can envisage possibilities and differences, and see these through.

Teaching for creativity, by contrast focuses on the child. Recent research work (Jeffrey and Woods, 2003) has highlighted an important approach in practices that foster creativity. This approach has been named 'learner inclusive'. In other words, giving the child many choices and a great deal of control over what they explore and how. It is, essentially, learner-centred (Jeffrey and Craft, 2004).

Research (Shallcross, 1981; Torrance, 1984; Woods, 1990, 1993, 1995; Halliwell, 1993; Edwards and Springate, 1995; Fryer, 1996; Hubbard, 1996; Woods and Jeffrey, 1996; Balke, 1997; Beetlestone, 1998; Craft, 2000; Kessler, 2000; Jeffrey and Woods, 2003) suggests that a teacher who is successful in stimulating children's creativity seems to do some or all of the following:

- Develops children's motivation to be creative.
- Encourages the development of purposeful outcomes across the curriculum.
- Fosters the study of any discipline in depth, developing children's knowledge of it, to enable them to go beyond their own immediate experiences and observations.

- Uses language to both stimulate and assess imaginativeness.
- Offers a clear curriculum and time structure to children but involves them in the creation of new routines when appropriate, reflecting on genuine alternatives.
- Provides an environment where children can go beyond what is expected and are rewarded for doing so.
- Helps children to find personal relevance in learning activities.
- Models the existence of alternatives in the way information is imparted, whilst also helping children to learn about and understand existing conventions.
- Encourages children to explore alternative ways of being and doing, celebrating where appropriate their courage to be different.
- Gives children enough time to incubate their ideas.

OFSTED (2003a, 2003b) would add to this the significance of: partnership and authentic relationships with the social, economic, cultural and physical environment.

What has been described here is what Jeffrey and Craft (2004) call an *inclusive approach* to fostering creativity; one which some would say is likely to foster *creative learning* – another term that has recently entered the discourse.

Exploratory work is being carried out by many practitioners and researchers to characterise 'creative learning'. Some European work (Jeffrey, 2003b, 2004) suggests that it involves learners in using their imagination and experience to develop learning, that it involves them strategically collaborating over tasks, contributing to the classroom pedagogy and to the curriculum, and it also involves them critically evaluating their own learning practices and teachers' performance (Jeffrey, 2001a). It offers them, in many ways, a form of apprenticeship. But we still have a long way to go though in characterising creative learning.

In the second wave of creativity, then, there have been common themes to many of the policy initiatives named earlier, such as social inclusion, the role of the arts, the raising of achievement, the exploration of leadership and the place of partnerships. And entwined with these policy changes prior to and during the second wave, has been a matched growth in interest in creativity within the research community.

Following a relatively fallow period from the 1970s until the late 1980s, the last part of the twentieth century saw a burgeoning of interest in creativity research as applied to education. Research foci included the conceptualising of creativity (Fryer, 1996; Craft, 1997, 2001, 2002), exploring how creativity could be fostered and maintained (Jeffrey, 2001a, 2001b), investigation of creativity in specific domains, such as information and communications technology (Leach, 2001), documenting creative teaching (Woods and Jeffrey, 1996) and exploring creative leadership (Imison, 2001, NCSL 2005). A major direction of research into creativity, both within education and beyond it, has been to contextualise it into a social psychological framework which recognises the important role of social structures and collaborative practices in fostering individual creativity (Rhyammar and Brolin, 1999; Jeffrey and Craft, 2001; Miell and Littleton, 2004) – in other words, to *situate* it.

Since the 1990s, research into creativity in education has focused more on the creativity of all learners, rather than purely the gifted and talented. The methodology for investigating creativity in education has also shifted, from large-scale studies aiming to measure creativity, toward ethnographic, qualitative approaches to research focusing on the actual site of operations and practice, again *situating* creativity in specifics of the underlying disciplines, and in the social and cultural values and practices of the particular setting. There has also been a move toward philosophical discussions around the nature of creativity (Craft, 2002).

This was – and is – quite distinct from the earlier climate, in its changed emphases on:

- ordinary creativity rather than genius.
- characterising, rather than measuring.
- the social system rather than the individual.
- encompassing views of creativity that include products but do not see these as necessary.

Tensions and dilemmas

There are some fundamental tensions and dilemmas inherent in developing creativity. The choice of 'fundamental' is deliberate for these are rather more than mere tensions between policy and practice, although these too pose serious challenges in perspective, disconnected curricula, and curriculum organisation, to name a few. But there are three *much more* fundamental challenges, bearing in mind that, in this third wave, the education of children must nurture the creativity that will determine their ability to survive and flourish in a chaotic world.

- *Culture*. There is growing evidence (for example, Ng, 2003; Nisbett, 2003) that creativity is manifested and defined differently according to culture. To what extent can and should we take account of this in a multicultural context? Answer: fundamentally and deeply. However there is little sign of this occurring at present.
- *Environment*. How does creativity impact on the wider environment? For the creativity we are experiencing is *marketised*. It is anchored in a global marketplace that has a powerful influence on values. Wants are substituted for needs, convenience lifestyles and image are increasingly seen as significant and form part of a 'throw-away' culture where make-do-and-mend are old-speak, and short shelf-life and built-in obsolescence is seen to be positive. The drive to innovate further becomes an end in itself. And this occurs against a rising global population and an increasing imbalance between nations in consumption of reducing world resources. How appropriate is this? What significance do we accord the *evaluation* of *the impact* of our ideas on others or on our wider environment? For to do so might mean seeing creativity in perhaps a more spiritual way, in terms of

fulfilment, individual or collective. And so it could also mean taking a different kind of existential slant on life (Craft, 2005).

• *Ethics*. This is of course related to the environmental point. We want to encourage children's choices, but in a wider social and ethical context. What kind of world do we create where the market is seen as God? And how can creativity be divorced from its ends? For creativity undoubtedly also has a darker side. The human imagination is capable of immense destruction as well as infinitely constructive possibilities. How do we balance these? The role of educators, both in and out of schools, is perhaps to encourage students to examine the possible wider effects of their own ideas and those of others, and to somehow, perhaps collectively, determine worth in the light of these. This, of course, means the balancing of conflicting perspectives and values – which may themselves be irreconcilable (Craft, 2005).

These three fundamental challenges clearly leave us with pedagogical challenges. For example – if creativity is culturally specific, how do we foster it in a multicultural classroom? And how do we rise to the direct and indirect challenges posed by creativity linked to the market? How far does creativity in the classroom reflect or challenge the status quo?

Implications of schools-based creativity for fostering creativity in HE

The dilemmas discussed in the section above are relevant to how we might nurture the life-wide creativity of all learners, not only in early education and schools, but in higher education also. At the heart of these dilemmas perhaps lies a question about what ends creativity is harnessed to; the wider social and environmental 'good' being one possibility. In a marketised culture and a globalised world, where economic development is seen as uni-directional, the possibility of creativity being harnessed to social justice may be eclipsed by other, less altruistic goals. In fostering the creativity of young people in higher education, the ends are perhaps more significant and tangible than they might appear to be with younger learners.

But there are other challenges, too. For example, we need to consider the question of how to progressively expand and extend our expectations of young people as creative beings. The framework developed for the school curriculum has the potential to provide a foundation for both further and higher education. How do we address continuity and progression in what is expected of learners as they travel through the education systems?

A changing context, then, and a challenging agenda for those working with children in schools. Characteristically our creativity leads us to the edge of our current knowledge, and amongst other things produces new problems and new solutions.

It was Albert Einstein who once said: 'The significant problems we face, cannot be solved at the same level of thinking we were at when we created them.' It is this task that educators face – whether in early education, school, further or higher education.

4 Interfering with the interference

An emergent perspective on creativity in higher education

Paul Tosey

Change: a context for creativity

In this chapter, I explore how we might frame questions about creativity in higher education (HE) through the perspective of complex adaptive systems, emphasising the concept of emergence. Emergence denotes the process through which novel ideas, social forms and patterns of behaviour arise in an uncoordinated way through human interaction. It is a powerful concept that can help us consider how creativity happens in practice.

higher education institutions and the people they employ are confronted daily by continuous change. There has never been a greater apparent need for creativity at all levels of the system in order to accomplish complex change while maintaining quality and standards. Yet the spaces for emergence in HE currently seem ill-matched to the issues of change that appear most urgent to address. Various features of HE, such as mechanisms for the maintenance of quality and standards, often appear to inhibit emergence and sit in tension with creativity.

Also some connotations of 'creativity', such as imagination, originality, unorthodoxy and fantasy, appear in tension with important cultural values in HE about respectability and rigour in knowledge generation; and with needs for conformity, standardisation, accountability and risk aversion in our institutions. While generating the outputs expected of us in HE undoubtedly involves creative processes, it is perhaps regarded more as a subset of innovation (as is implied by Hannan and Silver, 2002).

Here I explore the question of how to enhance conditions under which emergence seems more likely to occur, illustrated with examples from contemporary experience of working in the HE sector, particularly by removing or obstructing that which inhibits emergence. To adopt a phrase I have used elsewhere (Tosey, 1993), I argue the need to 'interfere with the interference' and consider potential strategies through which to achieve this.

Do we need to create creativity?

A well-known Congolese drummer, TaTitos, was asked how new compositions are created in that culture. TaTitos replied that there are three methods. In the first, a new piece of music is presented to someone in their dreams; in the second, musicians notice and build on mistakes they make while they are playing, and generate new variations from those errors; in the third, someone consciously constructs a new composition. However, TaTitos added, there are no known examples of successful composition using the third method.[1]

Discussions of creativity often focus on how individuals can be more creative. Why cannot our people be more innovative, or take more initiative? Why are the ideas coming forward for research or development projects so lacking in imagination? The perspective of complexity is more that creativity is latent or inherent in human systems. We all dream and we all make mistakes, but can we create and sustain conditions in which that capacity can flourish?

Last year a colleague and I were developing a new module on organisational change. The design was fine, but still relatively linear and un-integrated until one morning in the summer I awoke around 3 a.m. to find the metaphor of 'change as a drama' in my awareness. Luckily when I shared this metaphor with my colleague the next day, she welcomed it and we began to explore its possibilities together. Both the content and the process for the module quickly cohered around this central idea. Later we formalised this design through a written module outline that received approval at a Board of Studies. While this became a product recognisable to the formal systems of the institution, it feels important to honour the creative dreaming, the gift to the unconscious, and not to diminish or distort this by pretending that the metaphor was a rational product of my intellect.

This example also illustrates the way that creativity is triggered by constraining events or circumstances. We had already been given the task of designing and delivering the module in a timescale of just a few weeks. Had we been asked to design a module but not deliver it until we were ready, it would perhaps still be on the drawing board. This view of creativity does not entail a romantic notion of total artistic freedom in which constraints are negative; necessity is the mother of emergence as well as of invention.

Creativity is also social and collaborative. As with the Congolese drummers, connections and relations in which individuals are fully engaged are vital if dreams and mistakes are to become manifest as new forms. This steers us away from the dominance of the view that creativity is a matter of individual genius. However, in human systems, people are also skilled at creating conditions that inhibit or interfere with creativity. The management of human systems is often orientated towards predictability, control and rationality, thus inhibiting or interfering with emergence. UK HE, in common with many public, organisational worlds, seems to insist upon 'consciously constructed new compositions' – virtually every proposed new programme or module, and every research proposal, has to be fully justified and costed, and demonstrate to the satisfaction of the gatekeepers who will judge them (rationally and objectively) that they are more or less guaranteed to work.

We may not need to create 'creativity' so much as generate conditions in which it can flourish. The espoused need for creativity and innovation in HE is, it appears, in considerable tension with pressures in practice towards efficiency, certainty and conformity. Spaces in which dreams and mistakes stand a chance of taking hold and growing seem, to those who work in the sector, to be much constrained – ever smaller gaps in increasingly dense networks of formal structures and procedures – as evidenced, for example, by perceptions of teachers as to what inhibits creativity gathered through the imaginative curriculum project (see, this volume, Jackson, Chapter 1; Fryer, Chapter 7; Wisdom, Chapter 14).

Complexity and emergence

Complexity theory (see, for example Lewin, 1993; Reason and Goodwin, 1999; Stacey *et al.*, 2000) refers to a cluster of ways of thinking that have developed over the past decades from branches of 'new science' concerned with the behaviour of natural systems, such as Chaos Theory (Gleick, 1987), Dissipative Structure Theory (Prigogine and Stengers, 1984) and quantum physics (Hey and Walters, 2003). Waldrop (1992) offers an accessible introduction to complexity studies, especially through developments at the Santa Fe Institute[2] in New Mexico, which uses the following definition:

> Complexity refers to the condition of the universe which is integrated and yet too rich and varied for us to understand in simple common mechanistic or linear ways. We can understand many parts of the universe in these ways but the larger and more intricately related phenomena can only be understood by principles and patterns – not in detail. Complexity deals with the nature of emergence, innovation, learning and adaptation.
>
> (Santa Fé Group, 1996, cited in Battram, 1998: v)

Theories of complexity are fundamentally interdisciplinary, and are of contemporary interest in many fields. These include management (e.g. Lissack, 1999; Stacey *et al.*, 2000) and education (e.g. Fullan, 1999, 2003; Tosey, 2000; Fenwick, 2003; Cooper *et al.*, 2004; Haggis, 2004). Broadly, complexity offers a way of thinking about human systems.[3] Specifically, it offers a radical and innovative frame for professional educational practice, particularly away from the idea that leaders, managers or teachers are in control. It treats human systems as directly analogous to nature, which is rarely predictable and linear.

It is important to also note that this view is contentious. Some relevant issues are summarised by Houchin and MacLean (2005: 152), who suggest that, 'Our best use of complexity theory for understanding organization development may be as a metaphor giving us new insights... However, even that has to be treated with caution...'. Others (for example, Reason and Goodwin, 1999) argue that there is firm epistemological ground for applying the ideas of complexity to human systems.

The systems studied at Santa Fe are known as 'complex adaptive systems'. These systems consist of assemblies of 'agents' which interact with one another. It was found that computer models could simulate the behaviour of natural systems (such as flocking – Waldrop, 1992: 241) through quite simple rules of interaction. Yet, despite this apparent simplicity, the results of the interactions were unpredictable from knowledge of specific interactions between agents, a fundamental feature of complex adaptive systems. Such systems are also adaptive in the sense that they both respond to and proactively shape the environments or contexts in which they exist.

Human systems are considered more complex still (Stacey *et al.*, 2000), particularly because the 'agents' – people – are complex systems in their own right. Their interactions may not always be governed by simple rules, even though when interaction is observed the rules might be revealed as more simple than the agents themselves believe to be the case. Human beings also have intentionality and reflexivity (Reason and Goodwin, 1999); they can reflect awarely on events, can construct meaning, and can decide to (attempt to) ignore or change the rules.

Even so, human systems appear to display many of the characteristics of complex adaptive systems. In particular, coherent patterns of behaviour can arise from the apparently idiosyncratic interactions of random individuals. This property of complex systems, a phenomenon known as *emergence,* is highly significant. It refers to – 'the process by which patterns or global-level structures arise from interactive local-level processes. This "structure" or "pattern" cannot be understood or predicted from the behaviour or properties of the component units alone' (Mihata, 1997: 31).

Thus, in complex adaptive systems, large-scale effects can arise even though no single agent had intended to produce them – analogous to the way that TaTitos and his colleagues might build on a mistake to produce a new composition.

Authors such as Goldstein (1999) and Johnson (2001) offer helpful introductions to the notion of emergence. While emergence involves unpredictability, new forms coming out of apparently disconnected, even irrelevant, thoughts and sensations, and an inability to force or control the outcome, it does not seem to be a completely random thing. There are times when it is more likely than others, and there are conditions that appear to encourage it.

Conditions for emergence

Many people have struggled with the question of the conditions that foster emergence, as we could consider the presence or absence of such conditions as possible indicators of the propensity for creative change in an organisation. Drawing on much of the work in this field, Richard Seel (2002) has distilled a tentative list of seven conditions for facilitating emergence in human systems (see also Seel, 2005). These are:

* *Connectivity* – emergence is unlikely to occur in a fragmented world.
* *Diversity* – if there is not enough diversity in the system, it will be hard for different patterns to emerge.
* *Rate of information flow* – either information overload or too little information flow can make emergence unlikely.
* *Lack of inhibitors* – e.g. inappropriate power differentials, too much anxiety or threats to identity can all inhibit emergence.

- *Good constraints to action* – effective boundaries can enhance the possibility of emergence.
- *Positive intention* – a clear sense of purpose can influence the chances of emergence occurring.
- *Watchful anticipation* – while a clear sense of purpose can influence the chances of emergence occurring, a period of expectant waiting is often necessary to facilitate emergence.

I make reference to some of these conditions through reflections on experiences of creativity within an HE setting, focusing particularly on connectivity. As above, the emphasis will be on interfering with conditions that inhibit emergence.

Why should higher education institutions be creative places?

From a complexity perspective, HE institutions cannot help but be creative. They are full of capable people who are constantly using their ingenuity in interaction with others. However, there is also a paradox to address. As acknowledged above, structures and other conditions that may be regarded as inhibiting emergence are themselves the products of creativity. This highlights some of the difficulty with the term 'creativity'.

According to Stacey, organisations are best described as patterns of what he terms *complex responsive processes,* such that 'human futures are under perpetual construction through the detail of interactions between human bodies in the living present . . .' (Stacey, 2001: 6). Thus we can conceive of institutions as ever-changing conversations – patterns of gesture and response, meaning and commitment. If these interactions are rich and diverse, novel forms may emerge, and enable creative and adaptive change. If not, the institution may be doomed to repeat itself until it is so far out of alignment with its environment that it starts to exist within a time warp. The propensity of these conversations for generating novelty is crucial.

This view does entail some epistemological problems, which I want to acknowledge even though I will not attempt to examine them here. For example, it seems hard, without the wisdom of hindsight, to say which forms of novelty – and which forms of stability – are the more likely to represent creative, adaptive change.

The broad argument, however, is to regard human systems as directly analogous to evolving, ecological systems. The greater the tendency towards uniformity, and the less the appearance of random variations, the lower the adaptive capacity. The context in which the HE sector operates is likely to change in unpredictable ways over time. A lack of mutation and capacity to generate novelty will harm the chances of survival and prosperity.

A simple model developed by Stacey (Stacey *et al.*, 2000), the 'agreement and certainty' matrix, often referred to as the 'edge of chaos' diagram (see Figure 4.1) aims to encapsulate this idea. To give a simplified explanation of this, an organisation (or sector) that creates increasing agreement and certainty

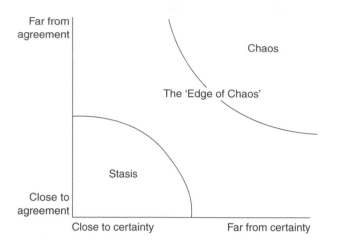

Figure 4.1 'Agreement and certainty' matrix (adapted from Stacey *et al.* 2000).

moves towards the bottom-left corner of the diagram. This is suitable in stable, known circumstances. Decreasing agreement and certainty, on the other hand, creates movement towards the zone of chaos to the top right. At the extreme there is too little commonality to hold an organisation together – for example, there may be no agreement on the basic purpose for its existence.

Stacey's argument is that, in an uncertain and changing world, organisations need the capacity to operate just at the margin of that area, far from agreement and certainty but without becoming wholly chaotic. This margin is known in complexity thinking (e.g. Waldrop 1992: 230) as 'the edge of chaos' (Fullan, 2003: 22, refers to the 'edge of order'). It is at this edge, where uncertainty, difference and risk-taking have more space to generate creative thinking and action, that the propensity for emergence is thought to be at its greatest.

All our domains of work involve self-determined events and pressures, and external forces that trigger needs for creativity – for example, financial viability and needs for funding; student feedback and external examiner reports; QA audits; Research Assessment Exercise scores; government policies for increasing and widening participation; the introduction of e-learning or personal development planning. For various reasons, mostly well-intended, the direction of our creative responses to these triggers in HE is often towards the zone of stasis. Houchin and MacLean (2005) argue that this happens because organisation functions as a *defence against anxiety*; rather than displaying the characteristics of natural complex adaptive systems, they suggest that human systems self-organise defensively towards stability.

To illustrate this, my institution recently went through its Institutional Audit managed by the Quality Assurance Agency. One comment,[4] in the context of a positive report, was to question the basis for variability in practices across the institution. This certainly sounds reasonable from a student's point of view – should not differences in practice, which can have real consequences for success or otherwise in study, have a sound institutional rationale behind them?

To use the statement as a trigger for reflection, however, is there also an underlying message about what types of differences are acceptable? Are differences fine where they can be rationalised, but not where they exist 'only' because of custom and practice? Because if we were to restrict acceptable difference to that which can be rationalised (and defended?), even more random errors would tend to be eliminated before they could grow into new compositions. Equally, it implies to me that the avenues for change become restricted largely to what is achievable through institutional-level agreements to vary policy.

This may contrast with Richard Seel's condition of 'watchful anticipation', such that it may be necessary to wait before the value of a new idea becomes evident and palpable, especially an idea that appears at odds with the prevailing stasis. The speed and pervasiveness of change confronting HE may lead us to reject a creative idea prematurely because it does not fit with the prevailing mind-set in the organisation, or because there are more pressing needs for our attention:

> If we want to learn anything we must pay attention to the information to be learned. And attention is a limited resource . . . a great deal of our time is committed to the tasks of surviving from one day to the next . . . To achieve creativity in an existing domain, there must be a surplus of attention available.
>
> (Csikszentmihalyi, 1997: 8)

Arguably, large-scale changes, like for example the contemporary system-wide development of personal development planning, require many individuals to have the time to develop, experiment, evaluate, learn from the experience and try again. In this context, watchful anticipation means that commitment is required over many years. Institutions need to provide enabling environments to encourage a multiplicity of creative ideas and practices, only some of which will work well.

In summary, HE institutions are necessarily creative places. However, from a complexity perspective it may be that the emphasis of our creativity is too often towards the zone of stasis on Stacey's 'agreement and certainty' matrix. In other words, we tend to use our creativity to converge and control. Michael Fullan shows us the direction we need to travel:

> Operating at the edge of chaos means also resisting the temptation to impose too much order . . . Policy makers will have to design policy levers which give them less control than they would like (they never had it anyway) in exchange for the potential of higher yield innovation and commitment on the ground.
>
> (2003: 26)

Good constraints

A complexity perspective reduces the risk of a romantic fallacy that polarises, say, creativity and bureaucracy, because it recognises that constraints enhance emergence. I recognise the contribution of constraints to creativity in HE practices with which I am involved, and acknowledge that I like working within constraints so that I am not overwhelmed by possibilities.

One example of a perceived constraint is the prevalence of frameworks of learning outcomes, programme specifications and the like. I know of colleagues who rail against this perceived tyranny, and I have sympathy with them sometimes. If learning outcomes are used as a very linear and literal device and have the effect of taking away the unknown, the adventure, the discovery, the risk, then it seems that education becomes a routine and programmed affair.

I like to think that in a Master's programme that I lead, we have not only embraced but also integrated learning outcomes, using them creatively (a possible indicator of our success in doing so was a good national Subject Review in 2000[5]). The process of specifying outcomes really challenged and helped me to be clearer about the educational aims I was working towards. But I maintain that we have managed to design spaces and opportunities for students to use and demonstrate their creativity, and that we recognise and reward their creativity through the forms of assessment we use within the constraints of the learning outcomes model.

An example of a 'good constraint' is the programme's use of learning contracts (Knowles, 1986). At first sight a learning contract format can look rigid and restrictive. Indeed it becomes so if used as an instrumental, tick box exercise, where the process of designing a contract becomes overly rational and task-driven, a product of thought without feeling or intuition. This can happen, for example, if students rush through as a defence against the anxiety of contemplating an ambiguous task.

In order to interfere with the propensity for a learning contract to be an interference to learning itself, our programme requires each person's contract to be negotiated with a small group of peers, through iterative meetings taking place at intervals over three days. We encourage these 'learning sets' to inquire, supportively and also with challenge, into each person's developmental needs and goals. The timescale gives opportunity for dreaming, such that the goal of the contract will often (as reported by students) emerge from the unconscious. Developmental tasks chosen by participants in the initial module (on theories of learning) are widely divergent and have included professional learning such as computer skills, but also salsa dancing and planting a tree. Used in this way, the learning contract becomes a discipline that supports creativity by channelling energy and focus, not a mechanism that obstructs it.

In summary, emergence is much more likely if there are some clear constraints to possible action. How do we interfere, then, with the propensity for a constraint to interfere with emergence? I suggest that:

- there is a significant difference between observing the spirit and the letter of apparent constraints (yet observing the spirit does not mean the letter can be ignored).

- it is possible to integrate and transcend both the literal demands of the constraint and the desire for an absence of constraints.
- dreaming, serendipity and the like can be complemented, refined and honed, but not replaced, by critical rationality. It is perhaps where rationality becomes too dominant that we need to worry.[6]

Connectivity

Early studies of emergence showed the importance of the right amount of 'connectivity' (Kauffman, 1996). It is not essential that everyone is connected to everyone else, indeed that is likely to inhibit emergence – modern network studies (e.g. Barabási, 2002; Watts, 2003) suggest that emergence is more likely where there are a few key connections between groups.

Teaching and learning in HE often restricts connectivity between staff and students. Student feedback tends to highlight personal contact with academic staff as very highly valued aspects of their experience. Yet for various reasons again – time, quantity of students, discomfort with personal, face-to-face contact with students – this connectivity is inhibited. The advantages of electronic contact are balanced against its propensity for student alienation, thus it cannot be assumed automatically to enhance connectivity.

Peer-to-peer connectivity between students is more commonly encouraged. Peer learning exists in many HE programmes (Boud *et al.*, 2001; our Masters programme is designed as a 'peer learning community', Heron, 1974), and again the use of e-learning to promote connectivity, using techniques such as chat rooms and discussion groups, seems to be increasing rapidly. Even so, except where a common task is expressly required or negotiated, connectivity between students is often peripheral and voluntary, not integral or task-led. The potential for collaborative learning often sits uneasily with the idea that, usually in HE, an individual's particular contribution should remain discernible. This is perhaps another idea with which we need to interfere in order to enhance emergence through connectivity between learners.

Compare the often constrained 'vertical' connections between staff and students with the rich variety of possibilities for lateral, peer connectivity amongst academics. Bodies such as the UK's Higher Education Academy (formerly the Learning & Teaching Support Network) have made great efforts in recent years to enhance connectivity within HE. There are now many more generic or subject-specific electronically linked networks of interest in UK higher education than there were five years ago. Paradoxically, while global connectivity has been vastly increased, local connectivity often seems less rich. I imagine that most HE professionals still work in environments in which informal contact is perceived as non-work; and in which the basic structure is the single-cell office.[7] I often seem to have more contact with people across the globe through electronic media in a day than I do with colleagues who work on the same floor.

Yet the prevalence of networks also illustrates the principle that there can be too much connectivity. For many of us, the quantity of such networks creates excessive information flow, which then potentially interferes with emergence. The sheer quantity of traffic arriving through discussion groups and networks can tip us over into chaos or cause us to not engage. This may then trigger a self-organising aspect of complex adaptive systems; we as individual agents are more selective about the messages we read or, if our passions and interests do not align enough with the time available, we resign from discussion groups. These individual decisions impact on the overall pattern of communication – some may flourish through this spontaneous pruning, others can lose diversity and become predictable, perhaps repeatedly relying upon the same agents as contributors.

Developing wider conversations

In tune with complexity thinking, I focus on creativity as a process through which locally developed new ideas and practices become engaged in, and are taken up through, wider conversations. So far I have considered aspects of emergence mainly within a teaching and learning context. While individual students may experience transformative learning from their engagement in an innovative programme, this can still make not one iota of difference to my institution or to the HE sector.

In the terms used by Watzlawick *et al.* (1974), innovative teaching and learning practice may still only represent 'first-order' change from the perspective of institutions and the HE sector. First-order change is essentially an adjustment within an existing set of alternatives, a move within an existing set of rules. This is contrasted with 'second-order' change, which transforms the rules themselves and so creates new possibilities. This represents some qualitative shift in the set of alternatives available and might involve some transformation in systems, or co-creation of a new environment.

Compared with the connectivity within our Masters programme, that between the programme and institutional systems within which it operates has been far more limited from the point of view of creativity. I reflected in an earlier paper (Tosey, 2000) on the extent to which I have filtered and suppressed its radical potential myself, aware, for example, that taking up a particular student suggestion could bring me into conflict with various university rules or procedures. I own that often I have responded as a representative of the wider system, articulating to students a rationale to explain why their suggestion is not possible – an example of my own capacity to elect to defend against anxiety.

At the same time I often felt frustrated that our programme practice, acknowledged as innovative and excellent by students, external examiners and quality reviews, remained an island. Many factors militate against spontaneous take-up of this practice by other programmes and by HE staff (quite apart from the 'not invented here' syndrome); programme structures that do not conform to institutional norms; the need for staff to possess specialist skills (e.g. in group facilitation); and very high demands on staff time and commitment. In view of this, it was perhaps naïve and arrogant to expect others to adopt similar practices spontaneously. In terms of complexity, here was a creative idea that represented difference, one that by all accepted indicators was excellent, but which failed to catch on.

Or *had* failed to do so. In 2004, this programme practice was the basis for a successful bid to HEFCE's Fund for the Development of Teaching and Learning (FDTL5) scheme, for a project designed to generate related practices across my institution at undergraduate level.[8] In other words, this project now represents an emergent, wider conversation, a connecting up of innovation within a single programme to the potential for change elsewhere. If this dialogue can generate more 'connectivity', it may have more chance of stimulating second-order change, at least within the organisation, and possibly acting as a catalyst for similar change in other institutions, which is the intention of the FDTL programme.

The project can itself be seen as an example of emergence through *constraints*, in that qualification for the FDTL5 scheme resulted from the 2000 QAA Subject Review,[9] a process regarded by many as a prime example of excessive HE bureaucracy. The principle of *connectivity* was also relevant. Price and Shaw (1998) note that, from a complexity perspective, we are concerned with the evolution not of genes, but of 'memes', ideas that catch on and flourish (or not). Rather than lead with a concept peculiar to our programme practice, like 'the peer learning community', we chose to focus on the meme 'enquiry-based learning' (EBL), which linked our bid to a wider, current conversation. This remained true to the programme, which we have always portrayed to students as enquiry-led, as well as echoing a theme in contemporary usage. The same meme is also being taken up by our university's Centre for Excellence in Teaching and Learning (CETL). A downside is that the meme 'EBL' may mask aspects of the *diversity* represented by the Masters programme. For example, the programme's emphasis on the emotional dimension of learning is particularly challenging (both as a meme, and in practice) for many HE staff, and seems not to sit in the foreground of thinking about EBL.

We believe our bid also engaged with a conversation that was of concern to the funders; that of how to promote 'transferability' of good educational practice. This was not something we foresaw, but emerged and became more significant through conversations at events for those developing bids. The project is predicated on experimentation with an enquiry-based approach to change, which is itself intended to be consistent with an emergent approach by supporting local users in co-creating developments that meet the educational needs of the context. We are aiming for this rather than the transfer of an existing 'best practice' because we suspect that the latter stance may also inhibit emergence. It is not easy to disseminate the creativity of others. All too often, policy-makers, managers, educational enhancement organisations and others make the mistake of believing that the main task in disseminating the ideas and products of innovation is to find something useful that someone has invented, and provide opportunities for people to learn about it. This is a very rational, benign, but naïve, theory of transformation. The real work of adaptation and transfer requires people to have the permission, support, time, motivation and energy to create their own local meaning and practice out of someone else's innovation.

As a postscript, the Educational Studies department to which the programme belonged no longer exists. The FDTL5 project is not the only phoenix that has arisen from the department's ashes, however, and from a complexity perspective, the demise of the department also represents an example of emergence; perhaps a more creative adaptation than its continued survival might have been.

Leading emergence: enabling creativity

What does this mean for those who are in positions of formal leadership in HE? More realistically, what are we going to do about this together? None of us are to blame, in that we are all tacitly and unawarely reproducing what Peter Scott-Morgan (1994) calls the 'unwritten rules' of our game. There is no villain of the piece who, if expelled, will allow us to be more creative.

If we are also all responsible and if, as I have argued, the answer is to seek to 'interfere with the interference', how do we do this? There is no master plan that represents any comprehensive answer to this – again, that would be incongruent with a complexity perspective. As Fullan (1999) and others have argued, rational strategic thinking has not worked and will not work. Complexity requires us to change our epistemological stance towards creativity and change; according to Stacey, there are no privileged observers, which means that we cannot stand outside our programmes or institutions and manipulate them, we can only influence through our participation:

> When one moves away from thinking that one has to manage the whole system, one pays attention to one's own participation in one's own local situation in the living present. Perhaps this humbler kind of 'management' is what the 'knowledge society' requires.
>
> (Stacey, 2001: 235)

I would add to this Fullan's (1999) emphasis on the moral nature of change agency. Enabling creativity is not a technical endeavour, to which complexity theories can be recruited just to help us be more sophisticated. It involves values, power, conflict and risk, and requires courage to pursue moral purpose.

With this in mind, and building on Stacey's message, let me offer three possibilities for interfering with the interference. First, there is an argument that there may be very little we can do. Whether or not we become more creative within institutions or within the sector, our efforts will mostly constitute first-order change; our destiny is more likely to be determined by second-order, macro economic and social changes. While I am not inclined to be as fatalistic as this, it is worth bearing in mind that we are part of a wider ecology and not privileged to determine our own fate. The positive value in this stance is in letting go of our striving to be more creative, because it is one of the paradoxes of complexity that 'action planning' or trying to find the answer can itself interfere with emergence. The message here is one of simplicity and humility: keep on working with quality at a local level, because it matters to those whom we serve, and have faith that it matters more widely too.

Second, in the sphere of organisational consulting Patricia Shaw presents 'the assumption that the activity of conversation itself is the key process through which forms of organizing are dynamically sustained and changed' (Shaw, 2002: 10). From this perspective, appropriate action consists of attending to our participation – engaging in, noticing and aiming to nudge, the unfolding meanings and energy. Price and Shaw (1998) argue, perhaps more reassuringly, that we can also work in more structured ways because it is possible to identify and change the 'unwritten rules' that so strongly shape a system's capacity for emergence. The message here is to work without plans but still to perceive our actions, conversations and contact with others as opportunities to stimulate and influence emergent memes, particularly by creating 'connectivity', and mindful of the principle that small changes can result in dramatic, large-scale effects.

Third, the ideas associated with complexity entail apparently counter-rational ideas. Seel's (2002) 'conditions for emergence' (Table 4.1) link in here by suggesting relevant types of action that would contrast with more traditional, linear ways of leading and following.

The message here is to challenge ourselves: are we operating through a command and control paradigm, rationalising our actions as being common sense or determined by the systems within which we work, when from an emergent perspective we may be neglecting to seek alternatives, or defending against anxiety?

In this spirit, I would invite you to consider experimenting locally with some relatively random actions, and to be curious enough to notice what happens as a result (or, alternatively, what continues not to happen as a result of not experimenting). This list may seem trivial as well as random, yet I imagine that some of these actions would involve risk and courage within our HE institutions today:

- Be seen having fun in the workplace by people for whom you are likely to be a role model.
- Redesign any aspect of a physical environment in which you work in a way that improves 'connectivity' between people.
- Read one of the following, and have a conversation (with anyone you choose) about what you would need to do to *avoid* putting any of it into practice: Bateson and Bateson's *Angels Fear* (1988); Fullan's *Change*

Table 4.1 Command and control versus emergent organisations (Seel, 2002)

Command and control paradigm	Emergent paradigm
Keep people in 'silos'	Build connectivity
Ensure everyone 'salutes the flag'	Encourage diversity
Manage communication initiatives	Have conversations in corridors
Blame people for failures	Learn from events
Make it clear who's in charge	Give everyone leadership opportunities
Tell people what to do	Tell people what not to do
Set objectives	Agree clear goals
Keep busy	Wait expectantly

Forces with a Vengeance (2003); Lao Tzu's *Tao te Ching* (1963); Price and Shaw's *Shifting the Patterns* (1998); Wheatley's 'Leadership and the New Science' (1999).

* Acknowledge, respect and build on someone else's creative idea before you decide to knock them down: as Yeats wrote, 'Tread softly because you tread on my dreams'.[10]

Having read the list, note the objections that arose whilst reading them – these are likely to embody the key 'unwritten rules' that are interfering with emergence. Aspects of anxiety and lack of time may well feature in these. And if you found no objections, then you are probably already adept at enabling dreams and mistakes to give rise to novel forms, and will have understood, better than I do, the applied dimension of what I have just been talking about. Please carry on interfering.

Notes

1 I heard this story during a training course in Neurolinguistic Programming offered by PPD Ltd. It originates in work by Grinder and DeLozier (1986), though does not appear in publication to my knowledge.

2 www.santafe.edu/

3 See also Zimmerman's article for an introduction to this model www.plexusinstitute.com/edgeware/archive/think/main_aides3.html.

4 'The team advises that the University consider more clearly defined methods to monitor variability with respect to the operation of quality assurance processes and the assessment of students across the University since some of the variation noted by the auditors appeared to be mainly the product of inherited custom and practice and insufficiently informed by University's published guidance on academic standards and quality management' www.qaa.ac.uk/reviews/ reports/ institutional/Surrey04/ summary.asp

5 Online, Available at: www.qaa.ac.uk/reviews/reports/subjReports.asp?subjID =9#S.

6 These general problems of the relations between conscious and unconscious processes are the subject of much writing by Gregory Bateson (Bateson, 1972; Bateson and Bateson, 1988).

7 I am indebted to Professor If Price, Sheffield Hallam University, for his thoughts on this issue – which emerged, incidentally, through a chance conversation.

8 www.som.surrey.ac.uk/learningtolearn;
www.escalate.ac.uk/index.cfm?action=resources.project&ID=1707.

9 At which time the Master's programme was within this institution's School of Educational Studies.

10 From 'He Wishes For The Cloths Of Heaven', *The Wind Among The Reeds* (1899).

5 Students' experiences of creativity

Martin Oliver, Bharat Shah, Chris McGoldrick and Margaret Edwards

Introduction

This chapter describes the first of two studies in two universities undertaken within the Imaginative Curriculum project whose purpose was to illuminate the way in which students and staff experience and understand creativity. In this chapter the views of students are examined.

Methodology

Given the lack of an established, commonly agreed framework for interpreting perceptions of creativity, an exploratory approach was adopted. Semi-structured interviews were conducted at two sites (the same institutions as studied in Chapter 6); in addition, one focus group was conducted using the same structure, to see whether interaction with other students would lead to further elaboration. Students were invited to explain what they thought 'creativity' was, to contextualise this by identifying and describing creative people or things (both within and outside of formal education), to discuss their experiences of creativity in the curriculum (and particularly assessment) and to speculate on whether they thought their course would develop their creativity in ways that might be useful to them in later life. A total of 25 students were interviewed (including four as part of the focus group). They were sampled so as to represent a broad spread of disciplines (including Anthropology, Architecture, Arts, Biomedicine, Clinical Psychology, Earth Sciences, Education, English, Fine Art, Geography, Humanities, Library and Information Sciences, Medicine, Molecular Biology, Psychical Sciences, Social Sciences and Urban Design). Participants were selected so as to provide an even distribution by gender, age (classified as 18–21 or mature; there was a slight imbalance towards the 18–21 age range) and year of study (first, second, third or postgraduate). The interviews were recorded and transcribed, and a constant comparative categorisation carried out to analyse the data. The categories that emerged from this are reported in the following section.

The study

Conceptions of creativity

When asked, many students found it hard to explain what they thought creativity was. Rather than giving one coherent, integrated account, they typically drew on a number of different discourses, often presenting contrasting or even inconsistent positions at different points in the interviews. Several attempted to dismiss their inconsistency by saying they were talking 'rubbish' or by being apologetic; others were hesitant in their responses.

Creativity was discussed not just in terms of what it was, but also in terms of how it worked or how 'intense' it was. These ideas have been grouped together, to show the contrasts that were present. Rather than being explicitly defined, creativity was typically described using ideas such as:

- *Freedom from routine* – not being bound by conventions, schedules or expectations.
- *An expression of imagination* – this was often associated with the idea of creativity as personal; it was also used to describe things that were done or invented 'in the head'.
- *Personal* – something that could only have been created by that person; linked to this was the idea that creativity was subjective.
- *Independence* – that it is associated with an escape from social conventions, rules or forms, and was thus primarily an act of individuals.
- *Risk* – something felt to be 'synonymous' with being creative.
- *Superficiality* – not always in a negative sense. This conception was primarily concerned with being free from having to justify decisions or creations.
- *Commonplace* – this suggests that everyone is creative, every day.
- *Infectious* – something that can be caught by being with others (teachers or students) who have it.

It was also felt that creativity could differ by degree.

- *Incremental* – this relatively common conception recognised a limit on creativity, suggesting that small improvements rather than a radical break with tradition are what should be expected. ('You can't be completely creative in what you do, cos there's a huge background to it, which you can only build on slowly.') This included the idea of bringing existing things up to date.
- *Original* – the sense that creativity was something more than just repetition. This was also associated with 'novelty', and the suggestion that what was created was in some way personal or a break from tradition, or with 'progress'. It was also associated with seeing a problem that others could not see, which allows new development to take place, or with serendipity, which prompts new connections to be drawn.
- *Radical* – the belief that something creative should be entirely new and original, being unique or 'groundbreaking', but certainly not 'obvious'.

The process of creativity was also discussed. These discussions drew on ideas such as the following:

* *Being struck by the muse* – 'something that you get at moments', outside of personal control ('you don't try and force it'), almost viral or like lightning.
* *Metacognition* – that being creative requires the ability 'to step back and look about what you've done, kind of a personal grace, almost.'
* *Escape from reality* – creativity was sometimes associated with a sense of detachment from day-to-day concerns; 'everything else leaves your mind and you're just in the moment.' Sometimes this seemed to be a side-effect; at others, this was presented as the point of being creative. This was generally associated with a sense of relief and with happiness.
* *Framed expression* – linked to the idea of incremental novelty, this conception suggested that to be creative involves working within some kind of framework. It suggests the idea of creating something that other people can *recognise* as being of a type. Where 'rules' were mentioned, these were usually seen as negative, in the sense of being rule-bound.

Nature or nurture?

As well as talking about what creativity was and how it worked, students described how they thought people 'had' it. Broadly, three models of creativity were used:

* *Innate* – something inherent to people, often something that is intuitive rather than (like a muscle) something to be activated or exercised. The capacity for creativity was not described as being the same for everyone, however.
* *Nurtured* – something that can be developed, perhaps through exercises or upbringing. One student suggested that creativity was all nurture, and that 'people can learn anything at all if we want to'.
* *A potential* – this combined nature and nurture by suggesting that people had some upper limit to their capacity for creativity, but that they could work towards achieving this. This was presented as a process of discovery.

These different models have implications for pedagogy. If students see creativity as innate, it makes little sense to teach it; if they see it as potential, then they may excuse themselves (or others) for poor performance on the basis of biology rather than effort. Nonetheless, they did see creativity as being associated with academic success – or at least, with success in some academic disciplines.

> I do think it is associated with intelligence. I think creative people are bright people. I don't think that all intelligent people are creative. But I think that all creative people are intelligent. I think you can be a professor of biology but not be necessarily be creative. But I think that if someone who's fantastic at the arts, or the music or drama or what have you I think, I would say, it was given that they were intelligent but not the other way around.

The conception of creativity as something that can be nurtured is where the notion of pedagogy becomes most important. Even here, however, the scope for teaching as a kind of intervention was seen as limited. Far more important, several students felt, was age. This reduced the value of any planned intervention in favour of deterministic, typically biological changes. However, students were not consistent on how they felt that things like age influenced creativity:

> I think it's harder to be creative when you're younger because you're not sure enough of yourself and I think its confidence as well to be creative. And I think that when for example you're a teenager or late teens any way of standing out is bad and being too creative is bad you know, you just want to be the same as everyone to fit in.

> I think all children are quite creative and kind of exploratory.

This inconsistency may result from the differences described above about what 'creativity' is. Where creativity was believed to be amenable to development (of a non-deterministic kind), study skills and other techniques related to learning were mentioned, but these were not considered to have great impact. Far more important, students felt, was wide life experience.

> If you are good at learning, you are more likely to take on new information and you can use that to expand your creativity. But it's not that much of a difference because there is a lot of creativity from the travelling and just experiences that's the main thing but there's a little bit from learning.

These perceptions raise questions about whether students will see any value in courses that claim to be about the development of creativity.

Creativity and role models

Since the concept of creativity was understood variously and used complexly by students, they were invited to identify and discuss individuals (both from within and outside of academia) whom they believed to be creative. This was intended to help them to elaborate the notion of creativity through reference to specific cases.

Outside of academia, an incredibly broad range of people were described. These included family, friends, sportsmen, musicians, people in the media and so on. The explanations offered were equally diverse, including:

- Being subversive, for example by rejecting convention.
- Not having had a traditional upbringing (so that their creativity arises from the lack of 'fit' with the dominant culture).
- Being able to 'read' social developments, so as to predict (and then influence) emerging trends.

Within academia, examples often focused on key figures from a field (Darwin, Einstein, Wegener, Hawking, etc.); such people were singled out for the 'leap' they made. Creative academics were also described in terms of creative pedagogies, such as making insightful but surprising links between areas of content. (The relationship between creativity and teaching is considered in more detail later.) However, there was a contrast between creativity and students' perceptions of academic professional identity. For example, a Medicine student suggested:

> If you've got someone who's quite dogmatic or someone who's only interested in basing things on an evidence and research basis it's just not going to happen.

Students made it clear that it was easier to assess the creativity of the dead, since there had usually been more time for their contribution to be recognised and valued.

Additionally, some students made it clear that, although such individuals might serve to exemplify what it meant to be creative, they were not 'role models' in the conventional sense because their example rarely inspired action.

> Watching something about somebody who is creative and then thinking, wow, they are amazing! But then it doesn't really normally go further forward. I kind of think wow, that day, and the next day I'm like yeah but I've got to do all this stuff. I think for me to suddenly be creative I'd have to [. . .] have a different lifestyle, so it's not going to happen. Not in the sense of being really creative.

Creativity outside of study

Another way of eliciting examples of creativity from students involved asking them about creativity outside of the context of their studies. The participants found this both easier and more positive than their discussion of creativity within the curriculum. Some comments identified things that students felt were creative. These included artistic activities (music, drawing, film, poetry, acting, etc.), cooking (when varying or working without recipes), competitive sports (focusing on tactics and out-manoeuvring opponents, or receiving cups, medals and awards), running a small business, making money, home improvements, playing practical jokes and so on.

> I'm quite creative in ways to get money. I mean I hate working. I hate work. No, I'm not lying about that. I hate working in pubs or offices or anything like that. And recently I've been doing the medical trials and stuff like that, so I get money for like sitting on my arse basically. [Laughs]

> I'd say my housemate Caroline is very creative because she plays practical jokes on my next door neighbours. Like putting gnomes in their garden.

The arts were so dominant as a point of reference that some participants felt the need to make their awareness of other contexts for creativity explicit.

> Creative is not just arts things.

Other comments were concerned with things students felt helped with creativity. These included physical exercise (as a way of reducing stress), being with creative people and reading or watching something inspiring. Some students suggested that study pressure was squeezing activities such as these out, either because it took up too much time or left students feeling tired. With cooking, for example, 'I'm busy and tired I don't want to experiment, I just want to do something that is simple and quick and done for me.' Creativity was seen by one student as something to be 'indulged'; it was an extra, and life and study would survive without it.

> Doing the degree appears to be about creating space rather than creative space.

There were also examples that focused on social or cultural contexts. One student talked about 'countries where it is less kind of regimented' in formal education, for example, citing pressure to perform for relentless examinations as something that impeded children's ability to develop their creativity. Others discussed friends and family, particularly the influence of parents, suggesting that being around people who were creative encouraged or inspired personal creativity (almost like a virus). Common to many of these examples was a concern with 'whether creativity is valued or is not valued' by those around you.

Motivation

The interviews were often animated, sometimes passionate; the topic was emotive, and students provided a rich picture of the ways in which creativity and motivations interacted. There were, for example, diverse reasons why students sought to be creative. Some concerned personal expression; others, competition or ambition. Some suggested that creativity arose from situations, such as problems that had no obvious solution. Other reasons were less expected, but entertainingly frank.

> Money makes me creative.

> Getting no sleep, drinking lots [laughs]. Cos in the middle of the night I find that I'm most creative. And alcohol induced I'm most creative.

Predominantly, however, it was felt that being creative made things more interesting and more satisfying, suggesting a positive link between experiences and creativity. This was not universal, however; some students saw creativity (and the expectation or valuing of creativity) as a source of great pressure, leading to anxiety and requiring courage to overcome.

> Anna used to introduce her own ideas into essays and then she would get a first, whereas I always felt frightened to do that so I didn't really do that very much.

> There's an infinite amount of possibilities; it's really, really daunting. [. . .], I'll do whatever I want and it might be something completely different, which is incredibly satisfying but it's terrifying as well.

By contrast, though, some saw it as comforting, almost therapeutic, or at the least, escapist.

> When I was about 14, I used to write a lot of poetry. And I wanted to be creative because it helped to understand a lot of what was going on in my head. And to get that feeling down on paper in that kind of way helps you to release feelings. [. . .] I guess it kind of gets you away from reality and provides this fantasy land that's just a break from normal life.

Students talked about being scared, feeling inadequate and even being concerned about becoming socially alienated. They also pointed out that when experiencing such feelings, or when feeling unhappy or depressed, people were less likely to be creative.

> I think people are happier when you don't deviate too much from the norm. Because creativity can sometimes be stuck together with being eccentric and being a bit bizarre and sometimes [people] don't like it when you're too creative. It can be threatening I think for other people who aren't as creative.

Creative teaching

Students explicitly discussed kinds of teaching that they considered to be creative and, in relation to this, identified things that they felt limited their scope or desire to be creative themselves.

Some comments were simple suggestions for teaching techniques that could be used to provide a contrast to current teaching. (Such contrasts typically portrayed current teaching as transmissive and dull; however, in context, it seems likely that this is a rhetorical description rather than a judgement about their courses.) Examples of techniques included role playing (by the teacher, not the students), debates and creating posters that were then presented to the class or displayed in a public place.

Students on vocational courses pointed to work placements, often as an explicit contrast to their academic study. They identified the people they encountered and the problems that arose in that situation as requiring the new solutions to be created, or existing ones to be adapted; it was also suggested that personal style could be expressed in such situations in a way that was not always possible within the formal educational component of the course.

> How am I being creative in my course? Well not academically, but we do [...] work three days a week, so when I'm at work I'm working with [clients]. Then you are being creative because you are tailoring an intervention to them and the changes that happen throughout time. So you're constantly modifying. It's not really creative because to some extent there is a protocol. I guess I'm most creative when I've got the protocol and I put a bit of myself into the [work] that I'm doing.

Some conventional forms of teaching were also felt to support creativity. These were inevitably dialogic, and focused on opportunities for discussion that addressed students' current understanding or beliefs. Some students did talk about free-for-all ideas generation sessions such as brainstorms, although there were also reservations about these:

> Everyone likes that. And you feel free to say whatever you want to say without having to back it up so yeah so that's sort of being creative. [...] Just thinking I can just say something, it's my idea, it's, maybe it's a bit off the wall and it isn't substantiated and in that informal setting you can do that, but [it's] nothing you would ever hand in on paper.

Generally, though, students discussed things with more obvious structure and purpose, akin in many ways to the conversational model of learning proposed by Laurillard (1993). Seminars and tutorials were mentioned several times, for example. One-to-one tutorials were felt to be particularly valuable, since there was scope to try out ideas without worrying about how peers might perceive you. Informal group work and projects were also identified positively, as were fieldwork, case studies and other situations in which the discussion focused on artefacts or situations. Other comments concerned qualities of the teacher, rather than techniques. For example:

> If a teacher is passionate about what they are talking about, what they are lecturing on then that really inspires the pupils I think.

Other things that were identified seemed to fall between values and techniques – providing encouragement, for example, giving examples or offering feedback. Whilst these are all techniques, it was the *use* of these (rather than just their existence) that was stressed. These were valued not just because they were present, but because they were introduced by the teacher in response to students' needs in an attentive, supportive way.

In addition to these practices that either are creative or which are felt to support creativity, students identified many things that limited or inhibited creativity. As before, some of these point to a perceived contrast between creativity and acceptable academic work:

> Our course is widely known to be academic, consult the literature, base your practice on the evidence, bang, bang, bang, tick all the boxes, thank you very much. So my view of our course is that it is a conveyor belt.

Several comments described similar situations, perhaps best summarised as 'rule bound'. It was not even that creativity was absent from these courses – however, it could be perceived as 'token' creativity, or creativity as a reward for enduring the 'proper' part of the course, which simply served to highlight by contrast the limitations on creativity within the curriculum. Other reasons tended to be more prosaic. Time, unsurprisingly, was mentioned repeatedly. For some, this meant that the schedule of the course meant that they could not wait for creativity 'to happen'; instead, they had to perform to deadlines (of which they generally felt there were too many) or to apparently arbitrary rules introduced for the convenience of the teacher, whether or not they felt inspired.

> My deadline would be my deadline, it would stop when I felt that I was finished, or I felt that I was happy, rather than because I've got to stop this piece of work now, I've got to wrap it up, because I've reached my word limit, or because the deadline is tomorrow and I've got no more time.

For others, this concerned the intensity of life, so that time cannot be set aside to be thoughtful and reflective. It was this sense of pressure, of being 'stressed out', that they felt inhibited their creativity, constantly forcing them to consider practicalities and details. As one student summarised, 'you need time and space in your mind to be creative and if your mind is full of studying and this that and the other then there's no space for it.'

Failings of lecturers were mentioned, but not extensively. If a lecturer was not inspiring, this would not prevent students being creative in their own studies (see below), for example. However, lecturers who were 'dogmatic' or rule-bound were felt to limit students' capacity to express their creativity.

Creative study

Just as students described creativity in their teachers' practices, they also discussed their own. They deemed this to be particularly important, since they felt it was learning, not teaching, that was central to their academic success; bad teaching might not inspire, but it did not prevent learning.

One particularly common strategy used by students involved making links across different contexts – for example, by applying principles learnt when studying a different discipline, by contrasting contemporary and historical perspectives on a topic, by expressing personal perspectives (something contrasted with accepting facts), creating artistic designs or images as part of study and so on. One student highlighted the whole area of interpreting texts as a creative endeavour:

> I think reading books means you go off into this other world of the book, which is not reality, so you are using the creativity of the writer. And also when you are writing about books you have to think about ideas about things and ideas about the book, is being creative.

Books were not the only resource deemed to help creativity; case studies and videos were mentioned too. The Internet was also mentioned, as much for the thought-provokingly unpredictable results of search engine rankings as for the volume of material available. Such comments did not tend to show the discriminating selection of resources that many information literacy courses now seek to inculcate, however (e.g. SCONUL, 1999).

> The Internet, I know it's quite general to everywhere but I think it can help to be quite creative. [. . .] For example, the other day I went on the Internet to do some research for an essay and I don't know, I typed in mirror, because that's what I'm doing my essay on, and there's like loads and loads of sites on 'mirror'. And I don't know it's just a fountain of knowledge really.

The environment in which study took place was felt to be important. Several students stressed the importance of comfort ('a big, comfortable chair or something'), and many identified 'distractions' such as music, exercise or a window to look out of as being important.

> I think breaking things up is relaxing – I need a mix of physical and mental – that for me helps the ideas along.

However, other participants spoke of exactly the same distractions in negative ways; the key to this was in whether the student had the *choice* to distract themselves in such ways. Similarly, both being alone (because it provided space to reflect) and being with others who were creative (because this inspired) were mentioned as things that supported creativity. These two areas combined to highlight a problem in the design of libraries:

> The architecture of the libraries – it doesn't work to be open plan – it's difficult to concentrate there. Talking things through – say new IT – can be a big help, but there are too few really quiet study areas where you can concentrate.

Although many students experienced limits or frustration over opportunities to express themselves creatively within their academic work, a few discussed the creative ways in which they 'played the game' of academic study. Some students talked explicitly about strategies for work avoidance, up to and including the deaths of fictitious relatives. Others talked about how they created an acceptable image of themselves in order to progress, with one student admitting, 'I just basically lied on my UCAS form.' Students sometimes said they felt shame about such incidents, but some seemed to take pride in what they had achieved; they were proud of their creativity, even if they felt some guilt about deceiving tutors.

Creativity and assessment

Assessment has long been recognised as being amongst the most important influences on learning (Biggs, 1999). Unsurprisingly, it was also considered vital to discussions about creativity. Criticisms of exams featured strongly in the interviews. These were typically described in ways that linked them to transmissive, rote-learning pedagogies (or at best to the application of standardised protocols), and these discussions stirred up considerable emotion.

> Having exams, for goodness sake, it makes me so mad, most people on my course have an average age of about 28, and that, I think I should mention that, that we have to go into an exam and give them back what they have given us in a year of lectures. I don't see why we have to do that when we've proved ourselves academically. And that is something as well because you just regurgitate information. Waste of time.

> My learning environment is that it is pretty much one, two, maybe three ways of approaching this but only three. So if you choose one of them within a framework you're alright. If you don't tell us about one of these then it's wrong.

Essays were felt to be better than exams, since they were seen as offering greater opportunity for personal expression. (This was not believed to hold true for essays under exam conditions, where time pressures were felt to limit opportunities for this.) It was suggested that students who valued creativity would opt for essay-based courses because of this. Other students only partially agreed, suggesting that although essays permitted self-expression the academic context limited opportunities to use imagination, because 'there is a set way to do it'. (This sense of frustration at having to conform to expectation pervaded many discussions of assessment and will be returned to below.) Some also felt that markers' expectations of authoritative writing meant that they could never move beyond exploring existing arguments and into creating their own interpretations:

> The idea of being creative when your trying to write an essay or something that you don't know about is very difficult because [...] you don't know enough about it, yeah. I think you need to be a bit of an expert perhaps to be creative, because you have to be able to draw a lot of things together and appraise them and then do something a bit more radical.

However, essay-based coursework was felt to support creativity through collaboration, as some students discussed the use of peer criticism to improve their work.

There were two broad reasons why exams were seen as a problem. The first relates back to one of the conceptions of creativity, in that such scheduled assessments were seen as being at odds with being struck by inspiration.

> It's also about spontaneity isn't it? So you can be creative and you've spent a month revising and your head is full of crap.

The second reason concerned forms of assessment. Students did not suggest that their work should not or could not be assessed, but they did express the opinion that alternative forms of assessment would be more appropriate. Suggestions included, for example:

- Being observed with clients or in the workplace, for vocational subjects.
- More coursework or project-based assignments.
- Expressive elements such as creative writing, graphic design, image/video/animation production, and so on.

Creativity, academia and the disciplines

In many students' comments there was a sense of frustration at a perceived conflict between being creative and being 'academic'. Many of the students experienced academic values as being controlling, conformist and inflexible, more concerned with producing 'clones' than supporting new ideas. These students framed their experience in terms of rote learning, spoon feeding and regurgitation.

Such criticisms are easy to sympathise with, but there were also comments that revealed a different side to students' experiences. There were complaints about being bound to topics and ideas raised by previous work, being restricted to using certain methods or protocols and being forced to use evidence rather than imagination.

> In my research project I'm addressing new questions trying to devise a theory but again it's tightly linked to what has gone before so I think you're stunted a bit. If you too creative that you are told that there's not enough basis to what you're saying and that you're talking rubbish.

This class of comment suggests a railing against *discipline*, the sanctioned forms of practice and participation that characterise particular academic 'tribes' (Becher, 1989). What this implies is that if Becher's characterisation is correct (and it is certainly widely accepted), then some students are opposed to what it means to be an academic. Without needing to resort to a value judgement, this simply reveals that there is a mismatch between what some students want and what higher education is currently like. (The politics of which party should be expected to concede ground are outside the scope of this chapter.)

It is important to point out that not all students were dissatisfied with their experience of academia. Indeed some came to appreciate the creative endeavour of academic work, even if they tempered this with the suggestion that it was somehow not for them:

> The more I learn about theories, even [...] strict academic ones are quite creative as well, the thoughts that they had.

> Geography is a discipline, it is very progressive and because of creativity, a hundred years ago, geography meant just exploring and mapping and through a process of creativity someone has decided that has to change [...] That's how it spread out into so many different disciplines from a very limited spectrum of things to encompassing so much. [...] So you can get cultural geography, you can look at ethnicity and how that affects people's perceptions on life and the way they live. And similarly it has also been pushed on the other side, the physical side of geography more. To more imaginative ways of looking at past, to try and reconstruct histories of climate and things like that. And that's the kind of creativity that keeps the discipline going and keeps it a worthwhile discipline, but that's the kind of thing that comes from the best geographers, not from undergraduates.

Students' experiences were, in fact, complex; their perception of the value of creativity depended on the teachers they had, their own history and the subjects they were involved in. Generally speaking, there was a perception that some disciplines were more creative (and consequently more valuing of creativity) than others; unsurprisingly, this was portrayed as a contrast between Arts at one extreme and abstract, rules-based subjects like Mathematics at the other, with Humanities being relatively creative ('it's based on one person's experiences') and the Sciences as well as many vocational subjects, such as Medicine or Engineering, being relatively constrained, rule-bound and 'more about learning facts'. Interestingly, one student suggested that this hierarchy of control and conformance explained the unequal value attached to different subjects:

> Dance and drama – you know, they're not necessarily academic subjects, they're certainly much more creative, but they're not given the same value as an academic course.

However, even within 'uncreative' disciplines, some students admitted they found ways to be creative, such as developing short-cuts or quicker approaches that helped them in their work.

Creativity and students' identities

Many of the discussions about creativity touched on how students see themselves, how they would like to be seen or how they thought academics would like them to be. Such concerns have a direct relevance to curriculum designers;

although some students would be sceptical that creativity can be 'taught' (see 'Nature or nurture?', page 45), studying for several years was felt to influence how students saw themselves.

> I've been doing my course for over two and half years now, so I guess it's involved me being creative and it's involved my mind developing so it's helped me become the person I am now.

As with all parts of this study, there were differences of opinion about how positive this experience was. Some students saw themselves as developing, increasing their capacity for creativity. For others, it was a struggle, confusing and unsettling even though it was productive.

> It's basically just conflicting personalities in one massive building. And it can get really jarring and you know its really exhausting. [. . .] I remember in the first year, why aren't I more like him, or why aren't I more like her. [. . .] The flip side of it is, that it is incredibly satisfying when you. . . I mean, it's really character building, when you get, you find your, your, your voice.

For some, academic study was a process through which this aspect of their personality was ground down.

> I don't think they want us to be radical. Clones of one another. We're all the same, people who are selected for the course. We're all very similar. Similar backgrounds, no-one's slightly wacky. They've selected people who are hard working, conscientious, will meet their deadlines, which are reliable, which isn't to me necessarily creative people.

The production of particular subjectivities (such as, in this case, 'the creative student') is an area usually considered in terms of individuals' self-expression; here, however, the combination of teaching, assessment and ethos is intended to produce certain sanctioned subjectivities in others. Holmes (2002), however, has talked about the production of 'graduateness' as an emergent identity, considering how students come to make claims about their 'graduateness' in a way that others (such as potential employers) choose to affirm or deny. His analysis identifies four kinds of outcomes to such identity-forming processes:

• Agreed identity (claimed and affirmed by others).
• Failed identity (claimed, but not affirmed).
• Imposed identity (not claimed, but affirmed by others).
• Indeterminate identity (neither claimed nor affirmed).

This provides a constructive set of analytical tools to explain some of the claims made by students. For example, those who railed against the discipline of their course might be seen as having a failed identity as a creative student (in that they claim to be, but this has not been affirmed by their teachers), or even an imposed identity (in that their teachers deny the relevance of their claims and instead affirm that they are something else, such as studious, wilful or lazy). This may explain some of the tensions experienced by students seeking to express themselves within the context of academic study.

Conclusions

Students' experiences of creativity in the curriculum are complex and often confusing. Participants typically drew on diverse, even inconsistent ideas about creativity to discuss their experiences, in some cases moving between incompatible positions in the same sentence. This suggests that creativity is something that students are not used to discussing and quite possibly lack a shared common frame of reference to interpret.

Nonetheless, the range of discourses used does throw some light upon the ways in which they might approach 'creative' learning. The aversion to constraints and deadlines, the denial of responsibility for instigating creativity (e.g. discourses of infection or being struck), talk of subversion and the wish to be free from routine or constraints all point to a desire to challenge the structures of formal courses. This may be an attempt to escape from the duties of study or disciplines of higher education, but it could equally reflect the difficulty some students expressed in reconciling their creativity with the need to produce assessments on demand. Some ideas (such as creativity within contexts, or as being incremental and commonplace) do fit well within structured notions of curricula, but generally, there seemed to be a desire for spaces within the course that were open to risk-taking, free from the need to justify decisions and where failure was an opportunity for learning rather than a problem.

The participants were able to discern things or people they felt were creative. However, these examples tended to operate as families with similarities, rather than as illustrations of some well-understood concept. Nevertheless, students were able to discern differences of kind (such as the nature/nurture discussion) and degree.

Although there were many students who gave examples of creativity in academic contexts, the picture that was painted in these accounts involved frustration, a sense of control and restriction, and a lack of value of creative endeavours. This was in contrast to their experiences outside of academia; interestingly, but worryingly, some students had come to understand this as a reflection that creativity was essentially different to 'academic-ness'. A significant majority of students had positive things to say about individual teachers, often without prompting, and lecturers were often identified as the things that most helped creativity; the problems they identified were mostly attributed to structures such as assessment conventions or the perceived hierarchy of subjects. Many were also able to identify opportunities to improve current practice, such as by the adoption of different assessment techniques.

Perhaps most interesting, though, are the tentative suggestions that even where creativity was not taught, not considered teachable and not valued in assessment, it was still relevant in defining how the students saw themselves.

The use of creativity as a discourse – currently so confused and inconsistent – becomes vital in this respect, since claims to an emergent creative identity can only be warranted if they can be articulated. In this sense, it may be possible that even a small change – helping students learn how to talk about creativity, particularly in the context of their study – would have an important effect, enabling students to lay claim to creativity in a way that currently eludes them within academic contexts.

6 Creativity and curricula in higher education

Academics' perspectives

Margaret Edwards, Chris McGoldrick and Martin Oliver

Introduction

The concept of creativity is contested and, as yet, imperfectly understood (Sternberg and Lubart, 1999; Osborne, 2003). Much current research is exploratory and little is currently written specifically about creative learning and teaching in the context of UK universities. Much of what does exist proceeds from the assumption that most students are capable of some creative work at some level; that creativity can contribute to the lives of individuals and societies; and that its encouragement among academics and students is a central part of universities' missions. This chapter synthesises discussions involving academics in two universities in order to explore their perspectives on creativity and the curriculum. The relationship between these is critical to understanding what higher education needs to do to create the spaces within its curricula to promote students' creativity. The diversity of views on these topics serves to illustrate the complexity of these concepts in practice. The structure of the study permits a number of comparative questions to be asked. For example, how much convergence or divergence is there in the views of lecturers in two very different institutions – a post-1992 university and a research-intensive Russell Group university; and between the disciplines that were represented?

Methodology

This research was undertaken between 2002–4, when the Imaginative Curriculum project commissioned two studies that examined academic teachers' views on creativity and the curriculum at Liverpool John Moores University (LJMU) (McGoldrick and Edwards, 2002) and University College London (UCL) (Oliver, 2002). Interviews were used to elicit perspectives and, to give consistency, a common semi-structured approach was adopted. Interviews were recorded and transcribed, then analysed by constant comparative categorisation. A total of 32 academic staff were interviewed, 14 from LJMU and 18 from UCL. The sample was designed to include a range of disciplines and of staff experience. The subjects represented include Architecture, Arts, Biomedical Sciences, Built Environment, Business Studies, Dentistry, Dutch, Education, Electrical Engineering, Engineering, English, French, Law, Library and Information

Science and Physics. Levels of responsibility for curriculum design (or re-design) varied from programme coordinators to junior teaching staff. Staff with a central support role in learning and teaching were also represented.

Findings

A context for conversation about the HE curriculum

Before attempting to explore the link between curricula and creativity, it is useful to provide some context about what academics thought 'curriculum' meant. Use varied widely, ranging from 'syllabus' and programme plans, to notions of the hidden curriculum, in which the social, cultural and political context (what some participants described as the 'fuzzier bits') was counted as part of what was taught. Predominantly, these notions of curriculum described plans of one kind or another; consequently, when talked about in this way, 'creativity' had to be interpreted as something that could be planned for, scheduled and anticipated.

However, one conception of the curriculum emerged that offered broader possibilities for understanding creativity. This was the idea of the 'lived' curriculum – this included talk about the curriculum as experienced in the classroom. The lived curriculum arose dynamically out of interactions with students:

> You've got to improvise – it's like a performance in a way. One in which the audience can heckle and change the ending [...] you just have to prepare as best you can and then cope.

Conceptions of creativity

'Creativity' was recognised to be a complex, contested concept that is poorly theorised, as acknowledged in many accounts (e.g. Czikszentmihalyi, 1999: 313). Some participants were aware of this complexity explicitly; for others, it manifested through the confused and sometimes inconsistent ways in which they used the concept. Examples of confusion arose in relation to the overlap between discourses of creativity and those about innovation, novelty, imagination and 'genius'.

This section attempts to identify common perceptions across disciplines. Some features of 'new-ness', for example, were present in all accounts, but it was recognised that the nature of the 'new' would be assessed according to criteria applied by academics within the disciplines.

Most participants considered that creativity included most of the following main features:

- *A quality of 'new-ness'* – 'Pastiche ... or straightforward copy', though newly-made, was not felt to be creative work (although it could be a precursor to it). However, what was no longer new in some particular context could be reconstructed imaginatively in others to produce a creative outcome.

- *Original* – This was, perhaps, the extreme end of the idea that creativity expressed 'new-ness'. It was suggested that creative work involved a 'certain excitement: the Eureka! feature'. It was felt to be 'different' and interesting for the producer and for those who encounter the work.
- *Related to traditions of work* – 'Creativity (is) not an individual – "I stand on the shoulders of giants" (attributed to Sir Isaac Newton) – or context-less achievement'.
- *A break with tradition* – For some, creativity was contrasted with received wisdom. Active language suggested that creativity was about ongoing processes rather than discrete decisions. The students were:

> Not ... having to produce according to some formula, they're ... having to think about things as they go – and I guess that's what I see as being the key to the creativity thing, not just going with the routine, safe, pedestrian options, but pushing the boundaries, trying things out, and if it seems sensible, really going for it ... it's a matter of us ... teaching in a different way than the one in which we were taught.

- *Different by degree* – Specific acts were judged as being more or less creative. At one extreme were works of genius, including anything 'which has far-reaching significance over time'. In contrast, one participant saw 'curriculum design at the ... weakly original end!'
- *Personally new* – Undergraduate attempts at creative work were, in general, considered to be less creatively significant than those produced by experienced academics, but it was considered important to give credit for trying to go beyond the boundaries of what a student had previously achieved.
- *Expressed through a product* – This could be a design, an essay or a model; Without some production, 'creativity remains at ... the imaginative idea level'.
- *Recognised* – There was doubt expressed that 'creative' work 'existed' without recognition. It was also felt that expertise in a domain was important in recognising creative work. In the context of university work, however, it was suggested that disciplinary tradition might also impede recognition of creativity. (This concept is clearly related to the idea of creativity being related to traditions of work.)
- *Useful* – 'It works – at least for the present.' However, it was recognised that there could be a planned and deliberate separation of practical purpose from experimental work at the 'prototype' stage. This was difficult ground and drew on the idea that creativity should be expressed through a product which had to 'work' in someway. For example, one participant criticised a particular student's design 'where imagination o'er leaped any technical resources [... This] was not judged to be creative, but over the top.'
- *Ethical* – Some participants felt that certain creativity ought to be seen as good not just in some general, abstract way, but by being linked to morality. For example, 'so-called creative accounting [could be] innovative ... exciting for the practitioners and so on', but was potentially destructive of

companies and livelihoods in the longer term. Consequently, some participants felt that 'it's our job to indicate limits' of acceptability.

- *Trivial* – Some participants felt that almost every act a person takes
  involves an act of creation; consequently, on this broad and inclusive interpretation, everyone is creative already.
- *Hard* – In contrast to the above assertion, some participants felt that 'depart-
  ing from familiar practice or cherished notions ... it's hard'. Thus an
  important part of encouraging student and academic creativity involved the
  motivation to develop imaginative ideas into creative work.
- *'Motherhood and apple pie'* – Very similar to the notion that creativity was
  trivial, this idea questions whether the concept of creativity had any dis-
  criminatory power. For example, one participant asserted: 'I should think
  everyone wants their students to be creative, rather than dull automata, so I
  should say that this ... is taken for granted. It'd be a bit like saying you
  want your students to be breathing at the end of the course.'

Generally, the renewed official interest in 'creativity' in education was given a
qualified welcome. It was felt to be 'unthreatening in the sense that good
teachers have always tried to stimulate ... creative work', although there was a
concern that 'there will be a try to SMART it'. SMART – Specific, Measurable,
Assessable, Realisable and Time-related – is an acronym commonly used to
judge whether some objective is manageable. It is widely advocated that learning objectives should be SMART, which has drawn criticism that those things
that are valuable but hard to measure will be neglected. Clearly, the same
concern about capturing the letter of the concept but losing its spirit was present
here.

Creativity and the individual

It is not necessarily a *feature of 'ability'* and may not be measured by university
assessment. The relationship between 'intelligence' and creativity is debated. High
intelligence and creative work are not necessarily associated, for example. Nickerson (1999) explores important dimensions of this debate.

Curriculum designs for creativity

Participants' comments suggested that creativity is unlikely to be incorporated
into curriculum designs unless it is explicitly valued either by students or by
influential academics in the discipline or department. There is little evidence in
participants' responses of the rational, structured design processes so prevalent
in the educational literature; instead course planning appears to involve orientation to norms (academic or cultural) rather than being a formal process of
designing from first principles. Typically, meeting needs, rather than analyti-
cally moving from course aims towards content and format, was more important. Needs were identified as familiarisation with the basic knowledge of the
discipline, generating student interest and consideration of the 'likely audi-

ence'. Other influences included the opinions of external examiners and colleagues.

Processes akin to constructive alignment (Biggs, 1999: 44–6) were noted, but in intent rather than in method. There was only one instance of formal design processes being used, and even here it was as a reflective aid when refining an existing course rather than to design a course from first principles: 'I have tried to think more about what I . . . want students to come away with at the end of the course, and try to work back from there'. Instead, participants described the majority of curriculum designs as being either a form of bricolage or an iterative process of refinement and readjustment. Curriculum design was thus seen as a creative act in its own right, although not necessarily one that promoted the creativity of students.

> I looked at it and delivered it for the first time, and I know what to change in the next year. So it's an incremental thing

In fact, such processes of re-design, rather than design per se, were what dominated discussions. Re-design happened informally and on an ongoing basis, in response to academics' experiences or student comments. More systematic changes arose from the five-year curriculum review process, especially when it was felt that the ongoing revisions had been so extensive that the curriculum looked as if it had been 'tweaked too often' and lost its coherence.

Institutional arrangements for student feedback were not felt to be particularly effective in either university. Students could regard them as 'an annoying routine', and academics rarely found this type of feedback helpful ('because . . . they just tick the numbers, and the numbers are arbitrary anyway – what does plus two mean?'). Student representatives on Boards of Study and informal feedback were found to be much more helpful. Generally, however, students tended to concentrate on details and 'not to be all that insightful about the whole curriculum'. Within this discussion a number of themes emerged:

Core knowledge – 'core' elements were identified as vital prerequisites for further study: 'to do [this subject], there's a certain core knowledge that you have to give to students . . . the concepts . . . and the maths to be able to apply and solve problems.' More generally, the 'core' was not seen as a logical pre-requisite, however, but as the result of social conventions, thus open to contestation: 'There are continual debates about what belongs in the core course and what doesn't, and it's an evolving organism for that reason.' This idea relates back to the notion that creativity 'has to be grounded', operating within a tradition: 'Accepting any curriculum is politically and value-driven . . . there's usually enough course team consensus [on] the foundations . . . [without which] students are not in a position to be creative in the context of their course'.

A personal act of sense-making – for some, the first step in designing a curriculum involved making sense of the discipline. This was particularly visible when faced with problems, such as designing for novel or controversial topics, or when an academic inherited a module on an unfamiliar topic and had to master new literature:

You have to fall back on your own creative processes. [This involves] a lot of brainstorming, actually. . . . You actually start asking quite deep and diffi- cult questions, like what classifies as [this category], how do you know – if nobody else is teaching this, why is nobody else teaching it? Is it something quite specialized that only my students are going to be interested in? Is it something that other people have found too difficult? Does it fall under, into other types of courses as maybe just a sub-category? You know, I mean, you ask, you ask questions – because absence is significant.

Internal orientation – this involved designing the curriculum to fit within a wider context, such as building on prerequisite modules or giving relevance to follow-on modules, taking account of existing offerings and departmental prac- tice, and focusing on the students and their needs. Generally, this was felt to be helpful in providing a grounding for design. Indeed, one participant focused on the difficulties of designing a 'widening access' module that was supposed to have no prerequisites. Internal orientation was not always positive, however; it could constrain creative practice by encouraging status quo.

External orientation – in addition to locating a module within the contexts of a course and department, most participants made comparisons with courses taught elsewhere. This process provided inspiration, developed a sense of the 'norm' within the curricular area being established, and located student resources. The location of the course in relation to others in the university, or to courses elsewhere in the world, were some of the more complex external orien- tations. Taking account of the needs of potential employers was also important.

Creating spaces – several participants noted how 'crammed' curricula tended to be, attempting to cover an ambitious range of topics. A recurrent theme in interviews was the need to replace some content with 'creative space' – areas of the curriculum where teacher and students felt able to try things out and negotiate what should be done, and how to do it. Such spaces created opportunities for 'more relaxed pedagogy and . . . discussion, workshop, individual feedback – you need this for deeper understandings'. Important features of such 'creative space' were that it should be enjoyable ('I'd want to make it fun!'), part of the course, but not so tightly assessed that risk-taking and the exploration of ideas were inhibited. Moreover, it was felt that the 'space' was not boundless. As a curricu- lum designer, 'your creative act is in trying to build in these spaces . . . in a way . . . which will still allow students to feel secure that there is a curriculum and that they aren't just in a free for all'.

Teaching for Creativity – slightly distinct from the design process were dis- cussions of the techniques that teachers associated with creativity. Several approaches were identified that were felt to support and build students' creativity:

- *Developing critical thinking* – this could be initiated with fairly simple tasks, then built upon. For example, one participant talked about the need to 'build in assessments and discussions which . . . from level 1 . . . question . . . official positions, from governments, pressure groups, academic writing'.

- *Encouraging lateral thinking and problem-working.*
- *Move between the university and 'outside'* – this could be achieved through the use of case studies, study visits, or hearing or working with external teachers, such as visiting specialists in the field or employers. The general principle was to 'get students outside classrooms ... with the chance to hear new voices ... and then critically review them ... [since] the business view can be uncritical'.
- *Give space for group work* – 'This can be informal working in a practical session – get students to report a summary of discussion orally – and at least once a year, include ... some assessed group work'.
- *Increase student confidence (in staff and student colleagues)* – fieldwork, off-site visits and social occasions were considered helpful to 'collegiality' and confidence. 'Without confidence in the context, creativity doesn't happen ... students *must* be confident in order to try new things ... I must harness developing confidence and foster enthusiasm – the two together – it's more interesting for me, too!'
- *Have fun!* – 'Most students (as I am) are averse to sitting and listening for long periods – 2-hour slots? Break them up with listen – activity – discuss – summary'; 'Brighten up dull walls ... could a small assessment involve 'doing a wall' with posters created from recent work?'

Generally, creativity was felt to be served by being able to draw on a wider repertoire of teaching approaches, rather than just relying on 'the cliché of lecture, seminar, lecture, seminar...'. Being forced, for example, to consider the needs of part-time students made one participant think in new ways about how a course could be taught. Similarly, one participant discussed the need for creativity when designing curricula that were intended to appeal to able students who had left university because of financial and other pressures. A number of these students were first-generation undergraduates with no family financial resources to draw upon, making part-time employment a necessity. Could the curriculum be designed in more flexible and creative ways in order assist them? It was felt that university space and systems could be used more flexibly, although there were considerable resource implications:

> What about the undergraduates who cannot come into the university in a conventional way – perhaps for financial reasons? It should be possible, for example, to come into laboratories at unconventional times – give them tutorial support. It is not satisfactory, but life is not satisfactory. However, it may be the best we can do for some students. ... Open learning is difficult for undergraduates – as we have found. ... We would also need more flexibility of exam opportunities. Further, pay as you go is more affordable for many students.

However, several participants noted that students did not always welcome new approaches to teaching. Students who lacked a grounding in 'core' parts of the course (particularly within science) often seemed to prefer academics to be 'teaching to what they can comfortably learn'. Further, the optimistic view that student creativity increased as autonomy was developed through the course was questioned. Some staff believed that students become encultured during their time at university, coming to expect the 'lecture/seminar' cliché to less comfortable alternatives. This sense of the conservative student may appear negative and perhaps even dismissive, but this was recognised as a sensible strategy on the part of students. Much effort is invested in learning the 'rules' that govern the programme, the 'hidden' curriculum, and once learnt students are reluctant to have these rules changed mid-study, which might have the effect of wiping out their investment of time in learning how to play the game.

> What I've found is because it's a final year course [. . .] and because of the department that it's in, the teaching methods in that department are very traditional. It's pretty much chalk and talk. And the students actually seem to prefer that. . . . The students in a sense are quite resistant to something that's quite different to the previous three years of teaching that they've had, and then also if you do something that's different, the students don't like it and they do badly then they get berated [laughs]. So I mean there's a kind of a – a sense of being worn down and saying, ok, I'll just do what everyone else does as well.

Assessment

Assessment appeared central to the whole issue of designing creative curricula. As one participant commented, 'If the assessment process is right, you can cope; creativity is encouraged'. What was 'right' about assessment was not only that it should be appropriate to course level and reliable with equitable standards, but that it should encourage 'student reflection on work, indicate areas for improvement . . . it is important not to destroy confidence – or encourage self-delusion. It's a delicate balancing act – the result may be disappointing, but feedback should point forwards.' Two further points were interesting. First, it was felt that 'divergent thinking [was] not encouraged in criteria-ridden assessment', yet creative work lacked credibility unless it were an explicit element of assessment. Second, assessment should be varied in order to give 'scope for different aptitudes' and encourage thinking in different ways.

A particular problem related to 'institutional practices . . . and a drive towards end-of-term exams', which it was felt 'are really not the best way of testing, especially in the higher levels, the skills we want students to learn and the kind of knowledge . . . that we want them to acquire'. However, proposals for replacing exams with other forms of assessment, or lowering their weighting, could result in 'pretty stiff resistance' at departmental or institutional level. This resulted in an interesting paradox:

> So it's really an interesting circular dilemma there. Yes, we privilege students' capacity to be creative, but no we don't let them show it to us in anything that counts.

The position did seem to vary by discipline. In Arts disciplines, exhibitions, portfolios and performances were used for assessment, and would be viewed by internal and external assessors. 'Mini-vivas' would give undergraduates an opportunity to comment upon their work and would be taped in final-year modules for external examiners. Outside Arts disciplines, more than one assessor would comment upon assessments that were specifically designed to incorporate creative work; these included oral presentations, poster demonstrations and role play.

Having a variety of assessment types was felt to be an important stimulus to creative work. Assessment was typically summative, concerned with 'solo performance' and characterized by exams or academic essays. Changes that participants sought to make included more formative assessment (work in progress that received feedback, and which was 'contributory – otherwise some students wouldn't do it') and having a greater variety of written and practical work (to include, for example, précis, report-writing, critiques of articles, group work and projects on topics negotiated with students).

Some respondents tried assessing creative work, but there were issues about defining what 'counts' as creativity in assessable ways.

> [Creativity] is not written into the learning objectives, but then again, it wouldn't be, would it? . . . But like all these things that are important, you can't pin it down – so we try to encourage it . . . but we don't necessarily give marks for it.

Given the problems of changing forms of assessment, one interim tactic was to subvert the conventional forms. One participant included questions with an element of creativity in summative examinations; another described how 'essays' could incorporate group work and discussion, at least at the thinking and planning stages. One participant tried to counter the 'power dynamics' of assessment by engaging in negotiations with final-year students about the assessment tasks and criteria. Some students were wary of this departure from more usual approaches within the discipline, but the end results were felt to include 'greater engagement' by students in 'their' topics, more transparency about assessment criteria and institutional processes and an opportunity for personal development.

A final observation in this section is from a participant who had assessed oral problem-working among groups in two universities. The comment illustrates that placing value on creativity can create problems, if this happens on a piecemeal basis. It highlights the importance of holistic courses, which allow students time and opportunities to develop areas which some can find difficult.

> In the first case, the students were raring to go – ideas were coming thick and fast . . . what emerged was an imaginative and well-designed working hypothesis. . . . Good teamwork was noticeable. In the second example (and I wouldn't say there was an ability difference from in the first case) . . . it just didn't work. Students were not used to brainstorming, to trying ideas for size. . . . It was

stilted and the students failed – dramatically – to communicate. A very plausible explanation for the difference seemed to lie in curricular content and assessment. Once you looked at the curriculum, you realized that group two . . . had sparse practice and no guidance in this sort of problem-working until final year – where was the preparation? You cannot expect students to draw things out of a hat . . . it's unfair.

Designing first-year courses

Experiences of design for first-year courses were similar at both institutions, but certain issues were felt more acutely at LJMU. There, most introductory courses had undergone significant redesign, largely in response to a perception that there was a growing mismatch between school/Further Education and university-level study, even when admission grades appeared to be constant. The criticism was not of the students per se but of their previous educational experience, which was felt to be unduly 'convergent', with one participant explaining that the 'crowded, heavily normative curriculum in schools [encouraged] superficial learning and regurgitation'. Independent study skills and basic numeracy and literacy were also felt to be a problem in some contexts.

'Collective brainstorming and a lot of heart-searching' had produced some proposals to change the situation; this was also felt to have a creative aspect. 'We tried to articulate fundamental values about society and . . . what is a university for?'

Some course teams had experimented with literacy and numeracy sessions for weaker students, but they were generally not well-attended, since students who were expected to attend felt stigmatised. Consequently, numeracy enhancement was built into the curriculum for all students and it was found that even better-prepared students benefited ('we just take them faster, further'). Problem-working was felt to increase understanding and motivation. As discussed earlier, designing to address particular problems could result in participants feeling more creative about their approach to teaching overall.

Designing final-year courses

The final-year curriculum typically combined some core study (often advanced applications of concepts and techniques) with student choice of modules and more independent study time. Academics felt that they often had greater freedom to draw upon their own research interests at this level.

The idea of creative space, discussed earlier, was felt to be particularly important here. Opportunities for discussion between staff and students were encouraged as 'students [are] more likely to have a better grasp of the discipline and insights from elsewhere . . . and more confidence to challenge you in informed ways'.

One lecturer spoke optimistically about students becoming more creative as they developed their autonomy throughout a course – but went on to reveal that her experience contradicted this, and that what seemed to happen was that students developed set expectations about what ought to happen which then limited what could be achieved:

> I would assume that I had greater creativity with the later years, because they've had some exposure to the university system and hopefully they've learnt how it works and that they're supposed to think for themselves. [Later that same interview] That's what I expected when I started out. And ... there are some who really are just really interested, want to think about things on different levels. But then there's a large majority who are just there to pass the exam. And they are the majority, as far as I can tell, and they really do prefer just for you to transfer information to them, then they go away, they do the past papers, and then they regurgitate it. So it ought – three years of university ought to mean they were mature enough and put in of their own effort outside lecture courses and practicals and what have you, that you could do something different, but in reality, I've not yet found that that's generally the case.

This sense of the conservative student may appear negative and perhaps even dismissive, but as the interview progressed it became clear that this was a sensible strategy on the part of students. As noted above, after learning how to study in a particular way, students are reluctant to have their successful study habits overturned by unfamiliar approaches to teaching. This was particularly acute in relation to assessment:

> How to assess is an obvious case. I think first year courses are quite amenable to different modes of assessment, in a way because students haven't yet learned how to do the standard things.

New assessment formats in the final year produced great anxiety – particularly when they were first introduced. Such changes render worthless many of the points of reference that enable students to judge their progress and prepare for forthcoming exams.

> If you change a course that exists, and the exam questions then become different, and students rely very heavily on past papers.

Thus designing final-year modules had to take account of 'a widening gap ... between students who are beginning to fly' in creative ways and those who could not cope with too much autonomy. It was generally felt that the final year should be a development of the previous years, rather than a quite different curriculum – for example, to achieve this, two course teams had introduced more 'mini-dissertation work at level 2' as a preparation for final-year study. Similarly, on a course where 'mini vivas' were expected, 'the preparation has come through levels 1 and 2'.

The organisational environment

Apparent throughout these interviews was the way that the wider context (academic, political and social) influenced the ways in which creativity was or was not taken up. Sometimes, these influences were quite general; some participants, for example, believed they were 'increasingly working in a culture which perhaps doesn't like failure', and since creativity may well involve risk-taking 'no-one wants to be seen to be a lecturer who's not able to ... be successful'. Other participants pointed to quite specific exercises of power and authority:

> There's someone I know who can't do what she wants with her course because other people keep interfering. There's real issues of power and control there, which I guess also relate to security. It's hard when you're a junior member of staff on a part-time contract; how do you turn round to a professor, and say, 'hang on, that's stupid, and this is my course so I'm not doing that?'

Issues of personal contracts and security were touched upon by several participants. There were real implications for creative teaching arising from the perceived need for self-preservation: 'the less security you have, the less willing you are to take risks'. Moreover, junior lecturers in particular experienced problems with inheriting courses designed by other people. Freedom to vary an inherited course could differ by the discipline, academics' knowledge of the curriculum area, confidence, inter-personal politics, and expectations of students and colleagues.

A more pressing problem for established staff was the perceived lack of resources – particularly time. One course leader, for example, felt caught between the desire not to over-commit colleagues to new course activities and his own time pressures, which meant that he could not 'carry it all single-handed'. Even if it were possible to bring in more teaching staff, this would lead to a fragmented structure where it would be 'hard to build in those creative spaces'. Material constraints, such as shortages of suitable accommodation or resources such as books and primary materials, were also felt to place limits on innovative work.

A very considerable discouragement to creative curricular design and student learning was felt to be the university's 'insistence on [semester-long] modules... there is no space, there is assessment crowding in and reduced opportunity for formative assessment – and – pat! that's finished. Students don't easily see linkages.' Similarly, pressures of accountability (both internal and through external audit) and the perception of managerialism restricting academic practice, not to mention the perceived resistance from some colleagues to 'debate and change' in general, were felt to be further discouragements to creativity.

Creativity and employability

Courses in both universities were also shaped by consideration of employment opportunities. However, the extent to which employers looked for employees whose creativity has been encouraged is open to question. Thrift (2000: 676), for example, argues that 'something new is happening to Western capitalism – not as new as some of its more evangelical proponents would argue, no doubt – but not just business as usual'. Moreover, the employability literature reports recruiters' aspirations for graduates who innovate and can be 'transformative' (Harvey, 1997). Whether the current emphasis on 'creative' recruits is style, an attribute which is only valued in fast-track recruitment or in the 'creative' industries, or an awakening to the realisation that in a fast-changing world, routine-dependency may not be enough, it seems that students will be emerging into a world in which their claims to creative work are becoming increasingly important.

Conclusions

These interviews illustrated the complexity of creativity, both generally and within the curriculum. In both universities, the risk of regarding 'creativity' complacently and un-analytically was identified. 'Of course . . . creativity is A Good Thing, . . . a universal aim.' The problem with this is that the concept is rendered benign but bland. However, participants in each university described absences and difficulties of creativity, as well as instances of creative curricular design and pedagogy. Encouraging creativity was felt to be a worthwhile goal. However, like many complex, qualitative achievements, it required conversation and reflection by academics and students upon the 'complex and contested' as part of curricular design, pedagogy and assessment.

There were many commonalities in conceptions of creativity, creative teaching and supporting creativity in learning, across both sites. However, the issue of meanings emerges once more. Did academics in mathematics departments 'mean' quite the same thing as those in arts departments when speaking about 'creativity' and 'the new', for example? An initial reaction might be negative, but the observation of the mathematician Poincaré (1970: 80) seems remarkably familiar: creative work produces some 'new combinations', but 'new' on its own was not the sole criterion of creativity; it also requires 'discernment', 'choice', 'not uselessness', 'beauty', 'harmony', elegance' and an 'aesthetic feeling . . . [that] surely belongs to emotional sensibility'. Perhaps the common ground between arts' and sciences' conceptions of 'creative' is more important than the distinctions.

Participants questioned three stereotypes. First, that 'creativity' was the prerogative of arts courses. Disciplines in both arts and sciences could go through creative bursts, perhaps in the early stages of their development, then become 'quite formulaic', or later become re-invigorated 'with the emergence of new paradigms'. Second, creativity was not necessarily associated with 'genius'. Craft (2001) explores the idea of 'small "c" creativity', which can enhance individual potential outside the genius range. Finally, neat distinctions in creative processes between arts and sciences were also questioned (see Yeomans, 1996; Feist, 1999: 283).

The strong prominence of assessment in this picture was no surprise. As Yorke (2002: 156) has observed, 'Assessment is ... a problematic issue for higher education [especially in the] extent to which intended learning outcomes can accommodate creative ... work by the student'. Participants identified several dilemmas in the assessment of creativity, and other complex student achievements:

- Students' creative work may be underestimated or dismissed within a domain because of lecturers' unrealistic expectations of developing creativity. Typically, undergraduate creative expression is different from that exhibited by experienced practitioners, and neither group is likely to include a Mozart. Moreover, an undergraduate whom we remember as pushing against conceptual boundaries some years ago may not be such a radical if we apply virtual fast forward and position her or him within the paradigms of the present.
- Creative work can challenge fixed conceptions of the discipline that may derive in part from academics having invested intellectual capital within it and an unwillingness to cede capital gain. Departure from 'imitation' of established ideas may be tolerated or even encouraged within the disciplinary culture of a department; or it may be blocked by gatekeepers who have 'cognitive dominance' in the socio-cultural context in which assessment takes place.
- Summative assessment by examination was felt to be a blunt instrument in the assessment of higher-level understandings and other student achievements, including creative work. Yet participants were, to an extent, 'bound into the belief by some professional bodies, employers... [and even] by conservative thinking internally that this is *the* credible form of assessment'. The way forward was felt to include a range of assessment forms, some of which would encourage divergence.
- The problems of under-assessment of creative work vied with concerns about SMART performance criteria and what has been described as 'an overenthusiastic search for fine-grained benchmarks' (Knight and Yorke, 2003) that might destroy the very creative qualities that academics wish to encourage.

Another recurrent complexity was the relationship between teachers and students. Whilst students were an obvious inspiration for many acts of particularly creative curriculum design, they were as often an impediment as a spur to reform.

Bourdieu and Passeron (1977) refer to the issue of cultural capital, which consists of a familiarity with the dominant culture in society, especially the ability to understand the use of educated language. In each institutional study, there were references to either explicit or 'hidden' curriculum adjustments to try to take account of some students' more difficult transitions to university. Creative undergraduate work can develop only where there is confidence in disciplinary knowledge, in the context in which students are working, and when they are interested and challenged. Some participants reported having made adjustments to the curriculum in response to this. Traditional 'teaching' has not been abandoned in favour of facilitation, since students were found less able to cope with the greater autonomy of facilitatory pedagogy, at least at first (see Northedge, 2003).

To summarise, a stressed academic, like a stressed student, is rarely creative. Slightly adjusting Thrift (2000: 688), it may help to consider: 'Is it possible for [a teacher] to achieve 'balance', to 'live lightly' – and be a change agent?' It was clear from this study that real, additional resources (rather than prescriptions from national and institutional centres) are needed to foster creativity and cope with more diverse student bodies. Lighter-touch accountabilities and sensitivity by evaluators to academics' expertise, especially in furthering complex learning such as creativity, might free spaces for collegiality and good learning. Lying behind all of this is the elusive idea of 'culture change', which might remove many of the normative barriers to the introduction of creativity. However, changing cultures is notoriously hard and time-consuming; perhaps, for the moment, it might be sufficient for course teams to create a context in which they, collectively, place value on creativity. Given the central role of creativity, one starting point might be to consider whether there is an over-teaching of content coupled with too little 'high gain [student] and low pain [academic] assessment' (Knight and Yorke, 2003). If systematic changes could begin to be made within complete programmes, rather than in a piecemeal manner, then it may be possible to begin opening up the creative spaces within the curriculum that so many of the participants in these studies seemed to be seeking.

7   Facilitating creativity in higher education

A brief account of National Teaching Fellows' views

Marilyn Fryer

Introduction

This chapter describes the results of a research study carried out by The Creativity Centre on behalf of the National Endowment for Science, Technology and the Arts (NESTA) and the Higher Education Academy (HEA). It explored the views of 94 National Teaching Fellows (NTFs) about creativity, teaching and learning in HE, via an email survey of 90 NTFs and interviews with a sub-sample of 21. The research questions (devised by NESTA and the HEA) are similar to those used by the author in *Project 1000*, a study of the views of 1,028 teachers and further education lecturers about creativity, teaching and learning (Fryer, 1989). Some of the *Project 1000* measures have also been used in this research. The results of the survey show that most Fellows are keen to develop students' creativity and are highly motivated to provide interesting and highly relevant teaching and learning experiences for their students. On the whole, their views about how creativity may be developed are quite congruent with the creativity literature. In contrast to the teachers and lecturers who took part in *Project 1000*, the NTFs are far less inclined to see creativity as a rare gift. The findings indicate a need to address the assessment of creativity in HE, especially the relationship between creative ability and academic achievement. Indeed, there is an urgent need to ascertain how many highly creative students fail to achieve academic success, as currently measured, and what steps need to be taken in the light of the findings. The results also suggest that it would be timely to examine HE provision with a view to creating provision that is geared more towards the future than the past.

Background literature

Here the aim is to briefly locate the results of this investigation in context rather than provide a comprehensive review of the literature on creativity, teaching and learning – which is vast and has been extensively reviewed elsewhere (for instance Stein, 1986; Fryer, 1989, 1996, 2003; Millar, 1995). So here, the focus is on the *views* of educators.

Prior to the mid-1970s, there were few studies of educators' views on creativity, and most of them focused on school teachers and were based on Torrance's

Ideal Pupil Checklist (Torrance, 1965, 1975). This measure was designed to discover teachers' *attitudes* to pupils' creative behaviour (for instance, Torrance, 1965; Schaefer, 1973) rather than to identify 'ideal pupils' per se. A popular measure, it is still used throughout the world (for instance, Von Eschenbach and Noland, 1981; Noland *et al.*, 1984; Ohuche, 1986; Fryer, 1989; Sharma Sen and Sharma, 2004).

From his original study of the attitudes of over 1,000 teachers in Germany, India, Greece, the Philippines and the USA, Torrance (1965) concluded that teachers in all five countries may be unduly punishing children who are good at guessing/estimating, those courageous in their convictions, emotionally sensitive children, intuitive thinkers, those who regress occasionally, visionary pupils and those who are unwilling to accept assertions without evidence. On the other hand, teachers may be unduly rewarding pupils for being courteous, doing work on time, being obedient, popular and willing to accept the judgements of authorities.

In 1976, a fairly comprehensive study of teachers' views on creativity was undertaken by Bjerstedt and colleagues in Malmö (Bjerstedt, 1976). A key aim was 'to explore via teacher opinions and classroom observation, teacher and student behaviours that can potentially influence creativity' (Eriksson, 1970). The study involved collecting the views of 292 educators via an unstructured questionnaire about creative ability and the steps they thought students should take to promote creative behaviour. This was followed by a more structured version administered to 360 'key teachers'. Also, 200 teachers were asked how they would respond to a range of hypothetical classroom situations.

The results of Bjerstedt's unstructured survey revealed that the most common definition of creative ability was 'independent work', followed by 'richness of ideas', 'originality' and 'the ability to combine'. A request to identify the characteristics of highly creative pupils was answered with 280 different responses, mostly embodying the notion of intellectual capacity, including 'flexible', 'full of ideas', 'keen to discuss things', 'curious' and 'conscious of problems'. According to the Swedish teachers, the distinguishing personality characteristics of creative pupils included 'independent', 'unconventional', 'open' and 'confident'. The pupils they considered creative were also described negatively: 'want to do everything differently', 'are a worrying element', 'do not co-operate', 'adjust badly to tuition' and 'listless at the prospect of some subjects'.

With regard to developing creativity, the Swedish teachers believed that practical subjects and Swedish offered the most scope, although they thought that creativity could be developed in any subject. They also thought creativity could best be promoted through 'free practical exercises and group work'. Like Torrance (1965), they believed that positive teacher attitudes were most important for facilitating creativity.

The Swedish study was followed by Fryer's *Project 1000*, a similar but larger-scale quantitative and qualitative investigation into the views of over 1,000 UK teachers and further-education lecturers about creativity, teaching and learning (for instance, Fryer 1989, 1996; Fryer and Collings, 1991). The teachers and lecturers who took part taught pupils and students in the 5–18+ age ranges, in every area of the curriculum.

Fryer's 1989 investigation employed a range of original scales and checklists, as well as the Torrance checklists. Her research focused on teachers' perceptions of creativity, their preferred ways of teaching, attitudes to creativity, the facilitation of creativity, any barriers and enablers they perceived and teachers' preferred means of assessing creativity.

Results revealed (for the first time, as far as is known) clear and highly significant differences in perceptions of creativity and preferred creativity assessment criteria, between male and female staff, and amongst those teaching different disciplines. In addition, the variables which best discriminate between teachers most and least motivated to facilitate creativity were revealed. These variables all demonstrated a willingness to take learners' needs into account.

Of particular interest was the finding that attitudes to, and perceptions about, creativity in education co-varied with preferred ways of teaching. This led to the proposition that these might be rooted in some kind of underlying value system linked to *person orientation* (as defined in Collings, 1978; Collings and Smithers, 1984). This proposition was supported by a later investigation (Fryer, 1994a).

Fryer included the Ideal Pupil Checklist (IDP) in her 1989 study, along with her own measures and Torrance's Personality Checklist. The latter is similar but not identical to the IDP. Fryer used it to find out how the teachers saw themselves and how this compared with pupil characteristics they wanted to encourage or discourage. She found that the UK teachers and lecturers in her sample valued most the students who were 'considerate' and 'socially well-adjusted'. The next most popular student attributes were 'self confidence', 'independence in thinking' and 'curiosity', each of which is implicated in creativity. Sharma Sen and Sharma (2004) later found that a small sample of Indian teachers ($n=28$) ranked pupils' 'self-confidence' and 'courage in convictions' third and fourth respectively, after 'socially skilled' and 'healthy' pupils. Since 1989, there have been a number of similar small-scale studies of school teachers' views (for instance Woods, 1995).

In *Project 1000*, the teachers did not see themselves as creative, but rather in terms of their sense of humour and social attributes. This is in keeping with the findings of Popescu-Nevianu and Cretsu (1986) who found that Romanian teachers didn't value initiative in themselves, but valued it highly in others.

Following a review of creativity, teaching and learning at Leeds Metropolitan University in 1992, the author led a small-scale comparative study in 1993/4 into creative and effective teaching, involving Leeds Metropolitan University and Lisbon Polytechnic (Fryer, 1994b). At this time both British and Portuguese staff were facing growing class sizes with limited resources. From the Portuguese team's comments, the British researchers had expected to find mainly didactic teaching in Lisbon. Instead, they found good examples of challenging and creative lessons as well as some similarities in how creativity was being addressed in both countries.

Internationally, an increasing number of universities offer creativity development courses (see for instance Fryer, 2003, 2006), and there have been a number of related initiatives (for instance, DfEE, 1999). However, until this study (and companion studies described in this book), there has been very little research into creativity in teaching and learning in HE.

The National Teaching Fellowship Scheme (NTFS) is designed to recognise and reward teachers and learning support staff for their excellence in teaching in HE. The awardees have been selected for (amongst other things) their ability to inspire their students and colleagues, as well as demonstrating a reflective approach to teaching and learning support. Yet little is known about their views on creativity and learning and how this affects their preferred ways of teaching.

Aims and objectives

The aims of the present investigation were to ascertain the views of National Teaching Fellows about creativity and learning, the effect they perceive this has on their teaching and the implications for teaching and learning in HE.

More specific objectives were to discover the following:

- How the NTFs envisage creativity.
- Whether they regard themselves as creative.
- What they think creativity involves in terms of their discipline.
- How they view the relationship (if any) between creativity, learning and academic achievement.
- What creativity involves with regard to their teaching.
- The extent to which they aim to teach in ways which develop student creativity.
- The relationship they perceive between teaching creatively and developing students' creativity.
- The factors they regard as enabling or inhibiting.
- Whether they assess the creativity of students' work and, if they do, how they go about it.
- How they communicate any creativity assessment requirements to students.
- Whether they regard the development of students' creativity as primarily for academic purposes or to prepare students for the wider world.
- Their views on the effect of the current expansion of HE on teaching, learning and the development of students' creativity.
- Which aspects of this provision they regard as helpful to developing students' creativity and which they see as inhibiting.

Methods

All 130 National Teaching Fellows appointed up to and including 2004 were invited to take part in the survey. The response rate was outstanding (72 per cent). The sample included 54 men and 40 women. From this sample, 90 completed an email questionnaire; 21 (11 females and ten males) took part in interviews. They represent a variety of disciplines, ages, kinds of institution and regions.

Results and discussion

This section includes comparisons with the results of the author's *Project 1000* research in 1989, involving teachers and HE lecturers. Although the two samples are not matched, both consist of educators; and both studies focus on the same objectives and share some common measures.

Perceptions of creativity

The Fellows were asked to indicate which items in Table 7.1 matched their perception of creativity. In line with the results of the 1989 study, *imagination* was most popular. *Original ideas* is also ranked highly – third in the present study and second in the previous one. *Seeing unusual connections* is ranked second in the current study and fourth in the earlier research. In the 1989 study, female respondents were significantly more likely to identify with *self-expression* as an aspect of creativity than were men ($p < 0.01$). In the present study, the data did not meet the necessary statistical conditions.

When asked to describe in words what creativity means to them, the Fellows emphasised different constructs which may be broadly categorised as:

- *thinking* (e.g. 'solving ill-structured problems in ways which show initiative').
- *doing* (e.g. 'developing, implementing and leading new things').
- *thinking and doing* (e.g. 'both the cerebral and the practical').
- *the arts* (e.g. 'artistic version of innovative').

Table 7.1 Aspects of creativity with which the NTFs identify ($n = 90$)

Aspect of creativity	%
Imagination	90.0
Seeing unusual connections	86.7
Combining ideas	80.0
Original ideas	80.0
Innovation	76.7
Thinking processes	72.2
Discovery	66.7
Invention	61.1
Generative thinking	53.3
Self-expression	52.2
Valuable ideas	52.2
Sudden inspiration	51.1
Analytical thinking	44.4
Awareness of beauty	25.6
Aesthetic products	21.1
Unconscious activities	21.1
Tangible products	18.9
Mysterious processes	14.4
Other	14.3

- *self-expression* (e.g. 'ability to express an innate aspect of your psyche').
- *creativity as a continuum* (e.g. 'at one extreme... great artists and scientists... At the other... ordinary people...'
- *context* (e.g. 'contextually-based innovation inspired by responding to specific and challenging problems').

Most NTFs (92.2 per cent) believe that creativity *can* be developed (compared with 89.6 per cent in 1989). However, there is a striking difference in the extent to which respondents see creativity as *a rare gift*. In *Project 1000*, 70.6 per cent agreed that it was, but in the present study 71.1 per cent *disagreed*. This could be because nowadays creativity is a 'hot topic'. In 1989, there was little emphasis on creative education in the UK, except in relation to giftedness.

Just under half the NTFs doubt whether men and women are creative in the same way. This question was not asked directly in 1989, but when that data was analysed in terms of gender, significant inter-group differences were revealed in male and female perceptions of creativity, how they preferred to assess it, and how they preferred to teach (Fryer, 1989; Fryer and Collings, 1991).

Similarly, just under half the sample are unsure as to whether people of different ethnic origins are creative in the same way, even though more than half the NTFs think that creativity is different in different cultures. There is no evidence that ethnicity has a bearing on creative ability, but there is evidence of some cultural differences in how creativity is perceived and expressed (for instance, Raina, 2004).

In the questionnaire, NTFs were asked to describe creativity in terms of their own discipline. Most of the answers could apply to any discipline. For example:

- Finding new ways of engaging with students; tapping into unconventional ways of assessing student learning (neuroscience).
- Originality; developing, producing, manufacturing; bringing about ideas and design solutions in different, unusual ways; to critically analyse, reflect and apply and develop ideas and attitudes (design history).
- Being able to conceptualise possible solutions to problems or explanations that are novel. Being able to select from a very wide range of possibilities a few that can credibly explain the past, present or future (information management).
- Finding new solutions (pharmacology).
- Putting apparently disparate things together or seeing the relevance of something in a new context.... [compared with] the highest level of creativity in physics, which is to see problems where no-one else does and to have the technical ability to express them in a way that is useful (in which they can be attacked) (physics).
- New theories, original work, seeing new applications for existing mathematics (maths).

In *Project 1000*, staff were not asked directly how creativity was perceived in their discipline. Instead, the data was analysed in terms of subjects taught. This revealed significant differences in views about creativity, teaching, learning and assessment among different subject specialists (Fryer, 1989, 1996; Fryer and Collings, 1991). In the present study, the smaller sample and lack of quantitative data makes such comparisons problematic.

Views about creativity, teaching and learning

Over 80 per cent of the NTFs think the capacity to be creative helps people to be successful, and 86 per cent believe this prepares students for the wider world. For example, one Fellow described how this impacts on people's lives:

> I think if you're creative you ... can imagine all sorts of scenarios and it helps you judge what your options are .... I do think it broadens your perspectives. It also makes you very good at multi-tasking.

Whilst 75 per cent of the NTFs believe that the capacity to be creative enhances academic performance, few (13.5 per cent) believe that the most academically successful students are also the most creative. This begs important questions, such as:

*   Do other things contribute more to academic success than the capacity to be creative? If so, are these desirable, especially given that over 80 per cent of the sample think developing students' creativity prepares them for the wider world?
*   Are some highly creative students not academically successful? If so, is assessment in HE failing them in some way?

It is worth noting that many successful and creative people have either dropped out of school or HE or have achieved unremarkable grades (for instance Safter, 1993). An observation by Torrance (2002a) is also relevant:

> Both Getzels and Jackson, and I found that between the populations on intelligence tests and creativity tests, there is only a 30% overlap. In studies of academic achievement, and in follow-up studies of creative behaviour, we found very little difference between the high IQ/not-so-high creativity, and the high creativity/not-so-high IQ. In fact, in most of my own studies, the high creativity/not so high IQ group achieved better than any other group. Thus we should make one of our missions that of getting research findings into practice.

Developing students' creativity

Most NTFs (93.3 per cent) believe that developing students' creativity is important and 90 per cent aim to develop student creativity using a variety of approaches which include:

1   Stimuli for imaginative thinking or heuristic strategies, e.g.:

- 'problem-based learning' (physics).
- 'games which set challenging problems... [encouraging] students to think of new approaches' (chartered surveyor).

2   Learning in a particular context or providing a context for creative work, e.g.:

- '[using] real life scenarios to encourage the adaptation of radiographic technique' (radiography).
- 'showing examples of creative thinking and solutions; providing reading and resources to extend thinking. . .' (graphic design).

3   Supportive factors such as the relationship between tutor and students, e.g.:

- 'strong encouragement with a friendly approach' (maths).
  'trying to remain open to unexpected responses' (law).

4   Personality characteristics

- 'helping students develop an approach to risk-taking' (medical education).
- '[building] self confidence' (neuroscience).

5   Teaching skills for use in creative work

- 'first developing the craft skills; then when they're established, encouraging them to play, confident that they can recover if it goes wrong' (education).
- 'working on students' strengths whilst improving their weaknesses' (pedagogy and psychology).

6   Setting tasks which require creativity:

- 'developing opportunities for creativity processes, solutions, journeys and application – briefs, seminars, essays, presentations.' (graphic design).
- 'setting creativity tasks and being as open as I can be' (building pathology).

7   Developing students' motivation:

- 'empower students so they feel they can have ownership and contribute usefully to discussions and debates' (psychobiology; health psychology).
- 'a person-centred approach to teaching, tapping into each individual's dreams, needs, aspirations, curiosity and motivation' (open learning).

At interview, two Fellows working in very different fields (construction management and nursing) each described how they had created *virtual work contexts* in their classrooms to make learning come alive for their students and enable them to see the relevance of their learning. The chartered surveyor had created a virtual construction site that students could use in an interactive way; he used games and simulations to make learning highly relevant for students. The nursing tutor recognises that nurses need to be problem solvers. He gives students real problems and the visual tools to interact with a computer programme that simulates an actual hospital, with access to typical patient records. He took this step because students had not been applying the theory they learned. Teaching had become too conceptual and theoretical. His new method enabled students to start with the practical and move to the theoretical.

Most NTFs are interested in developing students' creativity and some appear to be very skilled in this regard. Their strategies are mostly quite congruent with the literature (for instance, Torrance, 1962, 1995; Stein, 1974, 1975; Fryer, 1996, 2004; Beetlestone, 1998; Cropley, 2001; Millar, 2004). A few Fellows referred to the use of formal 'thinking techniques' such as lateral thinking, brainstorming or mind-mapping. It is not always necessary to resort to such techniques and programmes, although they may suggest useful strategies. In the late 1980s, the author and her colleagues devised and delivered a series of accredited modules and courses in applied creativity at undergraduate and postgraduate levels and for professional updating. These modules introduced students to the whole field of creativity research and development, and enabled them to evaluate the relevance of formal 'creativity programmes' and everyday, informal approaches to their own work (which often involved the facilitation of others' creativity). These courses were accessed by several thousand students, from a wide range of disciplines over a 15-year period. The students worked together on issues relevant to them. Most were professionals in health, social care, education or business. It might be worth considering whether courses like these could benefit students and whether better mechanisms are needed for exchanging ideas about creativity, teaching and learning in HE generally.

Supportive factors

The Fellows identified numerous factors that help them to develop students' creativity. These may be grouped as:

- NTFs' personal qualities.
- Their abilities, activities or experience.
- Students' qualities and contributions.
- Manageable workload.
- Nature of the discipline.
- Resources.
- The system and its procedures.
- The institution's or department's ethos.
- The NTF scheme.

NTFs' personal qualities

For example, tenacity, willingness to experiment, ability to use imagination, motivation, patience, willingness to take risks, courage, self-confidence. The personal characteristics they identified were almost all typical of creative people (see, for instance, Torrance, 1965; Stein, 1984).

Their abilities, activities or experience

For example, teaching styles, skills and experience, research experience.

Students' qualities and contributions

For example, students' motivation and enthusiasm, willingness to learn and be original, creativity.

Having a manageable workload

For example, small teaching groups, being a professor with low administration duties, a light timetable and opportunities for travel.

The nature of their discipline

For example, a discipline that lends itself to creative approaches.

Resources

For example, suitable resources, good library facilities, funding for innovation.

The system and its procedures

For example, control of the curriculum, flexibility of assessment, autonomy in selecting different teaching and assessment styles.

The institution's or department's ethos

For example, work ethic in which creativity is the norm, supportive peer groups, colleagues happy to experiment, inspiration from others, working in creative teams, having a supportive manager who values creativity, support of external examiner.

The importance of an enabling ethos was also mentioned at interview. For example, the family atmosphere generated in one institution was seen as making a very real difference and enabled staff and students to get to know one another well.

The NTF scheme

The other supportive factor mentioned at interview was the NTF scheme itself. This was seen as providing freedom, flexibility, space to be creative or opening up opportunities.

Given these findings, it's not surprising that most NTFs believe they are creative. What is particularly interesting is that many Fellows' descriptions of themselves as facilitators of creativity are congruent with those of the *Project 1000* teachers identified by means of discriminant analysis as *most keen to develop creativity* (Fryer, 1989, 1996; Fryer and Collings, 1991).

Students' learning styles and NTFs' teaching styles

Although most NTFs (80 per cent) said they were influenced by students' learning styles, this is not easy to take into account, except perhaps by allowing students more choice and significant autonomy in their learning. This is exactly what those Fellows who do address students' learning styles report doing, together with a willingness to be responsive to students.

A few NTFs expressed doubts about the validity of learning style theory. One difficulty with attempts to assess learning styles is that these can be categorised in different ways and categories overlap. Consider, for example, the 'holists' described by Pask and Scott (1972), the 'activists' of Honey and Mumford (1986) and the 'syllabus free' students described by Josephs and Smithers (1975). Also, some learning styles are thought to be more stable than others (Floyd, 1976). Scores on some styles can shift as individuals mature – on *impulsivity/reflectivity*, for example (Kagan, 1966).

Constraints on preferred ways of teaching

Fellows were asked to tick the factors they see as inhibiting their preferred way of teaching.

An 'excessive non-teaching workload' appears to offer the most immediate scope for a re-think and this could create more preparation time. Clearly, it would be worth considering how to deploy HE resources more effectively.

In the interview study, quite a few NTFs mentioned feeling constrained by the need for peer or institutional approval. For some, the RAE was a barrier – setting up tension in those who wanted both to teach imaginatively and produce high-quality research papers. One Fellow described the pressure he felt to conform to institutional norms along with a sense of isolation – as a result of questioning current teaching practice. Despite this, he chose to forge ahead with his goals. His experience is quite typical of highly creative people (for instance, Torrance, 2002b).

Assessing creativity in students' work

Results indicate insufficient comparability in how creativity is assessed. Just over one-third of the sample assessed students' creativity *informally*; just over one-quarter undertake some kind of *formal* assessment. Slightly less do both.

Table 7.2 Constraints on NTFs teaching (*n*=89)

Constraint	Valid %
Excessive non-teaching workload	38.2
Unsuitable accommodation	37.1
Inadequate preparation time	33.7
Over-large classes	31.5
Insufficient class contact time	29.2
Constraints imposed because of colleagues' requirements	22.5
Inadequate resources	19.1
Other constraints	25.5*

Note
*Other constraints comprised a mixture of structural, procedural and personal factors.

Informal assessment is carried out in various ways, not all satisfactory. Many find it difficult to operationalize creativity criteria. And what tutors seek as evidence of creativity appears to vary. Where criteria are stated, they include 'creativity' per se, 'innovative' or 'appropriate' solutions and 'novel ideas'. One approach is to penalise students for *lack* of creativity: 'If a scenario is given and the student ignores the contextual information, they wouldn't get credit for describing a rigid... technique.'

Where creativity is *formally assessed*, this is normally communicated to students, although some tutors acknowledge they do not communicate this as clearly as they might. Overall, a variety of means of assessment were used, with peer evaluation and group project assessment being popular in years that don't count towards degree classification. Again, criteria are not always explicitly stated. Alternatively, the 'usual HE criteria' are regarded as sufficient to incorporate creativity.

Where creativity criteria are stated, they include:

- going beyond boundaries.
- being prepared to take risks.
- innovation, innovative thinking.
- originality.
- entrepreneurship.
- problem-solving ability
- imaginative use of media within the context of the brief.
- initiative.
- inventiveness.
- sophistication.
- engagement, motivation.
- ability to analyse critically.
- creativity per se.

In both the interviews and email survey, some NTFs saw a tension between the constraints of degree requirements and the desire to assess (and/or develop) creativity, for example:

- 'being creative doesn't always fit with the criteria.'
- 'assessment limits student creativity. You can't let them be too open-ended, because they might not meet the assessment criteria.'

However, this tension doesn't necessarily stop NTFs expecting creativity from their students, even though about one-third of them see assessment as inhibiting students. A few Fellows don't have this problem; they ensure that assessment *requires* students to be creative.

Whilst assessing creativity necessarily involves some subjectivity, useful objective criteria do exist (for instance, Puccio, 1994; Fryer, 1996, 2000) along with objective measures, of which perhaps the best known are the Torrance Tests of Creative Thinking (TTCTs). The TTCTs have sometimes been criticised for not assessing creativity comprehensively. However, their role is not to do this, but to distinguish between different levels of creative-thinking ability. These tests are based on American norms, are easy to administer, but complex to score. The Creativity Centre has been developing alternative UK tests, which are yielding promising results. All measures have strengths and weaknesses, so a good solution is to use a range of methods. Overall, the research suggests the need for greater clarity and accountability in creativity assessment in HE.

Aspects of HE provision supporting students' creativity

The NTFs are really aware of the many factors that support student creativity, including the need for active involvement in learning, with group work as the preferred vehicle. Although group work offers considerable scope, it doesn't necessarily follow that 'working as a group' enables creativity. Highly creative students often prefer to work alone and get absorbed in work that interests them (Shallcross, 1985). The NTFs also mentioned staff teamwork, a *can-do* attitude and supportive senior management.

Aspects of HE provision inhibiting students' creativity

Almost all of the NTFs (95.5 per cent) thought that some aspects of HE provision inhibit students' creativity. Assessment was most frequently mentioned (by about one-third of the sample). Other concerns include poor teaching, over-large classes, managerialism, inadequate student funding and a stress on 'not failing' rather than freedom to think or take risks.

The impact of HE expansion on teaching and learning

Most, but not all, areas of HE are expanding and views about the impact varied. Some Fellows believed this was (or could be) positive, especially if well-funded. Interestingly, many staff realised that this was a situation demanding creativity – as they had to question how HE education needed to be delivered.

At interview, there was concern about 'factory farming students' and 'managerialism'. The effect of expansion on class sizes was a key concern because students who needed most support were getting less. Yet not all NTFs experienced problems, sometimes because their able and highly motivated students coped well in large groups, sometimes because the tutors were successfully tackling these problems. For example:

> I went from teaching 20 students overnight to teaching 150. With 20 students, we would tend to do lots of group work, a much more creative approach to learning. But when I had 150 students, all that had to cease. We've now got round that by. . . doing computer-based learning and tutorial support in small groups again.

A particular concern was that the expansion of student numbers was not being matched with additional resources, which suggests the need for a radical look at how teaching and learning are delivered and how resources in HE are best deployed.

Impact of HE expansion on developing student creativity

Again, responses varied along a continuum from positive to negative. At one extreme, expansion was seen as an exciting opportunity that could stimulate student creativity, given the growing diversity of students. Indeed, there was the prospect of creating really innovative teaching and learning experiences. At the other extreme, there was concern that institutions would retreat into managerialism and factory-farming solutions. Again, this leads to the view that it is time for a radical re-think about how HE provision can be improved in order to enhance student creativity.

Conclusions and recommendations

Most NTFs are highly motivated and keen to develop students' creativity. Their views on how student creativity may be developed and supported are generally quite congruent with the literature. Even though most of the NTFs see themselves as having more autonomy, flexibility and opportunities than their colleagues, many struggle with challenging working conditions. Questions need to be asked about the criteria for academic success. Do these encourage conformity and 'playing safe', for example? Do the criteria really reflect the needs of graduates in the twenty-first century? If not, how should they be changed? The assessment of creativity in HE needs to be addressed. Where creativity is assessed *informally*, students need to know this is happening and how it is being carried out. In some cases, greater clarity is also needed with regard to the *formal* assessment of creativity. A continuing dialogue would be valuable between staff who cope well with large numbers of students with diverse needs and staff who cope less well. It is clear that space, staff time, student time and other resources are not always being used entirely effectively. The results suggest that a further investigation is warranted to determine whether there are significant numbers of highly creative students who are not achieving high levels of academic success; and what steps need to be taken.

Although the NTFs' responses have provided a good picture of their views, it is not possible to say how this compares with the views of other HE staff. A survey of *their* views would provide a valuable comparison. On the whole, Fellows' responses highlight the fact that, despite some really innovative teaching, much HE provision is still geared to the previous century (and in some instances, the century before that!). There is a real opportunity to create provision geared to current and future needs. Enlightened Fellows have pointed the way forward; it is time to explore in more detail what future educational provision could and should be.

8 Developing subject perspectives on creativity in higher education

Norman Jackson and Malcolm Shaw

Importance of cultural domains

> creativity results from the interaction of a system composed of three elements: *a culture* that contains symbolic rules, *a person* who brings novelty into the symbolic domain, and a *field of experts* who recognize and validate the innovation. All three are necessary for a creative idea, product or discovery to take place.
>
> (Csikszentmihalyi, 1997: 6)

> creativity is any act, idea, or product that changes an existing domain into the new one. And the definition of a creative person is: someone whose thoughts or actions change a domain or establish a new one.
>
> (Csikszentmihalyi, 1997: 28)

The primary cultural domains in higher education are the disciplinary or subject fields (Becher, 1989) and Csikszentmihalyi's conceptions of creativity as being socially and culturally constructed within well defined domains underlie our attempt to explore whether:

- Creativity is an important part of being a biologist, lawyer, historian or any other discipline-based practitioner.
- Being creative means different things in different disciplinary contexts and the sites where creativity is accomplished; the means by which it is achieved and the results of creativity will also be different in different disciplines.
- Creativity is largely unrecognised and undervalued in many (perhaps most?) subjects studied in UK higher education.

Underlying our 'adventure' into disciplinary thinking and practice is a belief that to extend our understanding of creativity in higher education we have to elaborate the meanings of creativity and the way it is operationalised in each disciplinary field.

Two approaches were used in parallel to explore these propositions. First, 18 QAA Subject Benchmarking Statements were analysed by Shaw (2005) using a simple evaluation tool (Appendix 8.1) to identify both explicit and indirect references to aspects of students' learning that might be associated with creative thinking and behaviours. Simultaneously, email surveys were conducted in four disciplinary fields (Earth and Environmental Sciences, History, Engineering and Social Work) with the help of Higher Education Academy Subject Centres. Over 60 academics and field-based practitioners contributed to these surveys. The core questions used in the surveys are given below.

1   What does it mean to be creative in your subject?
2   What is it about your subject that stimulates/encourages teachers and students to be creative?
3   How do higher education teachers in your field help/enable students to be creative?
4   How do teachers in your field recognise and assess creativity?
5   What are the barriers to creativity?
6   Is creativity valued in your disciplinary field?

Responses to these questions were compiled into a transcript and the key ideas were extracted and synthesised in a series of working papers (Jackson, 2005a, 2005b, 2005c; Jackson and Burgess, 2005), which were returned to participants for validation, critical comment and further development. This chapter summarises the findings of these approaches to gaining disciplinary perspective on the meanings of creativity.[1]

What does 'being creative' mean to academics?

Emerging from Imaginative Curriculum discussions and studies is a growing consensus amongst academics as to the key features of creativity (in any context). The ideas most often associated with creativity are:

*   Being imaginative (*using imagination to think in ways that move us beyond the obvious, the known into the unknown, that see the world in different ways or from different perspectives, that take us outside the boxes we normally inhabit and lead to the generation of new ideas and novel interpretations*).
*   Being original (*making a contribution that adds to what already exists*). For example, doing/producing/performing (inventing, innovating, transferring and adapting).
*   Exploring for the purpose of discovery (*experimenting and taking risks, openness to new ideas and experiences typically linked to problem working*).
*   Using and combining thinking skills (*for example critical thinking to aid evaluation, synthesis and intuition to interpret and gain new insights and understandings*).
*   Communication – this is integral to the creative process (*for example, storytelling as a means of communicating meaning within the discipline*).

Our 'problem' is to understand what these things mean when they are operationalised in different subject contexts. Here are some examples of operationalisation. When academic teachers were asked the question, *'What does being creative mean when you design a course?'* (McGoldrick and Edwards, 2002; Oliver, 2002), responses included:

- Creativity as personal innovation – something that is new to individuals. This is often about the transfer and adaptation of ideas from one context to another.
- Creativity as working at and across the boundaries of acceptability in specific contexts: it involves exploring new territory and taking risks.
- Creativity as designs that promote the holistic idea of 'graduateness', that is, the capacity to connect and do things with what has been learnt and to utilise this knowledge to learn in other situations.
- Creativity as making sense out of complexity, that is, working with multiple, often conflicting factors, pressures, interests and constraints.
- Creativity as a process of narrative-making in order to present the 'real curriculum' in ways that conform to the regulatory expectations of how a curriculum should be framed.

In these few examples we can see representations of all the generic features of creativity – originality (working across the boundaries of acceptability; doing/producing new things; personal invention and innovation); use of imagination in designs to achieve a complex objective; exploration and risk-taking; making sense of complexity and story-telling. In contextualising and operationalising creativity in this way, we render the idea more accessible and meaningful to academics and students without devaluing it. On the contrary, creating meaning in this way allows us to celebrate the contribution made by creativity to professional achievement in teaching. The rest of this chapter will explore the extent to which such generic characteristics are exemplified, modified and extended in different disciplinary contexts.

Subject benchmarking statements and creativity

A preliminary review of 18 subject benchmark statements (Table 8.1) revealed that only seven subjects (Art and Design; Medicine; Geography; Dance; Drama and Performance; Engineering; Nursing; Business and Management) make any explicit mention of 'creativity' per se as a desirable feature of curricula in their discipline. A further four benchmarking statements merely suggest that their students should either be creative or should demonstrate the use of certain skills creatively (Architecture; English; Languages and Related Studies; Social Work). The other seven statements that were evaluated (Accounting; Education; Maths; Earth and Environmental Sciences; Biosciences; History; Chemistry) make no specific reference either to creativity as a concept or to students being creative. Only five of the statements (Nursing; Business and Management; Dance, Drama and Performance; Engineering; Social Work) go further by referring to creativity

Table 8.1 Frequency of references made in subject benchmark statements to the 18 possible indicators of creativity identified in the evaluation tool

A&D	13	EES	7	Hist	6
Eng	9	Med	7	LRS	6
SocW	9	Bios	6	Math	5
Arch	8	B&M	6	Ed	4
DDP	8	Chem	6	Geog	4
Nurs	8	E	6	Acc	3

Key
Accountancy (Acc); Architecture (Arch); Art and Design (A&D); Biosciences (Bios); Business and Management (B&M); Chemistry (Chem); Dance, Drama and Performance (DDP); Earth and Environmental Science (EES); Education Studies (Ed); Engineering (Eng); English (E); Geography (Geog); History (Hist); Language and Related Studies (LRS); Maths, Stats and Operational Res (Math); Medicine (Med); Nursing (Nurs); Social Work (SocW).

or creative outcomes in their benchmark assessment criteria for defining standards. Only one statement (Dance, Drama and Performance) treats creativity as an underlying principle of education and student development throughout the statement. If the benchmark statements represent the views of the field on what is valued in students' undergraduate learning, then it would appear that many subjects do not overtly see creativity as an idea that influences and shapes teaching, learning and assessment.

A second more detailed evaluation was undertaken to look for indirect evidence that the disciplinary community recognises and values creativity in students' learning and achievement using an analytical tool (Appendix 8.1) based on some of the indicators of students' creative engagements with higher education learning (Jackson, 2003) namely,

- Imagination and originality.
- Thinking abilities (particularly combining analytical rational thinking with divergent and associative thinking).
- Capacity to generate/evaluate ideas.
- Activities that enable students to be creative.

The analytical tool contains 18 possible indicators of creativity and, whilst the presence of an indicator does not guarantee that students are engaged in creative practice, at least it indicates that such practices are encouraged. Each subject benchmark statement was read and passages that could be associated with the elements of the tool were extracted from the statement and included in Column 3 of the table. The column was left blank if there was no reference to an indicator within the benchmark statement. The frequency count of indicators for each of the subjects is shown in Table 8.1.

A number of benchmark statements both mention creativity (or creative skills) and provide a range of indicators which suggest that opportunities exist for creativity to be practised (A&D, Eng, Arch, DDP, Nurs, SocW). Other benchmarking statements mention creativity, but seem to provide fewer opportunities for creative approaches to be practised (Med, Geog, LRS, E, B&M). Where a subject neither mentions creativity nor registers many indicators for its practice (Acc, Ed, Math, Hist, Chem, EES, Bios), then it would appear that the disciplinary community does not see creativity (or the way creativity is represented in the evaluation tool) as being important to undergraduate learning and learner development.

Divergent and convergent thinking is only specifically mentioned by two benchmark statements (Math, A&D) and similarly *Lateral thinking* only by two statements (Arch and Eng). *Taking risks and coping with failure* is only referred to by A&D. It is more encouraging that 11 subjects (Acc, EES, Eng, Hist, SocW, Med, Bios, Geog, A&D, Nurs, B&M, Ed) acknowledge the need to *operate in complex and ambiguous settings.* However this leaves four benchmarks (DDP, E, Chem, LRS) that do not mention any of the thinking abilities associated with a creative approach. Due to the general emptiness of this category, it is difficult to spot any emerging patterns within the different disciplines.

Indicators that students are expected to *generate and use their own ideas* are, if anything, more weakly represented in our benchmarks than the student thinking abilities described above. Only four benchmarks (DDP, A&D, B&M, LRS) specifically mention the need for *students to generate ideas*, only two (Arch, Ed) suggest that students should *reflect on ideas,* whereas three (Arch, Eng, A&D) see *review and evaluation of ideas* as relevant. The remaining 11 subject statements do not explicitly acknowledge the value of students' own ideas.

Imagination and originality: perhaps not surprisingly, since it is usually thought to be mainly within the ambit of postgraduate research awards, no subjects saw *development of new knowledge* as a relevant outcome for their students. Seven subjects (DDP, E, SocW, Math, A&D, Nurs, B&M) acknowledged *development of new practice* as pertinent. Only two subjects (Hist, E) suggested that *making new knowledge connections* was valuable. In this category *application of learning in new contexts* and *systematic process of enquiry* proved most popular with nine and 15 subjects registering respectively. Of note here is the failure of Acc and Ed to register at all in any of the five indicators in this category.

The strongest indicators in the *activities* category are *Skills*, with all subjects registering and *personal/interpersonal skills/personal development planning and reflection,* with all but Math registering. At the other end of the scale, *negotiated and experiential learning* was least subscribed, with only three subjects (DDP, Med, SocW). Whereas most subjects recognised problem-solving, only five (Chem, Eng, Math, A&D, Nurs) specifically distinguished *open-ended problem solving* as relevant. More problematic is *project/assignment work*, with seven subjects (Acc, E, Med, Math, Geog, B&M, Ed) not registering. It seems likely that the potential overlap of this indicator with *systematic process of enquiry* and with *Skills* may account for its apparent omission in some benchmarks. Finally, *negotiated, self and peer assessment* is recognised by eight subjects (Arch, EES, DDP, SocW, Med, Bios, A&D, LRS).

Preliminary conclusions

- Students' creative-thinking abilities are generally not addressed by subjects except for some acknowledgement of the need to operate in complex and ambiguous settings.
- Students' idea-generating capacities are least well covered, with only a small number of subjects registering any indicator.
- Student imagination and originality is poorly recognised, with the exception of 'systematic process of enquiry/research', which is well covered.
- The greatest attention is given to activities that have the potential for nurturing students' creativity. Most disciplines value 'project/ assignment work', 'personal/interpersonal skills and personal development planning/ reflection', but tend to neglect 'open-ended problem solving', 'negotiated and experiential learning' and 'negotiated, self and peer assessment'.

Academics' views on creativity in disciplines

The benchmarking statements suggest that creativity (or the thinking and behaviours that might be associated with being creative) is not something that the members of subject benchmarking groups were overly concerned with. There are a number of possible explanations for this. Benchmarking groups may have considered the idea of creativity, but it was either rejected as an explicit concept for undergraduate learning or it was considered to be implicit in the concepts for learning that are made explicit. Alternatively, the idea may have just been omitted by accident from many of the benchmarking discussions: or have been marginalised in the face of the primary concerns of the discipline. Or, as one Chair of a benchmarking group claimed, 'creativity was not part of the QAA criteria'. But it's hard to believe that a group of intelligent and caring professionals would omit something that they thought was important simply because the guidance was deficient. In the belief that omission was by accident rather than intentional, a second strategy was developed to engage HE teachers and a small number of non-academic practitioners in selected subjects more directly. Four subjects were chosen for the pilot study: Earth and Environmental Sciences, History, Engineering and Social Work. For each discipline, academics' views were gathered by email questionnaire and synthesised into a Working Paper (Jackson, 2005a, 2005b, 2005c; Jackson and Burgess, 2005). It is important to appreciate that these summaries represent the collective views of a small number of representatives in each field. No individual holds the range of perspectives offered and it remains to be seen whether the perspectives as a whole have currency when they are exposed to wider debate in the disciplinary community. The exercise must be viewed as an initial step in articulating the meanings of creativity in disciplines and the intention is to promote further discussion and expression within the community, rather than to claim definitive representation.

Acceptance that creativity is necessary to disciplinary learning and practice

From the responses, it is clear that most academics believe that creativity is necessary to being a practitioner in their discipline. But many academics felt that, although they as individuals believe that creativity is important, it was not really valued in their discipline beyond the rhetorical level – a view that is consistent with the evaluation of the benchmarking statements.

Sites for creativity

Sites for creative thinking and action appear to be available in most aspects of disciplinary practice. For example, in History the potential for creativity exists in the:

- Processes of knowledge-gathering, since the sources are numerous and generally disparate.
- Historians' awareness of the approaches offered by other human science disciplines and their applicability to the study of the past.
- Analysis of the information from the past, including critical evaluation of sources in a comparative context.
- Empathy and imaginative representation of the past, which is an essential component of the historical process.
- The process of writing and presentation of output, a vital part of communication in the discipline.

These sites can be connected through the idea of disciplinary problem working (see page 105).

Being original

Originality can be represented as *creating something new for and useful to the discipline*.

> The ability to form or formulate something that no one else has done before and that feels as if it has the proper relations of the parts to the whole.
>
> (Earth and Environmental Science)

It is connected to invention and innovation where these add something to the discipline. In history, originality is seen as the *invention* of: new approaches to historical problems; new techniques to gather and analyse data; new approaches to validate existing accounts and evidence of the past; new/alternative interpretations explanations and insights of events; re-interpretations of the evidence; new forms of history; new forms of communication and new forms of historical understanding providing insights into how the past has shaped the present. A key focus for originality in the discipline is advancing understanding.

Originality in the context of students' learning might be represented as a student producing work that is very different to everyone else's work, denoting that they had thought about something in a very different way to the other students (Edwards *et al.*, Chapter 6 of this book, use the quality of newness as a way of explaining originality in students, learning).

Making use of imagination

The use of imagination (the faculty or action of producing ideas, especially mental images of what is not present or has not been experienced) takes on particular meaning in the disciplinary context. Imagination as a thinking process acts as a source of personal inspiration, it stimulates curiosity and sustains motivation, it generates ideas from which creative solutions are selected and facilitates interpretations in situations which cannot be understood by facts or observations alone. The knowledge and intellectual cultures and concerns of the domain provide the essential context for imagination when an academic is engaged in disciplinary thinking and practice.

> Perhaps there is something unique in the way imagination is utilised when the imagination can access the domain specific knowledge and skills of an engineer. Perhaps there is also something significant about creativity in the way engineers are inspired to imagine by the technical problems they encounter and the economic constraints within which they work.
>
> (Engineering)

> Historical imagination, in the positive sense of the imagination is absolutely necessary to grasp the 'other' times and places under exploration, and the ability to convey both that difference and a personal understanding of it.
>
> (History)

> I believe most of the social sciences encourage/require creative thought – or at least imaginative thought; the ability to literally think outside the box . . . in both understanding and responding to constantly changing dynamics in whatever contexts people work.
>
> (Social Work)

There are suggestions that either the use of imagination is more acceptable in some disciplines (such as the soft sciences and humanities) and/or the nature of discipline inquiry positively encourages its use.

> The possibility for thinking imaginatively in our subjects is enormous. We are not so constrained as in the more analytically grounded sciences.
>
> (History)

The imaginations of academics and non-academic practitioners are stimulated by the needs, concerns, interests, experiences, problems, people and things they encounter in the disciplinary world they have chosen to make their own. For example:

> There are lots of contexts/situations within the disciplinary territory that excite interest and stimulate and capture the imaginations of teachers and students. The scale of what we work with from the nano- to the galactic from observations of how things happen as they happen to what happened 2.5 billion years ago. The awesome nature we can observe around us – volcanoes, hurricanes, earthquakes. The effects of what we do on our planet on our fellow human beings. Why we are here and how we got here.
>
> (Earth Science)

> Creativity means finding imaginative new ways of working with people who are referred or who come for help.
>
> (Social Work)

> It is the potential for infinite variety in working with human beings that can stimulate creativity. This can be sharpened by close encounters with poverty, and with emotional deprivation and abuse.
>
> (Social Work)

> Inspiration for creativity in the design of new products or processes can come from any source in the physical environment.
>
> (Engineering)

> In the world of creating buildings the possibilities are pretty endless. And the chance to influence an urban landscape can be incredibly inspiring.
>
> (Engineering)

Finding and thinking about complex problems

The great engine of academic creativity is intellectual curiosity – the desire to find out, understand, explain, prove or disprove something or simply to imagine something different. Curiosity leads academics to find/create problems that can only be visualised, formulated and worked upon by people who are immersed in the knowledge, thinking/reasoning and practice skills of the domain.

> Engineers find problems that could only be imagined and conceptualised by an engineer with their knowledge and technical background.
>
> (Engineering)

> It is often said that engineers are problem solvers. I would prefer to say they are problem creators.
>
> (Engineering)

Complex problems are complex because they contain many interconnected and interfering parts or complex processes or interactions. The dynamics of these problems are such that they are not amenable to reductionist and linear ways of thinking but must be envisaged as a whole.

> Engineers have to apply systems thinking to complex problems in order to think of the problem holistically – how the components of the system interact and relate to each other. They must balance costs, benefits, safety, quality, reliability, appearance and environmental impact. Balancing so many variables in finding solutions may be a distinctive feature of engineering problem working and an important driver for creativity.
>
> (Engineering)

> Problem working is focused on understanding and explaining complex (physical, chemical and biological) systems that have to be visualised and understood holistically.
>
> (Earth and Environmental Science)

Intellectual curiosity is stimulated by problems that are of two basic types. The first type of disciplinary problem working is concerned with resolving or mediating an issue or improving a condition or situation. In Engineering the problem might be framed in terms of the need to *design* or *invent* new processes and *adapt* existing processes and products so that they are better and/or more cost-effective (and therefore more useful and valuable to society) than anything currently available. In Earth and Environmental Sciences the problem might be framed around discovering and evaluating new mineral deposits or perhaps stopping a mine from polluting the environment. The social worker is primarily concerned with understanding and resolving or mediating the problems of his/her clients and improving their situations and life chances.

    The second type of problem originates when academics go in search of intellectually exciting and challenging possibilities or opportunities for problem working. The problem is inspired by academics' own interests and perceptions of need or possibility. This type of *exploration* characterises research and scholarship and the solution of abstract problems, which may not have any immediate application. The outcomes of this type of problem working are more useful to advancing understanding in the discipline.

> Creativity arises when one identifies an aspect of history or a subject previously uncovered, and sets out to portray it in one form or another. It also comes about during the portrayal process, as one considers the best mode of representation.
>
> (History)

Willingness to explore in order to discover

Academics recognise that being creative requires exploration, experimentation and taking risks. Although there are certainly situations where risk-taking and experimentation are kept to a minimum.

> It seems absolutely essential that in order to maintain creativity, we have to periodically move out of our own masses of fixed ideas into the unknown. In the earth sciences, we have the opportunity to do this simply by exploring our planet, and now, other planets. We must recognise that stimulus and surprises are important. We as individuals should try to break down the barriers that our own frameworks erect and allow ourselves to be open to surprises.
>
> (Earth and Environmental Science)

> During their work they may need to improvise what is seen as part of a solution but on the whole they need to be ultra conservative because people, money and resources are at stake and the engineer is employed to secure results and not to experiment or take risks.
>
> (Engineering)

Making sense of complexity

Regardless of the context for problem working, academics in all disciplines believe that creativity is something that is used in working with problems that are challenging, new, unpredictable and/or emergent. There is little need for creativity in routine, well-understood problem working situations.

> There is so much ambiguity and paradox in the complex systems that we are studying that their recognition stimulates our curiosity. Many of the problems we work with have no single solution: the possibility space of different solutions stimulates creative thinking.
>
> (Earth and Environmental Science)

> Given the many layers and how these layers interact and impact individuals and families, there are far too many factors, converging in far too complex a way, to simply apply a rational, left-brained approach to considering an individual or family's situation and providing an 'informed' response.
>
> (Social Work)

Imagination is important to interpretation particularly in circumstances where the evidence base does not permit interpretations that are based solely on factual evidence.

> Most of us like to feel that we can get pretty close to what happened and 'creativity' reminds us just how much we fill in the gaps in the evidence base for ourselves. We might do this based on contextual knowledge, comparable case

studies, the use of interdisciplinary tools or whatever, but at the end of the day we have 'created' elements of 'the past'. It's important to recognise this creativity because it forces us to consider that the picture of the past we put together, whilst based on evidence and contextual 'established' knowledge, is nonetheless rooted in interpretation. So we don't so much recreate History but create it, and this is a difference between the 'Past' and 'History'. The past happened, but history is what we create from what we know of the past.

(History)

The complexity of the world we study means that it is open to interpretation. Curiosity that drives the search for understanding is stimulated by the possibility space afforded by interpretations of what is encountered.

(Earth and Environmental Science)

Engineers have to solve problems, often on the basis of limited and possibly contradictory information. In situations of incomplete data imaginative use of pattern recognition and predictions based on similar situations must play a part in the thinking process.

(Engineering)

Imagination is essential for the construction of mental models, representations of reality that people use to understand specific phenomena, the basis of reasoning in all disciplines. For example, in Social Work imagination might be directed towards understanding the complex set of relationships and environmental conditions that have shaped a client's view of and attitudes to the world. In Engineering, mental modelling might be focused on how a construction would function under extreme weather conditions in the future. In disciplines like Earth Science and History, mental models have to be constructed in order to understand how something worked or happened in the past.

Thinking outside and transferring into the disciplinary box

While problems might be rooted in a particular discipline, ideas, ways of thinking or methodologies from other disciplines are often involved in creative acts. The blending and intelligent use of these different sources of knowledge and methodologies to solve particular problems is potentially another source of creativity.

The complexity of systems requires practitioners to think inter-disciplinary: the discipline is pre-disposed to borrowing/adapting/using ideas, constructs and methodologies from other subjects.

(Earth and Environmental Science)

Utilising insights/concepts/theories/methodologies from another context or discipline in order to approach and analyse a particular issue from a new perspective. Other 'disciplines' might include philosophy, anthropology, cultural studies, literature and art.

(History)

A curiosity about how discoveries or topics in almost any other discipline might be integrated into the engineering inventory, theory and vocabulary.

(Engineering)

Synthesis, making connections and seeing relationships

Because working with complex problems (systems) often involves working with multiple and incomplete data sets, the capacity to synthesise, make connections and see new patterns and relationships seems to be particularly important in sense-making (interpreting) and working towards better understandings and possible solutions to difficult problems.

Pushing analysis into synthesis, broader approaches to constraints and links to analogous systems are all involved here.

(Engineering)

Sense-making in many aspects of Earth and Environmental Science involves piecing together lots of disparate pieces of information to construct a coherent and believable story and/or to see emergent patterns of relationships. Capacities to synthesise complex and incomplete data sets in order to see and understand the whole requires both inductive and deductive thinking.

Communication

The communication of ideas, knowledge and deeper understandings are important dimensions of creativity. Communication may be part of the creative process and/or diffusion of the results of creativity. Disciplinary practitioners are creative in the way in which they communicate with each other and with people outside their disciplines.

Technology does change and with it the technical language changes. Quite unconsciously the engineering community will coin new terms and exploit metaphor and analogy. Sometimes, such linguistic innovations shift to other professions or even the public. Linguistic creativity is thus a trait amongst engineers.

(Engineering)

I would claim that the communication of science is a feat comparable to the ability of humans to transmit aesthetics through paintings or music that are from different centuries and cultures. ... we must hold up to the rest of the scientific world the tremendous success of earth scientists in communicating through different cultures and languages the concepts of space, time, stratigraphy and process, when we often have not even seen the same rocks or experienced the same phenomena. Thus, the scientific product – though very different in expression from the artistic product – resembles the arts because it accomplishes communication between human beings across generational and cultural gaps.

(Earth and Environmental Science)

The social worker cannot begin to understand and resolve a client's problems if he/she cannot communicate in ways that are meaningful and empathise with the client.

Teaching kids how to play and have fun offered plentiful creative opportunities, as did learning how to structure the more difficult times of the day. For instance, meal times were often hairy, and I made a habit of finding riddles or trivia questions to ask at the table to keep the boys amused. Certain activities were in themselves creative (e.g. arts and crafts), and I often felt in a 'creative zone' when using humour, negotiating a sanction, or just planning a shift. I enjoyed those shifts best when I felt a good, strong creative energy, and I think the kids responded best to that energy as well.

(Social Work)

Story-telling

Disciplinary cultures are largely based on writing using the language, symbols and images that have been developed to facilitate communication of knowledge and understanding. Story-writing and story-telling seem to be important parts of academics' creativity.

Story-telling is fundamentally about making sense of worlds past, present and future. It is profound curiosity that these worlds invoke that is the primary source of creative inspiration for many earth and environmental scientists. Story-telling is a way of theorising about the way the world works.

(Earth and Environmental Science)

Authority depends not upon the discovery of 'facts' but upon the construction of convincing and persuasive argument; and all argument is creative. The process of creating stories to explain the past is one of generating possible interpretations and testing these through the evidential record.

(History)

When working with problems that society is interested in, practitioners must communicate with people outside their discipline.

The selling of ideas and novel solutions to clients must also be part of the creative process of an engineer. In presenting a unique idea or novel solution to a technical problem the creative engineer must convince other people of its value and its technical and economic feasibility.

(Engineering)

The social worker's creativity is used to create the best conditions for his/her clients to tell their stories, and for those stories to be understood by others who can help resolve the problems. The social worker is a creator and illustrator of stories. They help clients tell their stories in ways that reveal their situations and problems in order for them to be understood/diagnosed and addressed. The social worker captures these stories in forms that are appropriate and necessary to present a client's case and argue for support on their behalf. Social workers have to imagine the situations of the people they are helping in order to understand their problems and needs.

> Working with people requires a degree of spontaneity, flexibility and fresh-ness in order to be effective, and I think creativity underlies these things. It's about being responsive to the person and situation (and yourself, to some degree) in the moment. Working with children and young people offered what I found to be a rich context for creatively solving problems, structuring time, or looking at situations.
>
> (Social Work)

Resourcefulness

In Social Work (and other disciplines that are focused on helping people) resolv-ing or mediating a client's problem will depend to a large extent on the social worker's ability to access and acquire resources (financial, material, professional expertise).

> At the most mundane level such things as getting money for a homeless family out of the benefits office at 4.15 p.m. on a Friday afternoon counts as pretty creative in my book! At a broader level, social workers work with few resources, often in hostile situations, with few hard and fast boundaries (except the law, social policy and procedures). All of this calls for creativity of a kind.
>
> (Social Work)

Interpretations

These pilot surveys suggest that there is general acceptance that creativity is widely recognised in disciplinary contexts. All participants identified things that they asso-ciate with being creative in the discipline, although there was considerable variation in the level of detail and elaboration of responses.

When set against the collective views of academics on creativity in each discipline, subject benchmarking statements give an incomplete and misleading view of the extent to which creativity features in disciplinary thinking and prac-tice. There are at least three possible reasons for this. First, and in mitigation, we might recognise that benchmarking statements are framed in terms of undergrad-uate learning, whereas the responses of academics in the study reported here are framed around their views of creativity in both academic and professional disciplinary practice; we may be dealing with different contexts and levels of creativity. But if one of the purposes of higher education is to prepare learners for professional practice in the field, then there should be a relationship between the two levels and contexts. Second, also in mitigation, we should recognise that the benchmarking statements represent the initial step in formulating a discipline view of what is important in students' higher education learning. Given the general absence of discussion about creativity in disciplines, it is not surprising that most benchmarking groups paid only cursory attention to its role in students' learning. The richer perspectives on creativity in the disciplines now being surfaced through these surveys can be used to evaluate and develop the benchmark statements when they are formally reviewed. Third, many academics report that creativity, while recognised in their discipline, is not really valued beyond the rhetorical level. So the limited recognition of creativity in benchmarking statements might simply reflect ambivalence to creativity in the disciplinary culture.

What is encouraging is that statements are generally supportive of active and engaged forms of learning within which students' creativity can be developed and demonstrated. Most disciplines value project/assignment work, personal/ interpersonal, skills and personal development planning/reflection, but tend to neglect open-ended problem solving, negotiated and experiential learning and negotiated, self- and peer-assessment.

Representations of creativity in disciplines

While being creative means particular things in disciplines, the following general patterns of meanings can be distinguished.

Originality – at the highest level of achievement, originality can be represented as *creating something new which is useful, recognised and incorporated into the culture of the discipline*. Originality is manifested in individual and collective acts of invention, innovation and adaptation that change the domain, and it is consistent with the definition of a creative person offered by Csikszentmihalyi (1997: 27): *'someone whose thoughts or actions change a domain, or establish a new one.'* But the concept of originality can't only apply to someone who changes a domain. Acts of personal invention or innovation that bring about localised cultural change, but which do not affect the domain as a whole, must also be viewed as creative. An example might be a new approach to teaching that is developed and adopted in a department, and then perhaps exported to other departments within and outside of the institution.

Imagination – 'seeing and developing new meanings of the world' (Thomas, 1999) lies at the heart of the creative academic enterprise and imagination is central to this ability. People working in a disciplinary setting imagine things that only they can imagine when their knowledge, understanding, interests and skills are engaged and stimulated by the things that matter to them in the disciplinary world they inhabit.

> Imagination – the mental capacity for experiencing, constructing, or manipulating 'mental imagery' (quasi-perceptual experience) is regarded as being

responsible for fantasy, inventiveness, idiosyncrasy, and creative, original, and insightful thought in general, and, sometimes, for a much wider range of mental activities dealing with the non-actual, such as supposing, pretending, *seeing as*, thinking of possibilities, and even being mistaken.

(Dictionary of Philosophy of the Mind)

Imagination is a capacity and a way of being that is central to the construction of new perceptual worlds that can only be imagined, not experienced.

Imagination is what makes our sensory experience meaningful, enabling us to interpret and make sense of it, whether from a conventional perspective or from a fresh, original, individual one. It is what makes perception more than the mere physical stimulation of sense organs. It also produces mental imagery, visual and otherwise, which is what makes it possible for us to think outside the confines of our present perceptual reality, to consider memories of the past and possibilities for the future, and to weigh alternatives against one another. Thus, imagination makes possible all our thinking about what is, what has been, and, perhaps most important, what might be.

(Nigel J.T. Thomas)

The core enterprise of the academy is to develop new knowledge and re-interpret existing knowledge. Much of our knowledge about the world has been created through direct observation, experience and careful measurement and recording of what we can observe and experience. But there are many things that we cannot experience, and to understand it in the way we have come to understand it we also have to *explore and see it* through our imaginations. Academics use their imaginations to:

- Generate ideas and possibilities (e.g. to find problems).
- Invent ways of exploring problems, complex situations and systems (e.g. thinking holistically, being resourceful, inventing new or adapting existing methodologies).
- Combine ideas and things in novel ways.
- Interpret and find novel solutions to problems and challenges. They fill in the gaps, synthesize, find patterns and connections, hypothesise and theorise, engage in sense-making that is not constrained by that which can be observed or proved.
- Construct and tell stories that explain and change the way people see the world.

Problem working – there are many sites and opportunities for creativity in disciplinary thinking and practice and these can be connected within different notions of problem working. While the nature of the problems and the way they are visualised and addressed varies from discipline to discipline, finding, formulating, exploring, interpreting and finding solutions to complex concrete or abstract problems is the key focus for creative thinking and action in all disciplinary contexts. Academics

Representation A

Mental representation of academics' creativity in problem working
combining inductive and deductive forms of thinking in novel ways

The taken for granted stock of problem working
knowledge that can be drawn upon in future
(origin of expertise drawn from experience?).

How do I communicate these ideas/solutions?
How do I persuade others that they are useful?

What are the possible/optimal solutions/
interpretations for the given circumstances?

What are the most useful solutions?

What is the nature of the problem(s)?
What sort of things can be done to
engage with/address the problem(s)?
What do I need to know?

How do I solve this problem?
What problems need to be solved?

Metalearning?

Solution-finding,
synthesising,
interpreting,
evaluating

Communicating

Exploring

Generating

Representation B

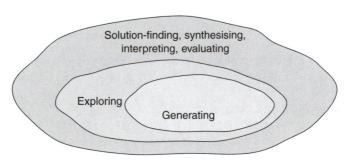

Solution-finding, synthesising,
interpreting, evaluating

Exploring

Generating

Figure 8.1 Representations of creative processes in disciplinary problem working contexts.

Note
(A) represents a problem working scenario that evolves more or less linearly over time. This form is typical of a major research project. Many problem working situations might require the cycle of generation–exploration–synthesis–solution-finding to be enacted over and over again. **(B)** represents a more integrated representation of the generation–exploration–synthesis–solution-finding cycle such as might be associated in problem working situations involving clients or patients.

believe that creativity is something that is used in working with problems that are challenging, new, unpredictable and/or emergent. There is little need for creativity in routine, well-understood problem working situations. Story-writing and story-telling, which enable complexity to be understood and communicated, are important parts of the creative process in all the disciplines studied.

Figure 8.1 provides a representation of creativity within the disciplinary field that is directed to problem working. Imagination is represented as the way academics combine different forms of thinking to find, formulate, explore and resolve the sorts of problems that are meaningful to them in their disciplinary settings. Imagination is grown from disciplinary understandings, stimulated by issues and events that are encountered and inspired by the things that inspire people in that disciplinary world. Imaginations might also be shaped by ideas and ways of thinking and behaving imported from other disciplines. Ultimately, the experience and learning gained from being creative by working with a problem in this way enters an individual's stock of metacognitive knowledge which can then be drawn upon to invent new problem working and learning strategies as the need emerges. The term metalearning has been used to represent this type of creativity (Jackson, 2004a).

Appendix 8.1

Example of the analytical tool used to evaluate subject benchmark statements for indications of support for creativity in students' learning. The complete set of analyses can be found at: http://www.heacademy.ac.uk/creativity.htm.

Indicators of Creativity in the History Subject Benchmark Statement

Categories for creativity	*Indicators of creativity*	*Specific indicators explicitly identified*
	Divergent and convergent thinking. Lateral thinking.	
1 Student thinking abilities	Operating in complex and ambiguous settings.	Interpretation of complex, ambiguous, conflicting and incomplete material. Capacity to consider and solve complex problems.
	Taking risks and coping with 'failure'. Generation of ideas.	
2 Student ideas	Reflection on ideas.	
	Review and evaluation of ideas. Development of new knowledge. Development of new practice(s).	

Categories for creativity	Indicators of creativity	Specific indicators explicitly identified
3 Student imagination and originality	Making of new knowledge connections. Transfer and application of learning in new contexts. Engages in systematic process of enquiry.	Empathy and imaginative insight. Skills of the researcher – to set tasks and solve problems.
	Open-ended problem solving Project/assignment work to plan/design/develop.	Ability to formulate questions and provide answers using valid and relevant evidence and argument.
4 Student activities with potential to promote creativity	Personal/interpersonal skills for teamwork/pdp/reflection.	Ability to work with others and have respect for their views. Reflect critically on the nature of their discipline.
	Skills: analysis, review, synthesis, evaluation. Negotiated and experiential learning. Negotiated, self and peer assessment.	Gather, sift, select, organise and synthesise large quantities of evidence.

Notes

1 The working papers and analysis of subject benchmark statements can be found at: www.heacademy.ac.uk/2762.htm.
2 www.calstatela.edu/faculty/nthomas/.

9   Views from the chalk face

Lecturers' and students' perspectives on the development of creativity in art and design

Ruth Dineen

Introduction

This chapter describes a study of lecturer and student views on creativity, under-taken in the field of art and design. The study, completed in 2004, involved over 100 students and 20 lecturers from FE and HE art and design courses in two institutions. The results provide useful insights into perceptions of creativity from a single discipline field, one which explicitly focuses on the creative individual and the development of their creative potential.

Methodology

Data was collected from 21 lecturers and 113 students at two art and design institutions. Participants were drawn from a broad range of subjects at FE and HE levels, including fine art, graphic design, ceramics and industrial design. The study group was selected to provide a spread of responses from foundation students through to final-year undergraduates.

All participants completed questionnaires (one for lecturing staff, one for students) which allowed for quantitative (tick box) answers and optional qualitative comments. Both students and lecturers were asked to define creativity in terms of their own practice. Students were asked to choose an art and design project which they had undertaken and to assess their creative development within it. Through the questionnaire responses they then identified which pedagogic and personal factors had assisted that creative development. In addition, they were asked to specify the two most significant factors for their creative success from a list which included physical environment, project organisation and scheduling, teaching styles or approaches, teaching methods, type of project, prior skills and knowledge, and approach to learning.

Lecturers were also asked to rate the significance of these factors for their students' creative success, and to identify the two most salient factors. Their questionnaire responses provided the basis for semi-structured, recorded interviews. Student and staff responses were categorised and compared to identify commonalities and differences of opinion among staff and between staff and students. The quantitative data provided further comparisons. The data were analysed via SPSS using chi-testing to assess significance.

In addition, each lecturer was requested to identify one or two students whose project work revealed high levels of creativity, and asked on what basis that judgement was made. Samples of that work were recorded both to provide evidence of the consistency (or otherwise) of lecturers' evaluation of creativity, and visual evidence that would support or extend understandings gained through questionnaire and interview responses.

The data are extensive and analysis is ongoing. However, several themes reoccur in the responses of both teachers and learners. For this account I am going to focus on the centrality of creativity, the importance of the teacher–student relationship, and the problematic nature of assessment. An overview of the qualitative data relating to these themes is presented here.

Perspectives on creativity

By their very nature, art and design deal with speculative and divergent ideas, the negotiation of uncertainties and ambiguities. The knowledge-base is contingent, moving across boundaries to make new connections. All of the lecturers interviewed for this study were practising artists/designers. They appeared to use their personal understandings of creative activity to inform their pedagogic practice, placing creativity at the centre of the curriculum and its delivery.

It is not surprising, therefore, that the development of learner creativity was considered by all of the lecturers to be the primary goal of art and design education. In the words of one interviewee, 'we must give [the students] the right conditions to find their own self and their most exciting minds'. A humanistic view of creativity prevailed, reflecting Carl Roger's belief that creativity is libidinous, made manifest by 'man's tendency to actualise himself, to become his potentialities' (Rogers, 1952: 35). Interviewees' definitions of creativity thus tended to focus on the route to self-actualisation: through 'originality, imagination and curiosity', 'empathy and understanding mediated through practice', 'taking risks and jumping into the unknown'. With powerful conviction, one lecturer suggested that:

> Creativity is imagination, fired by passion, underpinned by knowledge and skill. What is imagination? It is questioning, foolhardiness, a belief that you can actually move yourself to that [new] place; spirit, determination, and optimism. And passion? It means having an open mind, integrity and a courageous heart.

Many students defined creativity in similarly active terms, describing it as 'a form of release', 'spontaneous excitement', 'vast and endless', 'a flamboyant explosion of imagination and emotion. Something that builds up inside me to sporadically spill out into a piece of work.' One suggested succinctly that it was 'getting the inside of my head onto a page'; one spoke of 'the ability to express myself and my individuality through my work'; another defined it as 'freedom to develop in the way you choose, refining your skills and imagination'. Student responses were most frequently emotional or personal. They referred to self-expression and self-development, to expressing emotions or individuality, and to interpreting or communicating their viewpoint through imagination and intuition.

Other responses, from both staff and students, focused on originality and 'adventure', on the importance of 'seeing things differently', 'pushing boundaries', 'making connections' and working in ways which were 'wild', 'crazy' or 'unorthodox': 'It's about lateral thinking, distance from the origin, pushing all ideas good and bad with a belief in producing something of interest and desire.' The need to allow for the unexpected and to encourage open-minded approaches through experimentation, exploration and play was another common theme.

Similarly, all participants emphasised connections between creative expression and everyday life. Speaking of one, highly creative, student, a lecturer commented: 'She just knew how to interact with life. Everything that she delighted in, and everything that went on for her ended up in her workbook. That's the great thing about art and design, you live life and it comes out in the work.' Another was clear that 'by being a fully alive human being, your whole creativity flowers'. Creativity was held to 'relate to all areas of practice: intellectual, practical, material, social interaction, conversations ... it's ever-changing and ever-present'. Student definitions were often equally broad-based. One felt that, '[my creative work] expresses ideas, emotion, thoughts, humour, outlook, beliefs, love, hate, music ... a mixture of life experiences and imagination'; another simply stated, 'it's a way of observing the world'.

Several categories of definition emerged from the analysis of student responses. A small number were based on cognitive or motor skills. A much larger group related to imagination and self-expression, others to originality or to freedom from restraint. Most were inclusive, crossing the superimposed category boundaries. A first-year student, for example, suggested that 'creativity is using all your knowledge and skills, and then doing the impossible'.

All of the students were able to define creativity in relation to their own practice (and, by implication, themselves). Unlike the students in Oliver's study (see Chapter 5), their responses suggest that they view creativity as an innate and unproblematic aspect of their identity as learners, practitioners and individuals. This is perhaps partly to do with the UK art and design admissions procedure. In order to gain a place, students must demonstrate their creative potential through showing and discussing a portfolio of their work. To an extent, therefore, acceptance on to a course means that their creativity had been judged acceptable by the subject 'gatekeepers'. In Holmes' (2002) analysis (discussed more fully in Chapter 5 of this book), this would provide students with an 'agreed identity' in relation to their creativity, claimed by them and affirmed by others.

Students in this study also appear to be generally confident in their ability to realise their creative potential. Participants included the full range of ability levels, yet, when asked how creatively successful they had been in their current or last project, all ticked either 'very successful' or 'successful'. The assumption that this response might reflect not creative confidence but low aspirations on the part of learners or teachers is powerfully countered by interviewee responses and by the diversity and originality of the work itself.

The view of creativity expressed by participants in this study is extraordinarily all-embracing. It is seen as a defining factor of our humanity, and the wellspring of personal growth. Unless thwarted, it provides the motivation for self-actualisation, for the development of our innate potential. It is not limited by context but can manifest itself in all aspects of our lives. Creative potential is thus seen as a given; the task is 'to set up strategies that allow it to emerge, or to be confirmed'.

Teacher–student relationships

The pedagogic model that emerges from this holistic view of creativity does not appear to be discipline-dependent. Rather, it is based on a commitment to an 'emancipatory and transformative' education (Danvers, 2003: 47). One interviewee affirmed that her job was to 'tap in to the imagination and curiosity of the student, helping them access something that's deep inside themselves'. Lecturers stressed the need to 'make the students feel valued, for themselves and their own views, for everything they do', believing that art and design education 'is not just vocational training, it's the development of the whole person. I reinforce that, reiterate it throughout every single process that I teach'.

The teacher–student relationship was believed to be at the heart of this endeavour: '[it] is really important to show them you are interested in what they are doing, you care about it. It's to do with the relationship between them and us. That's the key.' Lecturers spoke of their role with often passionate conviction: 'to disseminate energy, express love, develop trust, allow them to stumble, to gain independence.'

The non-hierarchical nature of the relationship was frequently reiterated: 'it's about an attitude between staff and students. Both must be willing for things to go wrong ... for anything to happen'; 'my job is not to impose how I see the world. My job is to facilitate them to have the confidence to say what they as individuals want to say ... to feel they have something to contribute'. One lecturer stated explicitly that 'I don't teach, what I do is help people see, help them unlock what is already there. I know what helps people gain confidence ... I find the right buttons to push and then they start to push them for themselves.' Lecturers were also clear that 'it's not about putting your own ego forward. It isn't about "here I am", it's about "here's this idea, this problem, let's solve it"; it's about enthusiasm and delight.'

Students used similar words to describe the teaching approaches they encountered. A first-year BA student 'found the tutors welcoming, helpful and enthusiastic', commenting that 'they actually talk to you, rather than at you'. Another felt that 'the tutor's enthusiasm inspired me to think harder and become more creative'; a third commented that 'the tutor's attitude spurred me on to open all the doors of my creativity; it really inspired me to push myself and not hold back'. In the study, 97 per cent of the students considered that their creative success had been significantly and positively affected by the teaching styles they encountered. According to one interviewee, these were 'not to do with "success" or "non-success" [but about] getting them [the students] to enjoy themselves.

We are here to have fun, feeling enthusiastic, excited about the subject matter. That enthusiasm has to be there from the start; it comes from the teacher.'

Many students at foundation level commented on the differences between school and FE teaching approaches. They clearly relished being in an environment where 'creativity is considered important and is encouragingly taught by people who are passionate about it', and enjoyed the freedom of 'being given support without being spoon fed . . . like having an idea planted, then you grow on your own'.

Their lecturers emphasised the need to build confidence and trust, to 'nurture what they [the students] have and then give them a little bit more' and to 'be approachable'. They appeared to negotiate the subtleties of the staff–student relationship with considerable sensitivity: 'I feel I'd failed if students put up barriers, psychological walls. That can be tricky. It can be to do with something that's happened at home, or a previous bad experience. Sometimes you have to back off, give them a bit of leeway, a bit of space, and they might come back.' Empathy was felt to be key to success in this enterprise:

> I empathise with the difficulty of assimilating new information. I think they feel safe with someone who knows what it feels like. I emphasise that and my concern for them and their feelings. Then they are willing to look at additional options, to push themselves beyond a locked-in, mechanical attitude. And humour is used to break the ice, the tension, help them relax. It prevents the paralysis that can occur when they think 'I have to do this task'. The relationship dissipates that paralysis.

Comments by staff frequently echoed understandings of the relationship between teaching for creativity and creative teaching found elsewhere in this book. Stressing the importance of 'the right attitude and motivation on the teacher's part', one lecturer affirmed 'you have to be fully involved otherwise you fail [to reach] them'. Another provided an inspirational picture of art and design education:

> It was all to do with the staff-student relationship. It increased student motivation *and* staff motivation. The task could be dispiriting – almost mechanical. There's much more to us than that. The fact that we did it together made the students more responsive, and having an 'outside' client increased group cohesion – a common enemy! We were in this together and together we could do it. Staff involvement goes through the roof – I'm flying! Motivation [can] soar in the face of challenge.

Responses also affirm the collaborative nature of post-compulsory art and design education. Collaboration is encouraged not only within the teacher–student relationship but within and across the student cohort: 'We can teach them about 65 per cent if we're lucky – the rest comes from each other: testing things out on each other is absolutely fundamental. It's about collective energy'; 'It is nerve racking when you're reaching out for something that is quite unknown to you. I notice that in that sort of situation the students are very generous to each other. They are intrigued by what others achieve and that's really helpful.'

Most interviewees saw the ultimate aim of this teacher–learner partnership as student independence, reflecting a view of creativity as 'an intimate and individual thing. You can't say "this is creativity, now do it" because it has a unique pathway for each person.' Strategies were set up 'to make sure students meet their own challenge. You can't do it for them. Their outcome may be weak or strong but the pleasure is seeing their satisfaction at their own development.' There was a consensus that 'how to learn is the most important lesson we can teach. It's absolutely paramount. We want students to switch from the idea of information being delivered to them to gathering information for themselves ... becoming independent.' Students' responses suggest that they concur: nearly two-thirds mentioned the importance of independence for creative success. One student was unequivocal that their creative success was due to 'being able to work alone with personal enthusiasm and self-belief', reflecting the ambition of lecturing staff to 'give students empowerment, ownership of their creative potential'.

Assessment

There appears to be a close alignment between pedagogic aims and pedagogic methods in art and design education. At the centre of the curriculum and its delivery is the creative learner. Supportive, non-hierarchical teacher–student relationships are built up to encourage personal development and ultimate independence. However, interview responses suggest that this alignment of ends and means begins to break down when institutional systems are used to assess student progress. Lecturers raised concerns about the very nature of assessment:

'the culture is driven by assessment ... by auditors wanting to audit how many people have done how many things in a period of time. With creativity you can't say how many people have reached this creative potential over this period of time. It's not a tangible measurable structure, it's a subjective but [also] very real thing, which lies at the heart of human civilisation.

They suggested that formal assessment schemes inhibit experimentation, divergent thinking and risk-taking:

Students haven't got the feeling throughout the course that they can develop and go off down blind alleys. Creativity isn't a street that is bramble-free ... we need to allow students to actually get stuck in the brambles a bit more in order to find their own creativity and their own particular voice.

Staff were also concerned that formal assessment systems undermined student confidence and development:

I valued it when I had a chance to sit with every student, and had a chance to discuss [the work] with them. Paper assessment is not ideal for human beings. We need a pat, somebody to say to us 'well ok, you got a double E – but actually I feel you did your best and this element is particularly good'. For people to grow there needs to be personal interactive warmth ... that's what makes all of us prosper. That can't always be put on a piece of paper, especially not the subtlety.

Clear distinctions were drawn between informal or course-based diagnostic evaluations and institutional requirements for formal, summative assessment. The latter were generally viewed as demotivating, antipathetic to creative development. Conversely, all staff affirmed the value of diagnostic assessment:

Assessment (i.e. everything the student received during the [module], everything said by tutors, themselves and peers) is one of the greatest learning elements within the whole experience. It's not whether they got an A, B or C, it's about how did they respond to something, are they further down the road of understanding, how well did they contextualise things, how has that moved them forward?

This view of assessment parallels Cowan's proposal in Chapter 12 of this book that an assessment strategy should 'enable students to explore, experience and develop their own understanding of creativity and construct new meanings'. To this end, lecturers sought ways to subvert the imposed systems, to turn assessment into a collaborative and creative learning experience.

Primarily, lecturers encouraged students to redefine their notions of success and failure; '[we get them] to take risks with the way they are thinking, what they are making. I say to them "if it doesn't work then you learn as much from that as if it does". That idea of failing ... I hate that idea, it's a learning process – no right or wrong.' From the start students were expected to engage in this debate, to make their own judgements; 'the student evaluation doesn't have to justify their process or outcome – it could have been wrong, but the experience of doing it would enable them to get it right next time. Mistakes are always positive.'

Staff acknowledged the anxiety that this paradigm shift can cause. 'A lot of students are very scared when they start ... we take time out, take the pressure off ... [get them to] rely on intuition and trust.' They attempted to minimise fear through support and encouragement: 'I need to be there acting as the bridge between what they know and the unknown, the unfamiliar.' As one BA course director explained:

We attempt to make them aspire very high very early. It's dangerous. As long as you keep telling them that it's deep water and reassuring them that it'll get shallower then it's ok. If you keep aspirations high, nurture things, keep a close eye, it's amazing what people can achieve.

Student responses suggest that these strategies were working. One spoke of the necessity of 'being experimental and not being afraid to try new things. If you let go and don't hold back, I believe you're at your most exciting and creative.' Another considered that 'to be creative it helps to be around other creative people, to take account of their ideas, experiments and mistakes, to learn from these and from your own mistakes'. Several mentioned 'risk-taking' and the need for courage. Asked how she could have been more creatively successful, one first-year BA student replied, 'I should have been braver.'

Elsewhere in this book, Cowan and Balchin propose collaborative and con- sensual approaches to assessment. Interviewees in this study similarly stress the importance of having an evaluative dialogue with students; 'even if only to affirm that what they've done is a journey of experience, enriching their under- standing. That feedback is crucial; they cannot make any decisions [or] build on what they have learned if they don't have the opportunity to verbalise it.' At foundation level, students were required to reflect on their learning formally: 'they have to write down their thoughts about their own work – self-assessment, evaluation and reflection. They document what is going on in their everyday life – not just the art and design experience.' The system was less explicit on under- graduate courses, although all students were expected to keep workbooks or visual journals. These were used 'to provide evidence to see how they've developed and pushed the boundaries of what they've selected to do'.

Emphasising the non-hierarchical nature of this debate, one lecturer com- mented:

> I'm very honest at assessment. Then I ask them 'am I right or am I wrong? Forget the fact that I'm your tutor. What do you think?' I want them to eval- uate it. It doesn't really matter what I think. It's their understanding. At the end [of the course] they have to walk out and stand on their own two feet as independent thinkers.

Another explained: 'I'm more interested in them going on their journey rather than the grade. It's an ongoing discussion, we talk to students all the time . . . an informal assessment process.' Suggesting that 'assessment is one of the greatest learning elements within the whole experience', one lecturer outlined a discur- sive system where 'assessment is run with the students through critiques and dis- cussion groups; the students make a verbal presentation and the work is displayed'.

Several interviewees raised concerns that formal assessment tended, for prac- tical reasons, to focus on final outcomes rather than the journey taken by the student to reach their goal. This in turn was held to undermine deep learning, lessening student's engagement with 'what's underneath the iceberg [outcome], the two-thirds that supports it . . . you won't be doing the students any good if you just teach them how to make fascinating objects if they haven't got the mechanisms of creativity that took them there'. One foundation lecturer felt that outcomes were 'almost incidental' during the early stages of the course; another's comment suggested that the outcome and process were philosophically indivisible; 'within the project outcome they can see the process of thinking, of making, the places where they went wrong, the new things they've discovered;

how [the object] informs space, how space informs the object; having a project outcome substantiates the experience.'

To emphasise this interconnectivity, lecturers turned the entire creative process into an assessable outcome, using criteria such as 'breadth of experimentation', 'creativity and originality' and 'innovative use of media' to assess work-in-progress. An industrial design lecturer explained: 'we assess the brief, the specification, the range of ideas, the analysis, the solution and the evaluation of the solution. The marking scheme forces them [the students] to go through the whole process.' A similar breadth of approach was affirmed by other interviewees: 'we look at the research, creative development, time management and technical competence as well as their ability to discuss and evaluate and synthesise.'

Brief conclusions

A belief in the innate creative potential of the individual appears to be at the heart of the creative education studied here. This humanist approach has, it seems, given coherence to the pedagogic model used in post-compulsory UK art and design education. It can be seen to have influenced educational aims and aspirations, teacher motivation and engagement, attitudes to assessment and, significantly, to have shaped the relationship between teacher and learner.

The study was small-scale, and interpretation of the qualitative data unavoidably subjective. Nonetheless, participant responses suggest that lecturers and students in post-compulsory UK art and design education are not just 'talking the talk' but 'walking the walk', engaged in an energising and transformative experience of creative learning. Perhaps there are lessons here for the development of pedagogies to promote and facilitate students' creative potential in other disciplines.

10 Developing students' creativity

Searching for an appropriate pedagogy

Norman Jackson and Christine Sinclair

Introduction

> The search for ways to enhance creativity to help people develop more of
> their potential ... is a reasonable question in the absence of compelling
> evidence that such a search is futile.
>
> (Nickerson, 1999: 392)

The preceding chapters have elaborated teachers' and students' views of the
meanings of creativity in higher education contexts that are relevant to them.
The primary aim of this chapter is to help teachers and students to 'develop
more of their potential'. We are looking at (a) the potential of students to
develop their creativity and (b) the potential of teachers to develop strategies to
support this.

In order to do this, we have been through our own creative process: questioning, building on intuition, trying out ideas, connecting previously unconnected
resources. The results then had to be tempered with a more analytical approach:
evidencing, interpreting, refining, elaborating and then checking our ideas with
well-informed peers (John Cowan and John Biggs) who used their objectivity
and creativity to evaluate our thinking. It was very much a socially constructive
process.

We also want to provide practical support where we can, so we have been
engaged in selecting, exemplifying, suggesting resources, with a view to operationalising the most useful theories we have encountered (Appendix 10.2).
Because this has inevitably left a complex trail of thinking and writing that we
did not want to lose, we have incorporated some of the details in Appendix
10.1.

Our hope is that by elaborating the questions that have driven our search for
appropriate pedagogies, our responses to these questions, and our search for
theoretical underpinnings to substantiate our reasoning, we will help and encourage other teachers to engage in their own searches and sense-making. We have
embarked on a journey that we think will lead to creative development – and we
want to make our route explicit. We began our journey by asking what we thought
were important questions about creativity and its place in a higher education (Figure

10.1, column 1). Our responses to the questions (column 2) have been informed by the theoretical perspectives mentioned in the third column. In this way we have begun to extend and integrate various ideas from the literature and evolve our own thinking. Further elaboration of Table 10.1 can be seen in Appendix 10.1.

These themes are explored in the following section. The final section of the chapter concentrates on the last question and explores a model that may be helpful.

Features of creativity and creative people

Some characteristics of creativity

One of the problems with creativity is that it is difficult to understand and explain. Chapters 4–9 show the rich variety of perspectives on creativity of students and teachers in higher education. One of the purposes of our sense-making for teaching is to try to represent creativity in ways that can be operationalised.

In a list that was generated by the Imaginative Curriculum project, academics associated the following features with creativity and creative people (Jackson and Shaw, this volume, Chapter 8):

- Being imaginative, generating new ideas, thinking out of the boxes we normally inhabit, looking beyond the obvious, seeing the world in different ways so that it can be explored and understood better.
- Being original. This embodies:
  - the quality of newness, for example: inventing and producing new things or adapting things that someone else has invented; doing things no one has done before; and doing things that have been done before but differently;
  - the idea of significance – there are different levels and notions of significance but utility and value are integral to the idea.
- Exploring, experimenting and taking risks, i.e. processes for searching in order to find or discover often involves journeying into the unknown.
- Skills in critical thinking and synthesis – the ability to process and analyse data/situations/ideas/contexts and to see the world differently as a result.
- Communication – often through story-telling that helps people see the world you have created or helps you see the worlds of others.

These characteristics bear a striking resemblance to the characteristics of creativity recognised by the QCA (2004) and being promoted in schools (see Craft, this volume, Chapter 3). The QCA suggest that creativity involves pupils in: questioning and challenging; making connections, seeing relationships; envisaging what might be; exploring ideas and keeping options open; reflecting critically on ideas, actions and outcomes.

Furthermore, when the characteristics of creativity are operationalised in disciplinary practices (Jackson and Shaw, this volume, Chapter 8) they begin to

Table 10.1 The reasoning underlying our strategy for the development of students' creativity

Questions	Responses	Conceptual influences and relevant research
What are the creative abilities we want to develop?	Traits, abilities and characteristics of creative people and actions.	Perkins' (1981) six trait model of creativity coupled to Imaginative Curriculum findings.
	It depends what level they are at.	Taylor (1959) on levels of creative engagement and Dreyfus and Dreyfus (1986) on levels of skill acquisition.
		In HE – in this volume, Edwards *et al.*, Chapter 6, Fryer, Chapter 7, Jackson and Shaw, Chapter 8, Dineen, Chapter 9.
How do creative abilities at different levels fit into HE learning?	They form a set of abilities along with others required by successfully intelligent people. Success in a domain requires an appropriate balance of these.	Sternberg and Lubart's (1996) triarchy of abilities. De Corte's (2000) explanation of expertise in a domain. Taylor (1960) on levels of creative engagement. Dreyfus and Dreyfus (1986) and Dufresne *et al.* (1995) on the skills, knowledge and behaviour that move a person from novice to expert.
How does a person achieve a successful utilisation and balance of their own abilities?	Through self-regulated learning . . .	Zimmerman (2000) and Zimmerman and Schunk (2004).
How does a learner learn to self-regulate? What are the relationships and limits of self-regulation and cognitive apprenticeship with respect to creativity?	. . . supported with feedback to improve learning. Through cognitive apprenticeship. Some processes seem to be tacit and invisible or emerge when there is no focus. Nevertheless, creativity relies on other modes of thinking for its execution.	Nicol and MacFarlane-Dick (in press). Collins, *et al.* (1991).
What type of teaching and learning systems might encompass self-regulation and cognitive apprenticeship while promoting creativity?	One that emphasises and pays attention to the relationships between student, teacher and task.	Polanyi (1966) Schön (1983) and Claxton (1997). Dunne, in Jackson *et al.* (2004) adapted here specifically for creativity. Biggs' (2002, 2003) notion of constructive alignment.

resemble the features seen in generic models of creativity such as the well-known 'Snowflake' proposed by David Perkins (1981) which include:

- High tolerance for complexity, disorganisation and the messiness of life.
- Ability in problem finding and discovery modes of being.
- Mental mobility and ability to change perspectives.
- Willingness to take risks and the ability to accept and learn from mistakes.
- Skill in critical thinking, enabling ideas to be evaluated.
- Strong self-motivation and self-determination to accomplish goals.

The idea behind the snowflake model – that different individuals possess 'creative' traits or talents in different measures all contributing to their unique profile – is also relevant to our enquiry into supporting and developing creativity in students. This connects very nicely with the idea that creativity is part of a person's identity; their way of being and becoming (see Oliver *et al.*, this volume, Chapter 5 and Dineen, this volume, Chapter 9 to learn what students say).

Domains and levels where creativity is found

Creativity exists and operates on a continuum from inventions and interventions that change the world, through those that change a domain (like physics), to those that have local and personal significance: 'a sort of "personal effectiveness" in coping well with unknown territory and in recognising and making choices' (Craft, this volume, Chapter 3). In higher education, as in schools education, we are primarily concerned with the latter but we must aspire to prepare people to take on challenges at the level of creative change in their chosen field of endeavour.

It is important to recognise the significance of level; there will be differences in creative responses between those students who are just starting at university and those just leaving to go into employment. If universities are doing their job properly, when students complete their programme they should be able to apply their creativity at a more advanced level of complexity than when they started (i.e. they will have developed a number of creative abilities and be able to use these in combination with the knowledge and skills they have developed while at university). We consider that a higher education that has not achieved this has not fully developed students' potential. We certainly hope that they do not leave displaying *less* creativity than when they arrived or that they are less inclined to creative enterprise than before their higher education experience.

It is interesting to compare what writers about creativity and expertise say about level – and this comparison does anticipate and provide a link to our next question. An example of each is given in Table 10.2 – interestingly, both examples propose five 'steps'.

There are many interesting features about these two lists and it is instructive to try to map one on to the other. Here, however, we want to highlight two key points; about the conscious following of rules and the role of intuition.

Table 10.2 Steps in creativity, knowledge, understanding and skill acquisition

Taylor (1959) The Nature of Creative Process	*Dreyfus and Dreyfus (1986)* Mind Over Machine
Five levels of creative engagement (of an artist)	Five stages of skill acquisition from novice to expert
Primitive and intuitive expression – as in children and untrained adults.	**Novice** – following learned rules.
Academic and technical level – skills and techniques leading to expression.	**Advanced beginner** – knowing what to do in a particular situation.
Inventive level – experimentation with academic level, pushing boundaries.	**Competence** – recognising important factors in a complex situation and making decisions based on them.
Innovative level – breaking boundaries, being original, still based (unconsciously) on academic level.	**Proficiency** – intuitively responding to patterns.
Genius level – ideas defy explanation.	**Expertise** – knowing what to do, fluid performance.

In both schemes the fourth and fifth levels are associated with unconscious decision-making, but *only* after a person has gone through the earlier levels. While rule-following characterises the earlier stages, rule-bending/breaking and creating new rules characterises more advanced stages. Furthermore, Dreyfus and Dreyfus (1986: 36) claim that conscious use of rules by an expert can lead to 'regression to the skill of the novice, or, at best, the competent performer'. Experts operate at a level of high involvement, not rationally but intuitively.

Intuition appears at the very first level of the description of artistic engagement and in the final stages of the skill-acquisition model. Here it might seem that the coincidences between the models break down, but this is not necessarily so. We believe that intuition and insight are relevant in all situations and at all levels. People are creative and intuitive already because of existing experience (especially children perhaps) but to be creative and intuitive in a particular domain or a particular skilled practice depends on an earlier process of developing the skills and experiences of that practice.

We now want to investigate further the notion of the differences between expert and novice performance. We aim to make explicit some of the processes that need to support students' development towards the expert end of the spectrum.

Dufresne *et al.* (1995) provide a fascinating model of knowledge, cognition and learning developed to explain the differences in the way novices (students) and experts (e.g. teachers) store and use knowledge in a domain (their domain was physics) for the purpose of problem working. Their explanations and visual representations of the clustering and linking of different sorts of knowledge in different problem-working contexts for novices and experts are noteworthy for the way in which operations that we associate with creativity – like exploration and visualising and representing problems – are embedded within notions of analytical and reasoning processes.

Table 10.3 Summary of expert–novice differences in any domain (Dufresne *et al.*, 1995)

	Experts	*Novices*
Knowledge characteristics	Large store of domain-specific knowledge	Sparse knowledge set
	Knowledge richly interconnected and hierarchically structured	Disconnected and amorphous structure
	Integrated multiple representations	Poorly formed and unrelated representations
Problem-solving behaviour	Conceptual knowledge impacts problem-solving	Problem-solving largely independent of concepts
	Performs qualitative analysis	Manipulates equations
	Uses forward-looking concept-based strategies	Uses backward-looking means to ends techniques

Table 10.3 summarises some of the differences between experts and novices that cognitive research has studied and revealed (Dufresne *et al.*, 1995). We can perhaps begin to see how the creativity of an expert used to access and 'play' with the large stock of different sorts of knowledge will result in very different outcomes from the creativity of a novice with a smaller and more limited range of knowledge types.

Dufresne *et al.* (1995) refer to their own research in which they have shown that it is possible for students to learn how to develop 'expert-like' strategies. Does this mean that students are able to draw on their creativity and intuition at an earlier stage than we usually give them credit?

What does all this mean for higher education?

Creativity in the context of complex learning

Higher education prepares students for learning that is complex. John Biggs (in Jackson, 2002: 4) associates creativity with the extended abstract (EA) thinking skills like hypothesising, synthesising, reflecting, generating ideas, applying the known to 'far' domains, working with problems that do not have unique solutions. These are all outcomes that we hope to achieve from a higher education curriculum. These sorts of outcomes enable us to relate an existing principle to previously unseen problems and ultimately go beyond existing principles to discover new things (Biggs, 2003: 49).

But creative abilities do not stand in isolation. They have to be blended and connected to other sorts of ability and capacity. Indeed, the act of blending and utilising different abilities, knowledge and capacities to achieve a goal is itself a creative act. Sternberg and Lubart's (1995) triarchic model of abilities offers a perspective on the position of creativity with respect to other abilities that learners have to use:

> Successfully intelligent individuals succeed in part because they achieve a functional balance among a 'triarchy' of abilities: analytical abilities, which are used to analyze, evaluate, judge, compare and contrast; creative abilities, which are used to create, invent, discover, imagine; practical abilities, which are used to apply, utilize, implement, and activate. Successfully intelligent people are not necessarily high in all three of these abilities, but find a way effectively to exploit whatever patterns of abilities they may have.
>
> (Sternberg and Lubart, 1995)

This quotation provides a context in which to view abilities and it avoids a narrow stereotyping of creativity, because, as one respondent to our studies commented, it 'exceeds the idea generating technique'. It was clear from the responses of academics that this integrated view of creativity is more in tune with their notions of complex learning in the higher education context than lists of characteristics of creativity.

Sternberg and Williams (1996) point out that creativity must be appropriately balanced with analytic and practical skills:

> Everyone, even the most creative person you know, has better and worse ideas. Without well-developed analytic ability, the creative thinker is as likely to pursue bad ideas as to pursue good ones. The creative individual uses analytic ability to work out the implications of a creative idea and to test it. . . . The creative person uses practical ability to convince other people that an idea is worthy.
>
> (Sternberg and Williams, 1996: 3)

The key point that Sternberg and his colleagues are making is that there is a need for the blending and balancing of abilities to suit the context. The role for creativity will be different for different people, and different for the same person in different contexts. It will need to be supported appropriately by the other abilities if it is not to result in behaviour that stays at a simple level of 'zany' or 'off the wall'. Our job as educators is to create challenging situations for learning where learners are able to draw on and balance different abilities and discover for themselves how they can use their creativity in particular learning contexts. However, the final responsibility for engaging in this way rests with the learners themselves. This necessitates the development of learners who are independent and self-motivated and learning environments which encourage students to move from dependency to independency (Dineen, this volume, Chapter 9).

People who are successful and become expert in their chosen fields are good at drawing on and balancing their specialist knowledge, talents and abilities, and motivating themselves to achieve the goals that are subordinate to their chosen activities. De Corte's (2000: 253) explanation of expertise in a domain (in his context, mathematics) helps us to understand how they achieve this balance. He identifies four categories of aptitudes, namely:

- A well-organised and flexibly accessible domain-specific knowledge base.
- Heuristic strategies for problem analysis and transformation.

- Metacognitive knowledge and self-regulating beliefs.
- Positive beliefs, attitudes and emotions related to the domain.

We have already seen how the first two of these categories are transformed through different levels of practice. The third category gives us an indication of how this might happen. We are going to use the model of self-regulation developed by Zimmerman (2000) and others to help represent some of the complexity of how we achieve utilisation and integration of a repertoire of abilities in problem working.

Creativity and self-regulation

Being creative involves both conscious and deliberate acts and things that are done or understood which do not seem to be the product of deliberate thinking and action, for example the sudden insight or flash of inspiration. But people make decisions about thinking and behaving in certain ways in a particular situation, as a result of which new ideas, products and performances are more likely to emerge. They are regulating what they do through their knowledge of the domain and their previous experiences of working in the domain in similar situations or extrapolating what they know into a situation they are encountering for the first time. It seems relevant, therefore, to examine the well-researched model of self-regulation developed by Schunk and Zimmerman (Schunk and Zimmerman, 1994, 1997, 1998; Zimmerman, 2000; Zimmerman and Schunk, 2004), and others, to see how creativity might be involved in self-regulation and vice versa: 'self-regulation refers to metacognitive, behavioural and motivational processes and beliefs used to attain personal learning goals in specific contexts' (Zimmerman, 2000: 221).

For Zimmerman and colleagues, there are three sources of control underlying self-regulation: personal, behavioural and environmental. Each of these sources is also changing during learning, and each source must be self-monitored and adjusted using feedback mechanisms constructed by the learner. For more on this, see Zimmerman (2000: 222) and also Nicol and MacFarlane-Dick (in press), who consider what is required to support such a process. Highly self-regulated people are strategically flexible, environmentally resourceful and perceptive of personal agency. Creative people have these qualities in abundance, as we saw earlier.

There are three phases of self-regulation, all of which engage learners' processes and beliefs:

- *Forethought* – thinking about tasks, problems and contexts ahead of action.
- *Performance* – when ideas and strategies feed into actions as they happen.
- *Self-reflection* – replaying and mentally re-experiencing the performance.

Creative people will recognise some of the processes that will be engaged during these phases of self-regulation.

Forethought: Because of the beliefs they hold, creative people are good at using their imaginations to create projects that interest and motivate themselves; that give them a sense of purpose. They have an intense curiosity to understand and explore something that helps them turn things they have to do into things they want to do well. They set themselves challenging goals and are able to orient their goals towards mastering something as opposed to simply achieving an objective or fulfilling a task – they are as interested in the process as in the outcome. They are ambitious in their goal setting and imaginative and original in the strategies they employ to achieve their goals.

Performance: Self-observation will help a creative person to monitor performance and the conditions that surround and influence it. This process (also called 'reflection in action') enables people to adjust their actions and performance in response to their observations on the impact they are making. The performance is the place where creative ideas are turned into real things, e.g. writing, designs, constructions, performances, conversation, playing football, teaching!

Self-reflection: This phase combines imagination for re-experiencing the performance and perhaps considering how it might have been, with the more critical processes of evaluation and self-assessment.

Zimmerman and Schunk (2004) draw the distinction between proactive and reactive self-regulators. Reactive learners avoid forethought and attempt to regulate functioning during and after performance, whereas proactive learners engage in forethought in order to improve the quality of subsequent actions. It is tempting to speculate that it is the proactive self-regulators who are more likely to make use of their imaginations and creativity to achieve their goals.

Cognitive apprenticeship to support self-regulated learning

So far, we have identified some of the creative attributes and processes that we want to develop in students, along with the need to consider them in the contexts of their domains and levels. How does a learner learn to self-regulate and harness their creativity?

The short answer is through lots of experience and practice of self-regulating themselves and observing how others regulate themselves, including their teachers! We are suggesting that a good route to the development of self-regulatory capability and creative awareness and skills is through the process of a cognitive apprenticeship (Collins *et al.*, 1991). These authors explore traditional apprenticeship phases of modelling, scaffolding, fading and coaching, and consider how far the metaphor can be extended to cognitive work. They found three important differences:

- In cognitive apprenticeship, the process of carrying out a task to be learned is usually not so easily observable as in traditional craft-based apprenticeships, so the teacher's thinking must be made visible to the students and the student's thinking must be made visible to the teacher. By bringing these tacit processes into the open, students can observe, enact, and practise them with help from the teacher and from other students.

- In a traditional apprenticeship, tasks emerge naturally in the setting in which they are needed. Learning is entirely relevant and related to the situation in which it is needed. That is often not the case in higher education learning environments where so much learning is abstract and divorced from real-world environments. There are moves to create 'authentic' learning and these are helpful in making cognitive apprenticeship more meaningful and, we believe, more likely to promote creativity.
- In craft-based apprenticeships the skills are inherent to the task itself, e.g. carpentry, plumbing, etc. In cognitive apprenticeship the skills are intended to be transferable from one problem-working situation to another. This requires students to develop metacognitive and self-evaluation skills so that learners become able to generalise the skill, to learn when the skill is or is not applicable, and to transfer the skill independently when faced with novel situations.

The idea of creative apprenticeship has been developed and is successfully being applied in school education (Craft, this volume, Chapter 3). We are proposing that the sorts of creative development that higher education can support is best achieved through the model of cognitive apprenticeship.

Relationships between self-regulated learning, cognitive apprenticeship and creativity

For some readers, the above might appear *too* cognitive for a discussion about creativity. It might seem to ignore some of creativity's more esoteric aspects and also to deny the type of experiences that we can all recognise:

> the truth is that our ideas, and often our best, most ingenious ideas, do not arrive as the result of faultless chains of reasoning. They 'occur to us'. They 'pop into our heads'. They come out of the blue. When we are relaxed we operate very largely by intuition.
>
> (Claxton, 1997: 49)

Claxton believes that intuition has been inappropriately disdained, and describes 'a body of research which shows that intuition is more valuable and more trustworthy than we think' (Claxton, 1997: 50). In promoting self-regulation and cognitive apprenticeship, we are not denying the role of intuition – indeed, it has already emerged in our discussions about level. It is also very important to recognise that some creative processes seem to belong to the tacit dimension (Polanyi, 1966) and to result in professional decision-making that cannot be defined in textbooks. Here Donald Schön's (1983) ideas of reflection-in-action as performed by reflective practitioners usefully combine the notions of self-regulation and intuition. John Cowan's (1998) expansion of the distinctions between different types of reflection – for, in and on action – seem to correspond to the phases of forethought, performance and self-reflection that we have already discussed, without ruling out the notion that a creative practice may be occurring.

In all such artistic processes, including those which occur in educational situations, there are critical moments of feedback, of taking stock, of applying general principles (and of deliberately and consciously going against some accepted principles or criteria) all of which involve reflective thought and judgement.

(Cowan, 1998: 31)

So yes, creativity may sometimes be tacit and invisible (which may cause problems for assessment) and may appear to come 'out of the blue', but intuition, like imagination, tends to be balanced with critical thinking (a point also acknowledged by Claxton, 1997). It is not always (nor often) a case of either/or.

Effective teaching and learning systems

Dunne (in Jackson *et al.*, 2004) is developing a model for an effective teaching and learning system based on the best empirical evidence derived from a systematic review of the research literature that focused on the effects of reflection and action planning on students' learning outcomes – key components of self-regulation. The model highlights the complexity of the factors and interactions that influence students' learning outcomes.

We are making the assumption that these are important characteristics for most teacher-facilitated learning environments and therefore important in our own search for an appropriate pedagogy to support the development of students' creativity. The significance of this model is that it is grown from best empirical evidence of situations that had measurable beneficial impacts on students' learning, i.e. it is grown from teaching and learning practices that are known to be effective in achieving intended learning outcomes rather than theories of what effective practice ought to be:

> this model suggests that every learning and teaching situation . . . is underpinned by a complex set of conditions relating to the inter-relationship between student, teacher and task. It also suggests that any teacher, to gain maximum impact, must be deliberately aware of these relationships and the ways in which they are likely to impact on any kind of provision and any learner response. This could be of particular interest in the context of . . . innovation in general, where – for example – students may not be motivated to try out new ways of working, where they may not have adapted appropriate cognitive and metacognitive strategies, and may find this difficult without support, and may hence lose perceptions of efficacy – again impacting on motivation.

(Dunne, in Jackson *et al.*, 2004)

We would expect that the components of an effective teaching and learning system to support development of students' creativity would be connected and aligned in the sense of John Biggs' notion of constructive alignment (Biggs,

2002, 2003). One thing that we would like to emphasise in this complex set of relationships, is the crucial issue of teacher–student relationships (see Dineen, this volume, Chapter 9). A useful perspective on this was provided by one of our peer reviewers.

Learner characteristics	Teacher activity	Task
Any approach, or motivation towards a task, or learning in general is dependent on the learner's: • Attitudes/values towards learning *in general, or particular types of learning* or towards particular tasks. • Conceptions/beliefs of what it means to learn, to be a learner in any particular context. • Physical disposition, e.g. fatigue. • Possession of a repertoire of skills appropriate to the tasks. • Possession of a repertoire of cognitive strategies appropriate to performing any particular task. • Possession of metacognitive strategies, i.e. knowledge and awareness of their own cognitive processes. • Ability to actively control and manage their own cognitive and metacognitive processes (executive control). • Perceived self-efficacy.	Any approach, or motivation towards a task or learning in general is dependent on the teacher's mode of presentation of the academic task/learning processes/reflective approaches, and consolidation through: • Appropriate structuring of knowledge bases, dependent on a detailed knowledge of the academic content to be learned. • Attention to appropriate learning strategies for students, dependent on a knowledge of cognitive and metacognitive processes and how learners can be encouraged to use these. • Ability to predict and deal with variety of student's cognitive abilities, motivations, etc. • Ability to demonstrate and model approaches to required outcomes. • Ability to promote thinking through questioning and challenging. • Attention to written instructions and examples that reinforce spoken instructions. • Providing timely feedback, verbal and/or written, or computer-based. • Ability to match assessment to the intended learning outcomes.	Any approach, or motivation towards a task or learning in general is dependent on the teacher's: • Demands – level of difficulty. • Perceived appropriateness. • Manner of presentation. • Representation and opportunity provided for intended learning outcomes. • Modes of assessment and criteria that are matched to intended learning outcomes.

Figure 10.1 The complex interactions and interdependencies between teacher, learner and task. (Developed by Elisabeth Dunne from the results of a systematic review of the empirical evidence that reflection combined with recording and action planning improves students' achievement. (source Jackson *et al.*, 2004)).

My experience ... is that the relationship between tutor and student is of
critical importance, depends upon features which I have still to pinpoint and
seems to depend on those vital early exchanges which can make or break
the quality of the relationship. It's a relationship in which students feel able
to reveal and discuss innermost ways of thinking, and tutors can empathise
and at times demonstrate congruence, from their own experiences ... their
effect in initiation, rejection, doubts, acceptance, enthusiasm at the outset, is
critical to successful learning.

(John Cowan, pers. comm., 2005)

We can very readily relate this complex set of relationships and interdependencies to the idea of the cognitive apprenticeship (Collins *et al.*, 1991), the basis
for our pedagogic model to support development of students' creativity. Figure
10.2 attempts to contextualise the complex set of relationships identified by
Dunne (teacher–student–task – which we take to include environment and
context) within a model of a teaching and learning system that is purposefully
designed to promote students' creativity.

A strategy for developing students' creativity

The pedagogic model outlined above is a simple visual representation of a
complex process, set of conditions and relationships pertaining to the environment for learning. We need to convert this into something that can be operationalised by a teacher. Each teacher will search for and invent their own way of
doing this in a way that is appropriate for their context. Our search has led us to
the following assumption-led strategy.

* That higher education encourages the acquisition of domain-specific knowledge and skills. Students cannot be creative in a domain if they are not
  knowledgeable about the domain and/or if they don't care enough about the
  domain to want to achieve within it.
* If we want to develop students' creativity, we have first to develop our own
  understandings about what it means in the contexts for our teaching.
  Through such understanding we can be clearer about the types of creativity
  we want to encourage.
* A good way to help students learn about creativity is for a teacher to reveal
  their own creativity and show students what it means to them in their own
  practice, appreciating that this may be easier said than done.
* But showing students what it means is not enough. We have to help them
  articulate and construct their own meanings of creativity for the contexts in
  which they are studying and learning. And we have to show them that we
  value their understandings rather than simply our own. It is these perceptions that shape their beliefs and fuel their intrinsic motivations – widening
  the range of perceptions is perhaps the most important thing we can do as
  teachers to develop students' creativity. There are both individual and
  collective dimensions to meaning-making, which engages directly with the

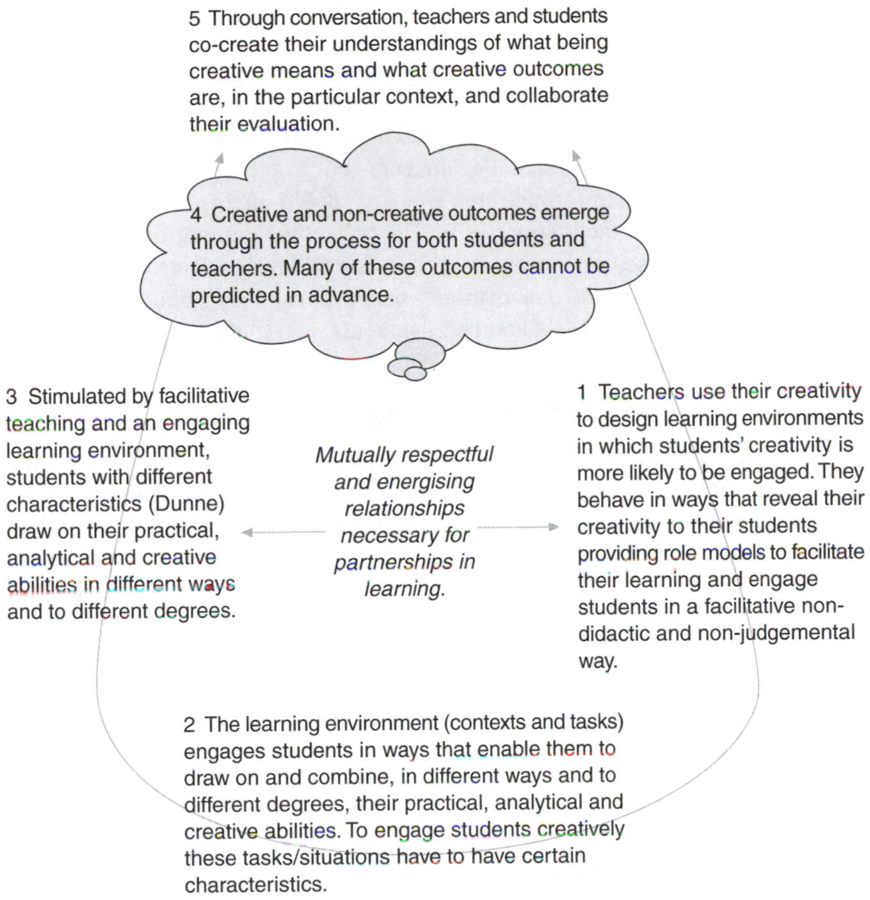

5 Through conversation, teachers and students co-create their understandings of what being creative means and what creative outcomes are, in the particular context, and collaborate their evaluation.

4 Creative and non-creative outcomes emerge through the process for both students and teachers. Many of these outcomes cannot be predicted in advance.

3 Stimulated by facilitative teaching and an engaging learning environment, students with different characteristics (Dunne) draw on their practical, analytical and creative abilities in different ways and to different degrees.

Mutually respectful and energising relationships necessary for partnerships in learning.

1 Teachers use their creativity to design learning environments in which students' creativity is more likely to be engaged. They behave in ways that reveal their creativity to their students providing role models to facilitate their learning and engage students in a facilitative non-didactic and non-judgemental way.

2 The learning environment (contexts and tasks) engages students in ways that enable them to draw on and combine, in different ways and to different degrees, their practical, analytical and creative abilities. To engage students creatively these tasks/situations have to have certain characteristics.

Figure 10.2 Model of a teaching and learning system designed to help students develop their creative potential. It embodies the complex set of relationships and interdependencies elaborated in the model by Dunne (Figure 10.1). The whole environment demands a self-regulating approach to learning, and teacher and students collaborate in cognitive apprenticeship (Collins *et al.*, 1991).

extended abstract field of creative outcomes (Biggs, 2003). The use of web logs can be helpful in engaging students and accumulating their understandings, and provides them with a practical illustration of how knowledge can be socially constructed.

- We have to give students opportunities to experience and practise their creativity by creating the curriculum spaces, conditions and experiences that are stimulating, relevant and authentic to their field of study. Challenging problem-working contexts provide favourable environments for practising to be creative.

- We might go further by introducing specific strategies for encouraging students to develop a repertoire of thinking skills that might help them to think freshly about the things that they have to give attention to.
- Finally, we need to develop students' capacity to recognise and capture their own creativities and help them make claims that can be substantiated. They have to be critical evaluators of their own creativity as it is manifested in the learning enterprises in which they are engaged.
- The feedback gained through this strategy should enable teachers to refine their thinking and facilitation skills. The collective learning of students and teacher can be used as a resource for learning and for students in the future.

This strategy is consistent and overlaps that proposed by John Cowan (this volume, Chapter 12) for the evaluation of students' creativity.

Information resources to support this strategy

A core purpose of the Imaginative Curriculum project is to develop information resources to help higher education teachers to think about and operationalise the idea of creativity. The repository for much of this information are the Imaginative Curriculum web pages. These pages are continually being updated so the resources that are identified in Appendix 10.2 will, with time, be extended. Indeed we hope that readers will contribute ideas and materials to the site.

Concluding remarks

In drawing this account of our search for an appropriate pedagogy to a close, we imagine that some readers will be disappointed by us not giving clear, unambiguous advice about how a higher education teacher might facilitate students' creative development. There are resources like the Sternberg and Williams (1996) e-booklet, the CASE creative thinking skills booklet edited by Caroline Baillie (see this volume, Chapter 11) and John Cowan's excellent description of a process (this volume, Chapter 12) that provide practical ideas and illustrations on how to facilitate and evaluate students' creativity. But we believe that the process of searching and constructing meanings and understandings is important in the development of personal pedagogies, so we have opted to provide an account of our own sense-making and a navigational aid to what we think are useful and stimulating resources, and leave the rest to the professional skills and imaginations of our readers.

Appendix 10.1

The reasoning underlying our strategy for the development of students' creativity in higher education

Important questions about the role of creativity in higher education	Our responses to these questions	Research influences and theoretical underpinnings	Pedagogic implications
Why should higher-education teachers try to develop the creative attributes and potential of their students?	Creativity is an important part of a person's identity and capability. It is central to being and becoming. Higher-education teachers have a moral obligation to develop students' potential so that they become successful and fulfilled learners and achievers throughout their lives in an increasingly fast-changing world.	Oliver et al. (this volume, Chapter 5) 'even where creativity was not taught, not considered teachable and not valued in assessment, it was still relevant in defining how the students saw themselves.' Barnett and Coate (2005) – to be successful in an age and world of uncertainty – the need to develop higher education curricula to embrace not just knowing and acting but also being.	Creativity has to be explicitly recognised and valued within the outcomes of a higher education. Teachers need to understand what creativity means in their disciplinary fields and to create learning environments and experiences so that students experience and learn to use their own creativity to accomplish their learning goals.
What are the creative abilities that higher-education might develop?	Creative abilities are traits and characteristics attributed to creative people or actions that lead to creative outcomes. A wide range of creative abilities are recognised in	Imaginative curriculum research has revealed a substantial list of abilities and capabilities that academics associate with creativity in disciplinary study and practice contexts (this volume, Edwards et al., Chapter 6; Fryer, Chapter 7; Jackson and Shaw, Chapter 8).	Higher education needs to systematically develop knowledge of creative abilities in different disciplinary domains and learning contexts (e.g. problem working or performing contexts). Each teacher needs to develop their

Appendix 10.1 *continued*

The reasoning underlying our strategy for the development of students' creativity in higher education

Important questions about the role of creativity in higher education	*Our responses to these questions*	*Research influences and theoretical underpinnings*	*Pedagogic implications*
	higher education and they vary from subject to subject and the contexts in which they are applied.	There are many syntheses of core creative abilities. Perkins' (1981) six trait model of creativity is one useful example.	understanding of their own creativity in their disciplinary field and working practices.
	Creative abilities are not used in isolation, they are integrated with other sorts of ability and competency.	Sternberg and Lubart (1996) develop the idea of a triarchy of abilities (analytical, creative and practical).	Using models of creativity appropriate for the discipline and context, teachers need to create learning environments and experiences that will enable
	Ultimately it is the blending of creative and other capabilities, driven by an individual's motivation and self-belief that makes them successful.	De Corte (2000) offers a useful explanation of expertise in a domain – experts are people who mastered a lot of knowledge and skill and who are highly successful at solving problems in the domain.	students to practice and develop the creative abilities that teachers think are important and also recognise those that students believe are important. These abilities will however be
		Biggs (2002) associates creativity with the extended abstract thinking skills outcomes of learning like hypothesising, reflecting, generating ideas, applying the known to 'far' domains', working with problems that do not have unique solutions.	integrated with more traditional academic abilities relating to critical thinking and the practice skills of the discipline.

If a person's creativity is intertwined with other sorts of thinking and abilities, what models of learning might provide us with a conceptual framework to help us understand how creativity features in students' learning behaviours and actions? How does a learner develop the complex learning behaviours, knowledge, skills, attitudes and beliefs that are embodied in the self-regulatory model of learning and being?

We believe that the development of the attributes, abilities, competencies and self-efficacy embodied in the self-regulation model is best achieved through a cognitive apprenticeship that enables students to

Learning, behaving and being is so complicated that it is helpful to have some conceptual reference points to guide the thinking and decisions of higher education teachers, and to help them understand how a pedagogic strategy might influence students. Higher education is good at developing a person's capacity for complex learning (which includes their creativity) typically in discipline-based contexts. Increasingly, HE has accepted responsibility for preparing students for a life of complex learning in contexts which are not discipline-based.

The models of self-regulated learning (e.g. Zimmerman, 2000 and Zimmerman and Schunk, 2004), provide us with a comprehensive framework to help us understand how creativity might be integrated with thinking, performance, motivations, goal setting and critical self-evaluation.

Self-regulation applies to all levels of expertise, from the novice to the expert.

Collins et al. (1991) provide clear and understandable explanations of the idea of cognitive apprenticeship into which concepts of creativity might be infused.

See also literature on tacit knowledge and intuitive thinking (Polanyi, 1966, Schön, 1983 and Dreyfus and Dreyfus, 1986).

Teachers would need to develop an understanding of self-regulation theory and test, through their own sense-making, whether it is relevant to their understandings and practice.

Teachers would need to be prepared to act as role models for students to reveal their own creativity within the teaching and learning contexts in which they work.

They would need to develop an understanding of the cognitive apprenticeship model of learner development and adapt the concept to their own disciplinary contexts and practices.

Appendix 10.1 *continued*

The reasoning underlying our strategy for the development of students' creativity in higher education

Important questions about the role of creativity in higher education	Our responses to these questions	Research influences and theoretical underpinnings	Pedagogic implications
	experience and understand their own self-regulatory behaviours. The literature on tacit processes underlying expertise is also relevant.		
What is entailed in cognitive apprenticeship?	Teacher – creating environment, providing a role model, formative feedback to aid development and self-regulation, coaching and guidance, stimulation. Learner – legitimate peripheral participation, doing, reflecting constructing meaning, using their creative abilities with other abilities and evaluating the effects.	Nicol and MacFarlane-Dick (in press). Various writers on social aspects of learning (e.g. Lave and Wenger, 1991 and Wells, 1999)	Teachers would need to develop an understanding of the sorts of learning environments that challenged and stimulated students' creativity and enabled them to learn through the cognitive apprenticeship model. Cognitive apprenticeship models could be developed in each discipline.

Who evaluates whether someone has been creative or something is creative? And how is evaluation accomplished?	Evaluation is important in the model of self-regulation. It is central to the production of creative outcomes, to the recognition of creativity and to the valuing of creativity within a field. To become creatively successful requires people to develop the ability to critically self-evaluate their own creativity. Developing this capability is therefore an important part of cognitive apprenticeship.	Csikszentmihalyi (1997) elaborates the social–cultural concept of creativity and discusses self-evaluative processes of creative people. Balchin (this volume, Chapter 13) describes the idea of consensual assessment and how it might be used in HE; Cowan (this volume, Chapter 12) describes a pedagogic process to aid development of students' self-evaluation capacities.	In a teaching and learning context every participant – learners and teachers – must be involved in developing understanding of creativity for its evaluation. It is through this process that students and teachers individually and collectively come to understand what creativity means and how it is operationalised in the particular settings in which it is being required. John Cowan (Chapter 12) provides a very useful pedagogic model for how this might be achieved.
What type of teaching and learning system will embody these forms of teaching for successful learning?	A teaching and learning system that is designed to develop students' creative potential should embody the characteristics outlined in this table.	Dunne, in Jackson et al. (2004), drawing on best scientific evidence, identifies the complex set of interdependencies (teacher–student–task) that result in successful learning. Our model of a teaching and learning system for development of students' creativity (Figure 10.2) embodies these characteristics and the reasoning in this table.	A teaching and learning system to develop students' creative potential must engage with the features of creativity and the pedagogies that are known to be effective in promoting creativity.

Appendix 10.2

Ideas and resources to help teachers develop their own strategies to develop students' creativities

Some ideas to help teachers developing their own understandings about what creativity means:

- Structured/facilitated group discussions with teaching colleagues, perhaps using the workshop framework provided at: www.heacademy. ac.uk/2804.htm.
- Self-evaluation of one's own courses or teaching practices using a tool to aid reflection: www.heacademy.ac.uk/3016.htm.
- Where they exist, reading one of the Working Papers that describe academics' perceptions of creativity in a discipline: www.heacademy. ac.uk/2762.htm.
- Reading the synthesis of discussions within the Imaginative Curriculum network or notes of workshops conducted on various themes: www.heacademy.ac.uk/2804.htm.
- Preparing a short, reflective, personal account of a teaching scenario (or other example of professional practice like disciplinary or pedagogic research, consultancy or applied practice) in which you feel you have been creative, and using this as the basis for analyzing meanings of creativity. Such an account could provide students with a relevant example of creativity in the practice of teaching. See examples produced by other teachers: www.heacademy.ac.uk/3016.htm.
- Joining the Imaginative Curriculum network and participating in network events and discussions: www.heacademy.ac.uk/1778.htm.
- Wiki sites – and if you can add to them, so much the better! (Wiki = a web application that allows users to add and edit content) en. wikipedia.org/wiki/Creativity and www.crinnology.com/ Main_Page.
- Qualifications and Curriculum Authority (QCA) website resources for school teachers includes review of research literature on creativity in education. www.ncaction.org.uk/creativity/about.htm.

Leading by example.
'The most powerful way to develop creativity in your students is to be a role model' (Sternberg and Williams, 1996). The best way of showing students that you value their creativity is to show them what it means to you in your own practice.

- Cognitive Apprenticeship: Making Things Visible. www.21learn.org/ arch/articles/brown_seely.html.
- 'How should I assess creativity?', this volume, Chapter 12. A practical illustration of cognitive apprenticeship in action.

Some ideas to help students develop their understandings of what creativity means.

The development of students' understandings of creativity is an ongoing process. They need to be able to capture their evolving perceptions and the teacher needs to facilitate the sharing and accumulation of perspectives across the group. This shared knowledge becomes an important resource for all involved in the process. Possible ways in which this might be achieved include:

- Structured/facilitated group discussions, perhaps using the question frame-work used by Oliver *et al.* in Chapter 5 of this book so that they can compare their results with what other students think.
- The strategy proposed by John Cowan in Chapter 12 of this book for engaging students in a creative discourse with professionals in their discipline.
- Where they exist, encouraging students to read part of the Working Papers that describe academics' perceptions of creativity in a discipline and facilitating discussion around these perceptions – is this the way students see the world?: www.heacademy.ac.uk/2762.htm.
- Developing a weblog around themes like: my creativity; using my imagination; synthesis.

Creating the conditions and experiences that will enable students to experience and practise being creative and be able to observe you and other students being creative.

What Conditions and Environment Could Support Teachers in

- *Finding Space for 'Creativity' in their Work with Curriculum* by Jo Tait (2002). Empirical study with useful reflective aid: www.heacademy. ac.uk/resources.asp?process=full_record&section=generic&id=59.
- *Designing for Creativity*, Norman Jackson (2002) www.heacademy. ac.uk/3018.htm.
- Imaginative curriculum guides for problem-based, enquiry-led, context-based game-play, role-play and simulations and enterprise: www.heacademy.ac.uk/3018.htm.
- Examples of personal accounts of teaching to promote students' creativity: www.heacademy.ac.uk/3016.htm.
- Higher Education Academy subject centre websites accessed via: www.heacademy.ac.uk.
- *How to Develop Student Creativity* by Robert Sternberg and Wendy Williams (1996):
  30-page practical guide framed around the investment theory of creativity. Provides an explanation of creativity and relates techniques you can use to choose creative environments, expose students to creative role models, and identify and surmount obstacles to creativity. Some of the techniques they explore include questioning assumption, encouraging idea generation, teaching self-responsibility, and using profiles of creative people.

- '*CASE Creativity in Art, Science and Engineering: How to Foster Creativity*' by Simon Dewulf and Caroline Baillie (1999). Sixty-four-page colour booklet which gives definitions of creativity, examines creative processes and creativity techniques and provides case studies of creative teaching. Available from the Higher Education Academy £5.
- *The Travelling Case: Creativity in Art, Science and Engineering. How to Foster Creative Thinking in Higher Education*'. Online., available at: www.heacademy.ac.uk/3271.htm.
- John Welford's Brainware Map for Creative Learning: www.jwelford. demon.co.uk/brainwaremap/.
- Leslie Owen Wilson's ideas and concepts used in her course – 'The creative teacher': www.uwsp.edu/education/lwilson/creativ/index.htm.

Some ideas to help students develop their creative-thinking skills.
The goal of many creative techniques is to achieve a shift in the perspectives associated with a problem or situation. Creative thinking techniques utilise a variety of tools and strategies to encourage this change in perspective and generate lots of ideas through divergent thinking processes. They might include the use of objects, sounds, images, habit-breaking strategies (challenging or inverting assumptions), imagination stimulators ('what if?'), search strategies (past experience and analogies or metaphors), analytical strategies (decomposition, problem reframing through 'how?' questions) and development strategies (compare and contrast, integrate). Idea-generating strategies are often linked to evaluative techniques to facilitate convergent or analytical thinking. The Imaginative Curriculum project explored four creative-thinking techniques (Creative problem solving, TRIZ, Medicine wheel and 'Mind and body' techniques) and their application to students' learning through a series of action research projects (Baillie, 2004 and this volume, Chapter 11).

- *The Travelling Case: Creativity in Art, Science and Engineering. How to Foster Creative Thinking in Higher Education,* edited by Caroline Baillie: www.heacademy.ac.uk.
- Innovation House (www.infinn.com/innovationhouse.html). Resources, tools, software, tutorials and information for creative thinking, lateral thinking, problem-solving, creativity and brainstorming.

Some resources to support questioning.

- A Questioning Toolkit from FromNowOn.org. a comprehensive set of strategies for asking essential questions; gives examples of the types of questions students can ask: fromnowon.org/nov97/toolkit.html.
- A framework for developing essential questions for student enquiry: fromnowon.org/sept96/questions.html.

Some ideas to help students develop their capacity to recognise and capture their own creativities and help them make claims that can be substantiated.

> The traditional principle of fair assessment, i.e. that all students are assessed in the same way and compared with each other through normative assessment on the same materials and individually, is inappropriate for the assessment of creative work. What has to be understood is that to treat everyone the same when people are so obviously different from each other is the very opposite of fairness. Instead, students are assessed in their performance against their potential and as a rule on the basis of negotiated learning agreements, largely on work presented by them in portfolios based on their own self-evaluation of their work. No two portfolios are the same and the assessment has to be criterion- and not norm-referenced.
>
> (Elton 2005)

- *Guide to Assessing Creativity,* Lewis Elton (2005).
- 'How should I assess creativity?', John Cowan, this volume, Chapter 12.

11 Enhancing students' creativity through creative-thinking techniques

Caroline Baillie

Why enhance creative thinking?

Teachers often pose the question: *how* can I help my students think more creatively, think up innovative solutions and perhaps even enhance their creative potential? However, we also need to think about *why* we want them to think creatively. I became interested in creative thinking as a way of helping engineering graduates solve problems for the world in innovative ways. To me, that means finding creative technical solutions to social and environmental problems – global problems, our problems. However, I am also concerned that we do not increase our effectiveness in destroying our planet or in killing each other with new and clever devices:

> the technologies which save us time and labour individually – that empower each of us – bind us collectively into a frenetic, mad race in which we often feel more caged by obligations and demands than before ... the people who succeed in this technologically hyper-charged environment make up a narrow elite that thrives on constant stimulus ... they usually don't think a lot about who they are, about what their ultimate aims are, or about the broader consequences of what they are doing.
>
> (Homer-Dixon, 2000: 102)

Homer-Dixon suggests that we need more ideas for solving technical and social problems but that societies cannot always supply the ingenuity they need at the right times and places. They face an 'ingenuity gap'. In the prologue to his book of the same name, Homer-Dixon discusses this gap which widens the 'already yawning gulfs' of wealth and opportunity within and between our societies. Homer-Dixon warns us of the 'dangerously self-indulgent and even delusional ... Western triumphalism'. In writing this chapter and in facilitating workshops that attempt to enhance creative thinking, it is important for me to first state my purpose and encourage others to do so also. Perhaps in taking a moment to reflect on our purpose, we will then be able to question it.

The Creative Universities project

In 2003, a group of university teachers and educational developers within the LTSN (Learning and Teaching Support Network of the UK) decided that we wanted to share the creative-thinking techniques we knew about with those who could use them in a responsible way to enhance the creative potential of their students and peers. We wanted to see whether we could investigate and share some of the 'know-how' about creative thinking that seemed to have been largely used to date by the private, and not the public, sector. We were funded by the LTSN to conduct a knowledge transfer experiment aimed at developing the creative capacity of 15 academics in a residential workshop, who would, in turn, share their know-how with others in their institution. The idea was to help academics to realise the potential of employing specific techniques to help their colleagues and students develop their creative potential. We asked four creative-thinking consultant practitioners to help our participants learn about their approaches to fostering creative thinking. We held a three-day experiential workshop which incorporated many fun, interactive exercises as well as social gatherings and music-making. We knew this would be a productive experience for the participants but what we hadn't realised was the huge power of this experience to wake up individuals to their true selves. I have never before experienced knock-on effects like those of that residential workshop. For months afterwards I was hearing third-hand about the participants having had 'life changing experiences'.

After the workshop we asked five volunteers from the group to become facilitators. Nine of the 15 volunteered and proposed that they would share the proposed fee so that all could participate. All nine selected one of the approaches to gain extra training and then tried to facilitate a workshop in an area of their choosing, with students or their colleagues. They used the same approaches that we had taught them. *The Travelling Case: How to Foster Creative Thinking in Higher Education*' (Baillie, 2003) describes in detail the experiences and the lessons learnt by each facilitator in their endeavours to foster creative thinking in others. In this chapter I briefly summarise the approaches used in the experiment, as well as the ideas that came from the participants about how to get the best out of these techniques in their particular teaching and learning contexts.

Creative problem-solving

All of the techniques we employed were based on the premise that they would be used in problem-solving. Participants engaged in creative-thinking exercises aimed at solving real problems. We worked with the essential framework of creative problem-solving that is described in *CASE: Creativity in Art, Science and Engineering* (Dewulf and Baillie, 1999). This is based on the following stages:

1   Preparation.
2   Question formulation, clarification and reformulation.

3   Purge, idea generation and incubation.
4   Idea clustering, evaluation and action planning.

There are many different versions of this scheme, split into four or five stages and different pathways but all have essentially the same stages.

Preparation

It's important to prepare for a creative session. The room needs to be set up so that it is as inspiring as possible – the most important elements are light, colour, flexibility in the use of space, comfort, warmth, music if desired and a good supply of goodies and drinks. You will also need a range of materials to encourage the notion of idea generation – flip-charts, post-it notes, marker pens, Blu-Tack and coloured stickers. Participants need to also be prepared for the session – depending on the context, they may be asked to bring along material, or do some prior reading.

Question formulation, clarification and reformulation

The problem to be solved needs to be examined from many perspectives. This can be a creative stage and allow for divergence of ideas if there is flexibility around the problem. It can also be a convergent stage if the exercise helps to refine our understanding of the problem, such that by the time it is well defined it is almost solved. The process helps us to frame a problem or problems in different ways and stops us from rushing off to start solving the 'wrong' problem.

Purge, idea generation and incubation

Before the idea-generation stage, it is useful to have a purge or 'brain dump' to clear the working memory and move ideas to the brain store (just like a computer) so as to leave space for processing ideas. If the working memory is too full, the same idea keeps coming to the forefront. Brainstorming is the most common purging method used. It is often considered to be a creative-thinking approach but it is too simple to get really innovative ideas if the group are a little fixated with certain solutions. A quiet round is a good idea; ask the participants to write down as many solutions as possible; one idea per post-it note.

At the idea-generation stage, we need to come up with as many varied ideas as possible. It is important to stick with the main two principles, originally attributed to Osborn, who developed brainstorming in the 1930s (Osborn, 1993):

•   Postpone your judgement.
•   Hitch-hike on the ideas of others.

There are many different techniques to enhance the quality and quantity of ideas generated. Participants can call out ideas or write them on post-it notes and stick them up. It is up to the judgement of the facilitator to see which approach feels right at the time. Inviting participants to write their ideas down on post it notes helps quieter participants to join in. The ideas need to be numbered – either on post-it notes or on a flipchart so that they can be easily selected at a later date. Once idea generation starts to dry up, another technique should be employed, so as to create as many ideas as possible.

Incubation can be at any stage during the process but, classically, after an initial sorting the ideas they can be developed – either by adding more information or by simply 'incubating' – resting, walking or sleeping!

Idea clustering, evaluation and action planning

Ideas can be evaluated in several ways, for example by using simple criteria to develop a rough cull or criteria that group ideas according to their feasibility and level of innovation. If the participants get this far in the time, they can use the time left to create a short plan for what comes next so that ideas taken from the workshop are more likely to get implemented.

Four approaches to creative thinking

Creative Problem Solving (CPS) techniques

The term 'Creative Problem Solving' or CPS is most often associated with the work of the Creative Education Foundation.[1] Many other companies have developed similar tools and principles and Fred Buining[2] joined us for the workshop. CPS is a 'toolkit' approach to creative thinking which often frustrates those people who believe that there is no way that you can 'teach' creativity but that it is an inherent quality of a person. However, the tools are based on ways of thinking and much practical research about what seems to work in helping people make lateral connections or interesting associations in their thoughts. By using these approaches you soon realise their potential in helping people 'think outside the box'. Once individuals or groups become used to some of the thinking suggested by the tools, they no longer need them and even develop their own tools.

The idea behind many of the random association methods of idea generation is that the brain has much stored information. If we can first purge what is in our working memory we will unlock the vast store that is available to us. If we then use methods to start the brain working and making connections – we can sometimes come up with ideas that we would not normally think of when analysing material in a linear manner. Such methods include assumption reversals and the flower technique. Other techniques rely on forcing us to think differently then linking back to the problem, for example using analogies (Hender *et al.*, 2001). Some examples of techniques used at the different stages are given below.

Question formulation

Usually there would be a problem owner who is asked to give a briefing of the problem. Everyone can ask questions for clarification – what are the barriers preventing easy solution of this problem? What cannot be changed? Everyone is asked to formulate a question from this briefing in the form 'How can we ...?' Each person writes a problem on a post-it note and these are then pinned up or written up on a flipchart. The most important words are circled by the problem owner and a reformulation takes place. The final problem statement is written up on a flipchart for all to see. It should be visible throughout the session.

Idea generation

Reversals. In the reversals technique, we are asked to reverse the problem, so a problem statement such as, 'How do we help students become motivated to learn?' might end up as 'How can we prevent students from being motivated to learn?' We are usually much better at coming up with negatives so we fill a flipchart full of ideas such as 'bore them to death in a lecture, close the windows, speak in a monotonous voice, never relate it to real life', etc. We then reverse each idea in turn to see if any useful ideas come from this. Often we end up describing our actual teaching situation, which is rather embarrassing but not very creative!

Analogies. Making an analogy with something is a method we often adopt in order to explain difficult concepts to students. Finding an analogy with familiar objects or concepts can help participants to generate ideas. As an example of applying the technique in higher education, a research student in one of my workshops was trying to find ideas about where to go next with a very difficult chemistry problem. She told us that the chemical reaction she was studying was similar to building a brick wall – and she wanted to do it more efficiently but we couldn't change the bricks, the cement or the bricklayers. We brainstormed ideas on how to help the bricklayers become happier so that they would do their job more effectively. Ideas that are first brainstormed have only a 'fuzzy' connection to the original problem – and do not have to be sensible. One idea we came up with was – 'make it more sunny so that they enjoy getting a sun tan whilst they work'. We then suggested that participants look at the ideas and go back to the problem and make stronger connections to the original briefing. This idea became 'use UV light to speed up the reaction'. The student did not know if this had been done before, but she had certainly not thought of it herself and it seemed feasible to her.

Flower technique. The question 'owner' is asked to choose one of the words of the problem statement and this is written in the middle of a flipchart. Everyone is asked to call out words which they associate with this. Each new word is written in a petal of the flower. After a couple of minutes use some wild cards: 'thinking of cartoons – what word comes to mind?' The zaniest idea from the flower is used as the basis for another round of idea generation. In this way we move from ideas that are obviously associated with the initial idea to ideas that are 'far away' and that one would not normally be associated with the original idea.

Evaluation and action planning

The Centre for the Development of Creative Thinking (COCD) suggest the use of evaluation criteria colours to help cluster ideas. They use a COCD Box in which common, feasible ideas (blue) are in the bottom-left, original, feasible ideas (red) are in the bottom-right and original, not yet feasible ideas (yellow) are in the top-right. Everyone gets a small number of yellow, red and blue stickers and they can select their favourite in each category or they can place their ideas in a COCD box drawn on flipchart paper.

Clustering. Ideas can also be clustered according to category so that similar ideas are not competing against one another for votes. Then participants choose their favourite five ideas based on novelty, appeal and feasibility. A count of hands for each idea will demonstrate the most popular.

Action planning

Action plan template. COCD suggest the use of the Wx5, Hx2 template – what, when, who, where, why, how, how much? Participants work in small groups to come up with a plan of how to execute the idea they have just generated.

Fast presentation. Another COCD tool is the fast presentation if time permits – where participants are given a short amount of time to think about the idea and action plan, what is the goal, what is the positive effect of the action plan, what are the negative effects, how can these be turned around and what are the expected gains?

We can see that at each stage of the CPS these techniques may well develop a whole new round of idea generation! As well as a technique on its own, the CPS approach can be combined with any of the techniques discussed below.

The groups using the CPS approach found it to be very powerful and productive. The structured format with flexibility and familiarity facilitates a high quality and high volume of ideas. It takes practice to understand when to use which technique and to read your group effectively, and it is important to be open-minded about the range of techniques you can draw from at each stage.

The medicine wheel

Cris de Groot of the 'Nowhere Foundation' introduced us to an ancient tool originating from the tribes of Native Americans. The medicine wheel represents a Mandala, which are used by many different tribes to help with thinking, meaning and existing. The wheel (Figure 11.1) symbolises a map of the cosmos. It promotes a holistic view of a problem and encourages participants to think about a problem from many different perspectives. It therefore helps us towards balance and wholeness in our problem working. It was used by the elders of the tribe – the medicine men – until about 1930 when it was opened to all. The main use was to help the tribe with a difficult decision. A circle was drawn on the ground and the tribe would put the issue in the centre for all to consider. The circle was segmented and labelled with words for different energy states and

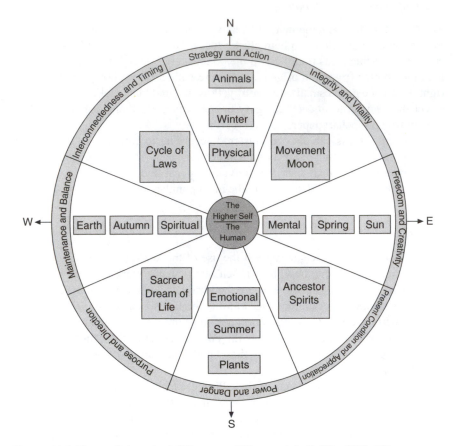

Figure 11.1 The medicine wheel (Filmore and Thomond, in Baillie, 2003: 20).

values, each of which would provide a different perspective through which the issue facing the tribe could be viewed.

The chiefs of various tribes take up positions based on their experience and wisdom in the tribe. These then become the 'wisdom council' and the wheel is used to decide on important matters that require coherence and widespread agreement. The technique works best when it is used for important issues to the members, and each person must stand in a place they truly believe in.

Starting in the East, the Heyokar tribe (known for riding into battle whilst sitting backwards on their horses to confuse the enemy) speak for freedom and creativity within the problem at hand. The responses are delivered clockwise. Each response begins with 'We are ... and we speak from ...' and each response ends with 'The ... chiefs have spoken'. It is a formal oratory, delivered to the council.

The tribes

Heyokar Chiefs: Freedom and creativity.
The Peace Chiefs: Present condition and appreciation.
The War Chiefs: Power and danger.
The Medicine Singer Chiefs: Purpose and direction.
The Women Chiefs: Harmony and balance (Maintenance and balance).
The Council Chiefs: Inter-relatedness (Interconnectedness) and timing.
The Hunter Worker Chiefs: Strategy and action.
The Law Dog Chiefs: Vitality, energy and integrity (Integrity and vitality).

At the end of the responses, the Wisdom Council vote on the issue as presented by each tribal chief, either 'I agree' or 'I am unsure'. This voting is done by the hand-signals of 'setting the sun' (agree), and of an unsettled sun (unsure). Any uncertainty is explained, discussed and reviewed. It is important that the responses are taken seriously and that each person sticks to the perspective of their own position.

The wheel can help teams to take a look at their 'whole self' and in this way can see behaviour patterns, and move to new ways of thinking. The Nowhere Foundation has developed the use of the medicine wheel and forces their clients to remain in tension with the energy that delivers creativity – rather than rushing to solutions. The ability to remain in a state of 'not knowing' is often the most elusive part of being creative. The wheel is most often used to help an organisation to look at their future. A group of 5–12 people might work together to assess the future of their organisation and consider it from different perspectives.

In applying the technique in higher education, one of the workshops discussed in *The Travelling Case* (Baillie, 2003) considered the problem 'How does the sustainability agenda interact with the luxury car industry now and in the future?' Small groups were asked to consider this problem from one of the perspectives around the wheel and to capture their ideas on post-it notes. Each group in turn (starting with the East) placed their notes on the large segment of a wheel drawn on a huge piece of paper on the floor. They then explained what they meant to the group, discussion followed and the process passed to the next group in a clockwise direction. As an example of the approach to problem solving, *the interconnectedness and timing* group considered the interconnections necessary to leverage influence for further work to make the luxury car industry see the economic, social and environmental benefits of sustainability. This proved a very useful way of approaching such a daunting task.

The process allows for a diversity of perspectives without conflict, encourages team-focused problem-solving and digs deep to the root of the problem. However, it is sometimes difficult for people to relate to the 'spiritual' undertones, and the headings are confusing for many. The medicine wheel can appear to be inappropriate for many of our participants' problems. They want tangible outcomes. This technique specifically puts the participants into a space of 'not knowing' and hence into a place of highly creative output. One recommendation from our facilitators was to change the titles on the wheel to suit your group's needs and to take the essence of the process whilst removing those parts which could put off participants. Doing this might also encourage a sense of ownership for the process.

Mind and body approaches

Mike Metelits, of the organisation 'Nothing Special', introduced us to the 'Mind and body' approach to creative thinking. The aim of these techniques is to help people be in touch with sensations in their bodies and to use them as well as their minds to help drive their needs in life. Recognising stress and tension that we may be carrying in our bodies (perhaps since childhood) is an acknowledged part of a psychotherapist's or chiropractor's work. Exercises involving deep breathing can increase awareness of the body and a feeling of being 'centred'. This is not an easy feeling to describe – but we can imagine it is one in which we feel 'comfortable in our skin' or balanced. The idea is that once we are aware of the feeling of being centred, then we can easily understand when we are pulled off-centre. We spend too much time with fruitless activities and thoughts dealing with being off-centre instead of on more productive and creative ones. The techniques can help to promote a general creative potential by freeing us of tensions; they are also intended to promote confidence and encourage deeper insights. Some of the basic approaches are as follows – each exercise is followed by a group debrief, in which participants are encouraged to discuss the physical feelings associated with exercises.

First, stand and breathe in a relaxed and open manner – find your own feeling of 'being centred' to gauge more accurately when ideas put us 'off-centre'.

In pairs, the idea for the next stage is to move into each other's personal space – slowly and considerately, maintaining eye contact throughout.

One person can push the other gently to apply different pressures from the side and front. The partner at this stage can ask questions about a problem or issue that is in focus. Switching to cognitive mode causes a lack of centredness. Variations to the questions and stresses added to this situation help us understand how we separate cognitive and sensory issues.

These approaches are often the most difficult for participants to relate to – and the least structured and rational. They are also the ones which would take the most time to learn how to facilitate and also to have an effect. As such they generally produce either the most significant result or none at all because the person is too blocked to cope with the foreign feelings that they evoke. One of our participants found that in situations where it was not going to be possible to use the whole technique, using some aspects as a warm-up and focusing exercise were invaluable.

The main advice from our facilitators for these techniques was that you need to think through purpose and context well. Students may need to lose stress but may not be in a position to appreciate the technique. To properly understand the technique needs time and practice. Participants may tend to want to ask questions about every technique and lose the body connection – focusing only on the mind. This approach can work well if judgement is suspended in the warm-up phase of the workshop.

TRIZ

TRIZ stands for *Teoriya Resheniya Izobreatatelskikh Zadatch*, a Russian acronym, approximately translated as *Theory of Inventive Problem Solving*. Genrich Altshuller began to share ideas with fellow thinkers of different disciplines and started to see patterns in the thinking which crossed disciplinary boundaries. TRIZ research started in 1946 when he began to study successful patents to find out what it was that caused the innovation in thinking to occur. There have been over 1,500 person years of research into TRIZ and over 2.5 million patents have been and still are being analysed. The main result was that patterns or principles seemed to be duplicated in many different problem scenarios in many different disciplines. A basic set of 40 principles seemed to relate to most problems. There is also a strong indication that the strongest solution renders unwanted or harmful effects into useful resources (much like nature, which uses all of its waste products instead of discarding them). It seems also that the strongest solutions overcome conflicts or trade-offs. The trade-offs have been collated in a 'contradiction matrix' which suggests which of the 40 inventive principles have been used for the strongest solutions to similar problems. A further finding was that technological change appears to be predictable and future trends of evolution have been identified.

Simon Dewulf and Darrell Mann, of Creax Company, Belgium, worked with us to help participants experience TRIZ. The following principles of TRIZ were elaborated:

1   Ideality – increasing benefits whilst eliminating cost and harm. You can work backwards from the 'Ideal Final Result' to something which is achievable now with minimal addition and optimal use of resources.
2   Functionality – identifying the purpose and effects of each element. Mapping a specific function to a generic function so that solutions from all areas can be shared (knowledge database). The example Simon and Darrell like to use is that of 'removing water'. Once this has become the generic problem 'move liquid' there are 33 methods for moving the water suggested.

The principles and tools combine to help individuals and groups brainstorm with many people before them who have solved similar problems. If the specific problem can be framed in a generic way, then one of the TRIZ tools may be employed to come up with creative ideas. The generic solution can then be translated back to the specific. The individuals' creativity is still needed to make these transitions to and from the generic.

For those who find the 'Mind and body' system described above frustrating – the order and structure of TRIZ provides a relief. To those who naturally come up with ideas it can seem constraining. Simon and Darrell are keen to point out that finding a solution is like searching for hidden treasure on an island. Brainstorming is akin to looking all over the island whereas using TRIZ helps you know where to begin looking once you have identified the island and the fact that there is treasure there to be found. Learning to use TRIZ properly can take some time but once you start to use it, it does help to develop ways of thinking that naturally become part of your creative problem-solving approach.

Summary of key lessons and the implications for teaching to facilitate creative thinking

The techniques above were applied to workshops with students and staff in a whole variety of disciplines and contexts across higher education. Creative problem-solving was used with product design staff and students, disability services and architecture students, HE teachers, managers and staff and education developers. The medicine wheel was used with research students in manufacturing sciences and electrical engineering students. 'Mind and body' techniques were used with urban design staff and students, library staff, art and design students and industrial design students. TRIZ was used with computing technology and product design staff and students, and with art and design students.

As shown from the above list, it was not the case that the more systematic techniques were applied to technical disciplines and the more intangible methods to artistic disciplines, as we might have assumed that the students would respond better to these respective approaches. In fact, very little that the facilitators reported of their experience related to the background discipline. It was clear that the acceptance of the more esoteric techniques such as 'Mind and body' were more related to personality and background than discipline. It was found that TRIZ is sometimes perceived as so complex that it is hard to introduce to younger students. The relative success of the different techniques was not 'measured', but rather evaluated qualitatively. We were not interested in the absolute number of ideas generated by these techniques but in the quality of ideas and thinking that we saw being developed in staff and students. The reports from our facilitators were unanimous – these approaches will help to foster creative thinking in many varied contexts. However, they learnt very quickly some of the lessons needed to help them optimise the potential of these techniques to enhance the creative potential, rather than forge even more blocks for the participants. The following sections give a summary of the suggestions made by our facilitators after they had learnt some key lessons in implementing these techniques.

Facilitation

A good facilitator will determine the success of the techniques and approaches. As with all educational approaches, the tool is only as good as the craftsperson using it. Sometimes it seems as if one technique does not work in a particular context when in fact, given a different facilitator, it may have been the perfect choice. The facilitator must try to match the technique to the problem and to the participants, and be sensitive enough to shift the focus flexibly as the session demands. One important factor in running a good session is to manage energy levels – to keep the group 'up'. It is important that facilitators are confident in their approach, and have hope and belief in the process, commitment to the technique and offer trust to participants. One of the facilitator's key roles is to be able to make connections between 'fuzzy' ideas and the problem. When trying to help students to see the connections it becomes important to offer examples in ways of thinking. This 'lateral thinking' often takes some practice. Facilitators need to be outside the process and not involved in the debate and must relinquish control – one of the hardest qualities for a teacher! It is best to move around the space and make it seem effortless – make people feel special and empowered, yet grounded.

Conditions

Creative potential may be blocked by the presence of important external and internal barriers (Dewulf and Baillie, 1999). Internal barriers such as those causing someone to avoid taking risks or to be held back by fear will be developed by the participants' backgrounds – there is little that can be done about this in the workshop other than to help individuals become aware of their own blocks. We have a much better chance of controlling external conditions and the environment in which we are working. We can use these to set up the *optimal tension zone* of our participants which will be different for each person. Our goal should be to try to increase the chances for all participants of reaching this zone. We can generate support for the workshop or creative training session within the department or degree programme so that participants feel that it is an important part of their work. We can also create a room which inspires – use of space, maximising the senses, use of sound, light, colour.

Participants

In our project, we tried to uncover those elements that keep participants enthralled, excited, motivated and engaged in sessions. One of the factors described above – energy management of the group – is key. In order to do this, it is necessary to 'read' your group and keep the dissenters under control. They might find the process very difficult and resist because they feel silly, possibly putting others off in the process. Motivation established at the outset is essential – the group needs to see the relevance of the work, so an emphasis on problem ownership might help. The problem-solving process needs to be democratic so that all participants are engaged and alert, feeling at once listened to and in control. The group size is important – when working with large groups it may be necessary to break these down into smaller groups for some of the creative exercises – however, the management of energy and suspension of disbelief needs to be maintained throughout. If working with tutors or peer tutors they will need training before being successful.

Problems

It is useful for students to learn how to be creative by trying to solve problems that mean something to them. However, when the intention is to develop the creative thinking of a group it is probably better not to have a really difficult problem to work on. It is important to gain some 'quick wins' so that the group starts to feel that they are in fact being very creative and enhance their confidence. This will help ideas to flow better. It is often useful to work with a problem owner who describes the briefing at the start of the session but who must not interrupt the session if it appears to be moving off the point. Group ownership is also important so that everyone feels that they care about the problem being solved. This can be developed in the early stages by the reformulation exercises described above where the group gets to re-write the problem in their own words.

Process

A good facilitator will be able to select a technique that will work at the onset, and change to another as necessary. Techniques that break mind sets are important and a balance of divergent and convergent processes works well. The skills of selecting techniques will come with time. It is essential that the facilitator is able to be humble and to admit when a technique is not working. It is also important to time the stages, know at which point to move on, allow for flexibility to suit the process and the participants' needs and expectations and allow for breaks.

At the start, the use of icebreakers is essential. The one thing that all the trainers and lecturers involved in this project stressed was that it was best to mix and match techniques and approaches rather than to stick to one method in a ritualistic manner. Some very cognitive techniques such as TRIZ can cause ownership of the problem to be lost if not carefully managed. Random approaches such as the use of abstract representation using finger paintings, for example, can forge the link to personal feelings and ownership that may be needed for buy-in to ideas. However, sometimes the opposite is true – some participants will find the random approaches too 'hit and miss' and will be relieved when entering a TRIZ phase. It is important for participants to understand that all ideas are valued so that they feel part of the process. The continual feedback, rewards and praise are all part of the energy management. Fun needs to be maintained at all times, but it has to be balanced with perceived and real productivity. The company Idea Factory in the UK once told me that when running workshops in the UK compared to the USA they had to take out '50% of the fun' otherwise UK participants would not take it seriously!

Facilitating creative thinking in education

In our first publication (Dewulf and Baillie, 1999), we attempted to discuss principles that might be applied to foster creative thinking generally in teaching and learning – ways in which we as teachers could provide stimulus to students and counter the effects of previous barriers. In this chapter we have described the approaches taken within a UK-wide experiment to foster creative thinking in universities. We focused on specific techniques that may be employed to help students and staff solve problems in more creative ways. We have detailed the way in which they might be used and we have presented a condensed version of the lessons learnt about their potential usefulness by facilitators working in many different contexts and disciplines. It is clear that in many areas it will not be possible to incorporate entire workshops as discussed above. However the principles of these methods are strong and may be adapted to suit many different contexts. Within any lesson/workshop plan it might be possible to ask staff/ students to take part in a short creative exercise and to solve problems related to their current studies or responsibilities. Any of the techniques described above can be used as a whole method or in a mix-and-match mode.

There are no rules to creative thinking – however, the skill of the facilitator is to create the atmosphere that is conducive to idea generation, as well as selecting the most appropriate technique, for the participants, in their context and with their particular problems to solve. Avoiding risk-taking is one of the biggest barriers to creative thinking, but exploiting some of these tried and tested techniques is worth the anxiety felt in the first few sessions. Creative potential will increase not only in your students but in yourself.

Notes

1 www.creativeeducationfoundation.org/.
2 Centre for the Development of Creative Thinking (COCD), the Netherlands.

12 How should I assess creativity?

John Cowan

Introduction

My background, as far as assessing creativity is concerned, is distinctly hetero-geneous. In my academic career, I have had to engage with this challenge in many different disciplinary settings. I have assessed creativity in my original discipline of engineering (Cowan, 1981a, 2004a), in my second academic career in the social sciences, but also in architecture, in design in a College of Art, in PGCertHEs, in mathematics and – admittedly briefly in each case – in a course on dance, in modules on theology, and in the design of a module on osteopathic education. In other words, I claim that my thinking in what follows is reasonably multi-disciplinary.

Originally, I had in mind to simply reflect around the challenge as I see it and then to advance my own somewhat individualistic blueprint for an approach which I sincerely believe is at least an advance on the status quo. However, while the process of writing was proceeding, so too was an unfold-ing public conversation about the assessment of creativity in the Imaginative Curriculum network. Three of the papers that emerged from that debate were so in tune with my thinking and the writing that I had already completed, that I felt somewhat nonplussed and uncertain about how to acknowledge and refer to them. I certainly wanted to make use of them, because they reinforced my suggested approach so strongly and endorsed or clarified the thoughts I had already assembled. I felt it would be wrong to plagiarise, even with adequate acknowledgement, since the writings spoke for their views more effectively than any paraphrasing of mine could do. Eventually, I decided to extract key quotations from these papers and incorporate them in an appendix (12.1), so that readers who share with me in the dilemmas that are presented by the chal-lenge to assess creativity, should encounter some positive, definite, authorita-tive and independent statements on the subject, before venturing with me into my somewhat innovative and certainly individual proposal. In deciding to present their shrewd thinking in this way, I was minded of the tale of the encounter between those bitter antagonists, Whistler and Wilde. During this discussion, Wilde was moved to admit grudgingly, 'I wish I had said that' – to which Whistler replied scathingly, 'You will, Oscar, you will.'

Finally, I should emphasise that – despite what I have just explained – this chapter is very much a personal statement. So its citations are almost entirely corroboratory references to my own work. It is thus virtually bereft of the profusion of cross-references that are increasingly expected of us, if our academic writing is to be seen as respectable and to be respected.

The challenge presented if, or when, we seek to assess creativity

Assessing creativity by the process

Of all the cognitive abilities, synthesis or creativity is arguably the most difficult to assess. We can determine and hence assess what someone knows, simply by asking a question which calls for the *knowledge* concerned to be given in the answer. We can judge *understanding*, by asking a question that calls for a response which explains or rewords that which the learner knows and claims to understand. We can assess the ability to apply understanding, by getting the learner to apply the particular understanding in question, and to leave a trail, in one form or another, which shows how they have been tackling the applying, and how that led them to the end product of that *application*.

Moving (for convenience) further up a familiar taxonomy of cognitive abilities, we come to *analysis*, which is rather more difficult to assess – but only slightly so. For analysis, almost by definition, tends to follow a fairly definite process, even if it is a distinctly personal algorithm. This approach, even if not explicit in the record of the analysing, is capable of being described by the learner as 'their method', for they should know what they were doing and how they do it. That claim can readily be checked against the overt evidence that they generated as they progressed through their analysis, since the evidence in the trail that they have left can then or later be amplified, if necessary.

Not so with *creativity*. For many of us, the heart of the creative process is often the sudden insight or idea, the 'blue flash' out of which the germ of an idea emerges. That inspiration may come about as a reaction to an earlier and now obviously unsuitable idea; or from thoughtful mulling through the elements of the problem that confronts us; or by adaptation of a remembered solution; or by responding to the prompt of a colleague or to an innocent question from them; or from translation of a familiar solution into an entirely new context, or even through systematic reasoning. And at one time or another, a creative person may find their route to creativity in any of these ways, or perhaps in another manner that I have not mentioned.

The multiplicity and often the suddenness of the possible approaches to being creative therefore complicate the business of assessing the process – because the creative process, for any learner, is unpredictable and difficult to capture. It is even often quite difficult for the creative person to capture and describe. I have listened to many recorded protocols in which students were talking out their thoughts aloud as they solved problems which I had set for them, often calling upon them to be creative, in some way (Cowan, 1977, 1980a; Brohn and Cowan, 1977). Time and time again, these recordings produced two forms of sound that conveyed very little detailed information. There would be the expletive when something went wrong, or when an error was spotted. And there would be the strangled cry of success when a penny dropped, or when a blue flash illuminated a feasible solution. Even drawing upon the recorded protocol, the nature of the creative thinking then occurring was insufficiently defined for me to formulate a full account, let alone assessment, of the speaker's creativity.

Assessing creativity is a problem with a number of dimensions. The process is highly personal, it varies from challenge to challenge, and often has at its heart a flash of inspiration which is extremely difficult for the creative problem-solver to capture for themselves. Another and more fundamental problem about assessing the creative process for academic purposes is that creativity (under-standably?) tends to be judged, within society, in terms of products that are seen to be creative and are rated as commendable for that reason. Yet often it is in the experiences of failure and frustration that the creative ability is honed and developed.

Assessing creativity by the product

What happens, then, if we assess on the basis of the product of the creative process? Surely a creative product is evidence of a creative mind in action? Assessment by product is the common approach across disciplines and levels of ability. We usually assess someone's ability to apply understanding by the product of their efforts. We can make a fair stab at assessing their ability to analyse from the evidence of the final analysis that they produce and present. In contrast, the creative process often takes place without much recorded evidence of what was going on in the creator's head, and with what *is* available being ambiguous and perhaps misleading. So it would seem that assessing creativity by product is the solution we should adopt.

Nevertheless, this is not as simple as it may seem. For that which appears a brilliantly original and creative product may simply (and quite legitimately) be something which was recycled (not plagiarised) from a piece of prior creativity generated either by this person, or by someone else. It may have arisen from imitation, adaptation or recall – all modestly creative, admittedly, but not quite meriting the assessment rating for top- standard creativity (whatever that is) that the product appeared to merit on first appearance. To make a considered and comprehensive judgement of the extent to which a product is creative, the judge of that potential creativity surely needs some awareness of how the innovatory product was conceived. Of course, the person best placed to make such an informed judgement is the creative person, themselves.

However, in academia at present and in the past, teachers have mainly relied entirely upon their own judgement of the created product to provide the basis for their assessment of the producer's creativity. Assessors strive to eliminate imita-tion, adaptation or recall, by engaging the students who are to be assessed on a task which should be new to them, and one in relation to which they have had little or no prior and relevant experience. It should be a problem for which they will not be recalling solutions, produced for a similar problem by other creative people, whose efforts can be imitated or adapted. It will be a situation rather unlike those that they will encounter in the professional life wherein they will, it is to be hoped, continue to demonstrate a creative approach, and interact formatively with peers and others while so doing. The yearning remains to find ways to identify the process of creativity in sufficient detail to make an assessment of it in relation to the product, and vice versa.

Relation of student-centred learning to the self-assessment of creativity

At the time of writing, and certainly in the UK, several forces combine powerfully to urge higher education to move markedly and swiftly towards student-centred activity for learning. This goal is, for a start, pedagogically desirable, especially in respect of the nurturing of higher-level abilities. It is economically essential, as numbers and student/staff ratios escalate while resourcing suffers attrition for a similar reason. It is socially desirable, if higher education is to be accessible to, and effective for, learners of greatly varied prior experience, learning styles and abilities.

It is perhaps less obvious that there is another factor which is strengthening the emphasis on student-centred learning and self-assessment. This is the stress that the quality-assurance 'industry' is placing on the design, provision and delivery of fully aligned curricula. In programme specifications and delivery, teachers are expected to specify their intended learning outcomes – which in relation to our current topic would entail encapsulating in generic terms what this highly individual and variable creativity will look like, once it is achieved. Teachers are also expected to design and to justify pedagogically the learning activities that they deliver, and in which, in this case, the creative ability should be purposefully nurtured and developed. And they should specify methods and standards of assessment, which will be used to judge the achievement of the learning outcomes – in this case, creative outcomes. In all of this process, the outcomes, activities and assessment should be as well-aligned as possible – which means, in other words, that they should be compatible. This is a demand to which all disciplines are nowadays expected to make an adequate response.

Even in the relatively recent past, reasonable alignment has been relatively rare; in most disciplines, mismatches in alignment represent clear weaknesses in curriculum design. Assessment has often rewarded regurgitation and the following of instructions, rather than the deep and creative thinking that featured rhetorically in the corresponding learning outcomes. Learning activities have often simply allowed students to *practise* abilities, without necessarily *developing* them – with the result that the able have demonstrated and confirmed their ability, and the less-able have demonstrated their inability. And so there have been, and in many cases still are, stark discrepancies in the links between these three aspects of our curricula, between which we should expect alignment (Figure 12.1a).

However the concentration, through various quality assurance initiatives, on identifying and minimising aspects of lack of alignment is having the interesting result (Cowan, 2004b) that there is movement from aligned elements, as they should be in Figure 12.1a, to what I will call integrated elements. The first such move is already apparent in some thoughtful curriculum designs, where the detailed plan and documentation for well-aligned assessment features explicit and well-designed tasks and clearly explained criteria and standards. In effect this then renders the statement of learning outcomes virtually redundant, since they are spelt out accurately and in full in the scheme for assessment. This intermediate transformation is illustrated diagrammatically as two partially integrated elements (Figure 12.1b and 12.1c).

If the designed activity for learning is open-ended and not overly directive, it behoves the learner who has to be active within such a situation to monitor, if not ensure, alignment between the two remaining elements – their learning as it progresses, and the intended and assessed outcomes. Consequently, the progression towards full integration will naturally move further. The self-directed learner, with an eye on institutional assessment, will see an advantage in early formative *self*-assessment, whether or not that is formalised and encouraged. This self-assessing learner, as we have seen in many schemes over the past 20 years or so (e.g. Boud, 1995), will *direct* their learning towards the intended learning outcomes, according to the declared values and standards. In addition, the self-assessing learner will further *manage* their learning on a day-to-day basis, to achieve as best possible the desired outcomes and standards (Boyd and Cowan, 1986). Hence the two remaining block elements are, or can be, in effect, fully integrated as in Figure 12.1d.

What implications could this then have for the assessment of creativity, in programmes or modules where the nurturing and exercise of creativity are

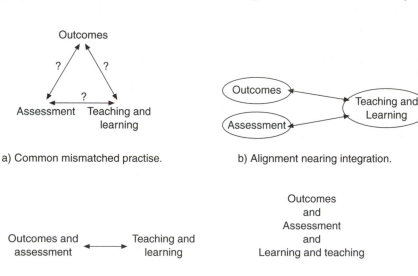

a) Common mismatched practise.

b) Alignment nearing integration.

c) Two elements integrated.

d) Full integration into student-centred learning.

Figure 12.1 From alignment to integration.

valued, and where the precise definition of that creativity might heretically be left un-specified at the outset? It would then feature, not as *intended* learning outcomes, but rather (at the conclusion of the learning experience), as *achieved* learning outcomes.

These thoughts have led me to a number of rhetorical questions with whose answers the writings of experts (Appendix 12.1) may assist us, as we review my plan for assessing creativity and creative work.

Plan for assessing students' creativity

Outline

The plan that I set out here is an amalgam of significant elements of practice that have already featured effectively for me, and for my undergraduate students, in validated programmes. They have simply not hitherto been brought together, in one scheme. Before outlining it in detail, I offer a description of the end product that I have in mind, for those who like to know, as I do, where they are going before they start. Each student will assemble what may at first sight appear somewhat like a portfolio, but is rather a self-assessment. A portfolio is a collection of a person's work, showing its strengths and variety, and enabling the reader or viewer to make their own judgement of overall merit. In contrast, a self-assessment contains and presents the following elements:

- A definition of what the person being assessed (whom I shall call 'the learner') means by 'creativity'.
- A clear statement of the achievement and/or development in creative ability to which the learner aspired in respect of undertaking the period of study or development wherein creativity is being assessed. This statement is to be amplified by an indication of the standards or levels against which the learner has decided to judge that creativity, as it was displayed and developed during the period of studies in question.
- An indication of the sources from which the learner has drawn information from which to assemble their judgement of their performance and development.
- The information which then emerged and informed the learner's judgement.
- The making of that judgement.
- The judgement in qualitative terms, perhaps under various headings.

In my plan, the learner will present this assembled collection of items for audit (meaning scrutiny of the rigour of the self-assessment). The assessors will not make their own judgements of the learner's creativity from the documents before them. Rather, they will decide if they are sufficiently persuaded by the learner's making of their judgement to endorse the learner's self-assessment of their own creative processes, thinking and outcomes, made against the learner's chosen and stated criteria, and following the method of judging which the learner has outlined. They will then simply confirm that the learner's self-assessment is (or is not) objectively established by the information the learner has assembled for that purpose, and the way it has been used.

The primary purpose of this strategy is to enable students to explore, experience and develop their own understanding of creativity and to construct new meanings in the context of their programme and disciplinary field of study. In so doing, it embodies the suggestions made by Oliver *et al.* in Chapter 5 of this book where they conclude that 'claims to an emergent creative ability can only be warranted if they can be articulated'. The role of the teacher is to create the conditions that facilitate this type of learning and to help students develop their capacity to recognise, represent and evaluate their own creativity. How, then, could we who are in the business of assessing creativity go about such a process of audited self-assessment? I offer below my plan, amplified as a sequence of steps, and accompanied by some comments in italics on the rationale for them. I leave it to you to refer to the experts' statements (Appendix 12.1) which I believe often explicitly support what I propose, and to the accounts of practice on which my plan is based (Appendix 12.2).

My plan

I now invite you to identify any parts of the plan that follows, which might have something to offer your practice – and any features that you can improve.

Step 1: I would introduce the process by reassuring the learners (preferring that term, now, rather than 'students') about the genuine flexibility of the programme. I would if possible bring in some of last year's learners, to confirm what I am telling the new cohort, which is that what they are asked to decide within the process which they will follow will be open at any stage to revision, refinement or total rejection and change by them.

Rationale: Development is an iterative process, in which the experiences of one iteration should inform the progression into the next one.

Comment: This step was a key feature in the three main programme developments I have instanced, and for the CPD pilot (Cowan and Westwood, in press), for all of which I have had responsibility, and which featured self-assessment.

Step 2: I would begin the process by helping the learners to define what they mean by creativity and the features of creative work in their discipline, at this point in time.

Rationale: If you don't know where you're going, any bus will do. Conversely, if the learner is clear about their intended goal, they will purposefully direct and manage their learning and their development accordingly.

With this end in view, I would plan and facilitate a 90-minute workshop in which learners (working in, and splitting tasks within, groups) will be prepared to go out individually, each to question one of a variety of resource people. The interviewees (selected and approached by the interviewers) are to include established professionals in the learners' discipline and outwith it, postgraduate students and recent graduates in employment, employers and representatives of relevant professional bodies. I would structure and facilitate a business-like task in which views and advice, which relate to our purpose, are in-gathered, digested, and re-assembled within the small groups, with interchange across the larger class group. These group discussions, and even the group summaries on a flipchart, would be simply a means to an end – for the individual. For, finally, each learner will draft their own definitions and explanations of what this creative ability should entail. This statement is to be drafted on a personal and individual basis, of which each writer has ownership and understanding.

Comment: I have run this workshop to greatest effect with first-year undergraduates, who were to go on to produce open-ended assignment work, and would be expected to self-assess it before submission.

Step 3: Similarly to the approach of the activity in Step 2, I would help the learners to produce their first drafts of personal standards and targets.

Rationale: We cannot make judgements of performance (and development) without descriptors against which to judge performances and development.

I would now offer a second workshop, following on from the first one, and on similar lines. In this activity, I would help the learners to draw upon and mull over the advice and examples given to them and their peers in their various enquiries. Such a discursive process might be informed by (but need not conform to) the demands of the qualification (Framework for Higher Education Qualifications or Scottish Credit and Qualification Framework), enhanced subject benchmarking statements that engage with the idea of creativity, or accounts of the meaning of creativity in different disciplines (Jackson and Shaw, this volume, Chapter 8).

Accordingly, and again after discussions in groups, students should individually draft performance scales in respect of their discipline area. These should spell out standards of performance and development, in terms and with inherent standards which the learners will have declared to peers and discussed with them, as with their teachers and other professionals in their discipline. This consultation definitely does not preclude the selection of personal targets and standards that may differ from the general view in the class. Nor should there be any element of 'second guessing' of the staff position. However, each learner should have identified any such differences, and rationalised them, for inclusion in their justification of the chosen targets and standards that will feature in their final self-evaluation.

Comment: This workshop, too, has been a feature of some of my work with students of social sciences, and combined studies (or general studies) students.

Step 4: I would set the learners off to engage reflectively in the creative activity, whatever it is, which is central in their study programme.

During this period I would expect the learners to maintain a reflective journal. This should focus on the creative process, but not as a diary. Each entry should begin by posing a question about the process in hand – a question for which the learner at the time of writing has not articulated the answer, and for which the learner feels that even a part answer would be of value to them, in progressing their development. I'm assuming that this will be a strange task for them, so I would not ask them to tackle it without first having been shown examples taken from a different discipline, wherein students would have been learning and developing reflectively. They would have the opportunity to discuss and question these reflective accounts. Thereafter, in their first journal entry, I will ask my learners to think through their answers to the question – 'How should I tackle the next programme task which calls upon me to be creative?' This reflection should happen early on, without the learners knowing at that point the nature of the specific demand they will confront in the first given task. Their self-advice must therefore be in general terms.

Journals will be commented upon, confidentially, by a teacher or tutor. The commenter will express no overt judgements, nor will they offer tutorial suggestions on its content. They will merely ask facilitative questions where they have noted a non sequitur, or failure to explore options, or the need to consider implications, or the absence of an indication of how decisions will be reached. The comments will mainly take the form of questions that the learner might usefully consider – with perhaps a brief mention of why the questions are worth considering.

Rationale: Those who take time to think in generic terms about how they do things are likely to become more effective in that activity; and those who are effective in doing demanding tasks tend to have the ability to stand back, if and when they so wish, and identify what they do, and how, and why (Cowan, 1986, 1998).

Comment: Such facilitative commenting has been a central element in my approach to developing capabilities in a variety of discipline areas for over 20 years.

The learners will now encounter a specific task for the first time, and will begin to tackle it. The form of tuition provided by me would be in accordance with traditional approaches in the discipline, those that would be described as 'good teaching practice' – but will naturally vary from discipline to discipline.

Whether or not it would normally be a feature of established practice, learners will take part regularly in group 'crits', as practised in architecture and the creative arts. In these sessions, learners will critically appraise a piece of their work in progress, after which peers and tutors will offer comment, with an emphasis on reasoned and constructive judgements of that work. In presenting these judgements, speakers will be expected to describe and explain the sound standards against which they make judgements. In addition, a few sessions (which will be arranged in the same format) will focus on the *approaches* which learners are following, in attempting to be creative and to enhance their creativity; and, again, peers and tutors will attempt to offer reasoned and constructive suggestions, this time on method rather than product.

Learners will encounter the concept that judgements, whether formative or summative, can be made in qualitative terms and against what we will call a 'sound standard' descriptor. It will specify a standard midway between a bare Pass and Distinction. This descriptor will be framed without using value words. For example, rather than specifying a standard in terms of '*thorough* consideration of options', a 'sound standard' descriptor might specify that standard as featuring 'at least three distinct and competitive options having been conceived and explored for feasibility'. The making of what will be qualitative judgements will be facilitated by discussions in class of supplied examples of 'finished work', which are in some ways stronger than the 'sound standard' against which they are to be judged, and in some ways weaker.

Comment: I have used this approach with students of social sciences with great effect in raising targets and standards, and hastening assimilation of intended learning outcomes.

Throughout the duration of the creative work that constitutes the main part of the programme for the learners, they will continue to keep a weekly journal, concentrating after the first entry upon such questions as, 'What have I learnt recently about being more creative than before?', or 'What do I need to do to develop in my creativity – and how?' – or some such general question of their choice, concentrating on their immediate priorities for the creative process and activity.

Step 5: Making changes.
Rationale: As we engage more and more and deeply with processes and standards, so does our thinking develop and so do our aspirations and intentions refine. The programme and its practices should recognise that, encourage it and build upon it.

During the programme, learners (as already explained) will be free to make any changes they wish in definitions, statements of standards or personal aspirations – provided these are reasoned and recorded in their journals. From time to time I will explicitly encourage them to do so.

Comment: This, again, was a strong feature of all three major developments I have listed in Appendix 12.2.

Step 6: Assessment.
Learners will assemble the following in their self-assessment:

- Their definition of creativity, and their specification of the appropriate standards against which they think their creativity, and development of it, should be judged.
- The sources of information – data, work produced, feedback, journal entries or whatever – upon which they have drawn to inform their judgement.
- A summary of the relevant items they have in-gathered.
- A description of their understanding of their own creativity and the way it was manifested during the module; and of the enhancement of that ability during the module. This should draw upon the items in their collection, and be framed in the same terms as their definition and statements of standards – against which it can then be set, and compared.
- The explanation of how they reached the judgements in their self-assessment.

Most of the items in the collection will not be self-sufficient; they will need to be corroborated by or with other items. Let's not call these items 'evidence', for that term has connotations for me of courts of law, where 'evidence' must be indubitable. Similarly, I'm avoiding 'data' as much as possible, as it's not really the term I would naturally use to describe the items in a personal collection.

Many of the items will only be strong enough to influence judgement validly when they corroborate and amplify each other. Items will come from reasoned judgements and advice from peers or tutors, from reflective journals and the comments thereon, from observations of changes in practice associated with enhancement of creativity, and from the evidence of work in progress or completed, as much as of end results. Learners will be encouraged to use these to establish the best that they can be. Consequently the risks that they took, creatively, but which led to failures, need only be featured if the learner feels that they reflect worthwhile or effective handling of the creative process.

The self-assessments will be audited (scrutinised) in the first instance by peers who will be charged to turn back any assessment that does not follow the specified procedure and embody its features. In that case, learners will then have the opportunity to re-assemble their self-assessment, if they so wish.

Self-assessments will finally be audited by assessors who do not know the learner's current work, and must authenticate the process of assessment and the learner's consequent judgement from the self-assessment collection itself. The auditing assessor will simply:

- Check that the learner's criteria and descriptors of standards are comprehensible.
- Check that the data and items used in informing the learner's judgement do indeed objectively justify the assessment the learner has reached, according to the method of making judgements which is described.

Learners will then proceed to the next stage in their studies, or to seek employment, bearing an audited assessment of how well they can perform in terms of values and standards that they have chosen. These values, demanding or otherwise, will be transparent in the self-assessment, and so are then open to judgement by employers, others – and self. If the university system demands marks or grades for this subject, then class and teacher together can and will negotiate a defensible way to convert qualitative judgements into marks or grades.

Some closing thoughts

Within higher education, we can and should only make a contribution to the business of continuing to develop a person's creative abilities. That development will continue throughout their professional life, by which time the learner will have come to understand the meaning of being self-directed in the employment environment, and will need to self-assess – first for formative reasons and then, on occasions, summatively. Surely we should anticipate that demand, by providing an education in which the necessary ability for self-assessment is itself introduced and nurtured? Will that not be furnished most effectively within a special type of teacher–student relationship in which both learn together to co-create understanding, values and awareness?

The person nearest to the creativity is the creator. It surely then makes sense to move the assessing activity and responsibility as near as possible to the person who is best informed, provided the outcome is then declared? In addition, the emphasis in my suggested approach is more on formative than summative assessment, and on its impact on learning and development. Maybe that is no bad thing?

Perhaps also, we would profit from giving more attention to the tasks within which we nurture and assess creativity? (Cowan 1981, 2004a)

Many years ago, I used to introduce quartets of first-year students of civil engineering to the concept and challenge of designing. I gave them some balsa wood or spaghetti and sticky tape, and challenged them to build towers or bridges or whatever, to a given problem specification. They were to be judged by the ratio of the load carried before collapse to the weight of the model structure. No marks were to be awarded, but the competition was intense. When I first offered this activity, I noted sadly that the designs were hastily conceived, and indeed that many were pathetic, often unable to support their own weight. So eventually I changed the task. I challenged them to design and fabricate *two* structures that were to be fundamentally different, though to the same problem specification. The structures each had to have one major feature which was not the same as in the other model. And a group was judged on the *poorer* of their two models. This completely changed the group behaviour, in four ways:

- They spent much longer thinking through their analyses, before selecting plans and beginning fabrication.
- There were hardly any pathetic models, which could not support their own weight.
- The winning 'poorer' models were distinctly better than the winning models of a few years earlier, when the same problem had been set, but judged in the old way.
- There seemed to be more conversation within the groups, both during the event and after the testing, about 'how to do it'.

With these observations in mind, I repeat and close these comments on the suggestion that perhaps we should give more attention to the tasks within which we nurture and assess creativity. That will entail much greater and more sophisticated creativity on our parts than feature in my primitive example from the early weeks of a first-year programme.

Could this plan succeed?

Of course it could succeed; I know it can work, because I have almost followed it already. It certainly contains no elements which I have not featured effectively in undergraduate programmes, with success and without problems. You will make your own judgement about the extent to that it embodies the advice and views of our three experts. For my own part, I find it difficult to see any major point in their advice that is not embodied in my plan more effectively than in the status quo of assessing creativity. I don't claim it's a perfect plan – but simply that it represents a real step forward.

It can be supported by other strong arguments:

- Most of the main features in this plan featured in the example described in my second group of references in Appendix 12.2. This was approved 20 years ago as 25 per cent of the programme in the penultimate year of a degree programme, which was accredited by a professional body not known for its liberal approach.
- Around the same time, if not earlier, several Scandinavian universities with project-orientation programmes dispensed with final-year assessment altogether. Once the first cohort had moved into practice and proved their ability, subsequent graduates did not experience much difficulty being employed on the basis of what they were, what they had done, and how well they interviewed.

Why is this scheme not in use in at least some UK programmes, then? Bluntly, the first reason is that I am a retired part-time lecturer, and no longer a senior member of any course team. Another reason is that to put this plan into service would call for a course team to be willing to examine practice elsewhere, and consciously to take risks in delivering something in a style for which they have not hitherto been responsible. It also calls for a validation panel to take risks in the same way. To achieve all of that, frankly, would call for an influential leader of the innovation who would not only have conviction and resilience – but also tactical *nous*. For, in my experience of launching innovations in higher education, the secret of success is to have piloted what you plan, and to know that it can work; to have carried your students with you into seeking enhancement in their learning from what you plan; and in confronting the sceptics tactically, rather than on the basis of reasoned arguments, which I have found will seldom impress staunch sceptics.

Appendix 12.1

Conversations in an evolving debate

This appendix contains a synthesis of mail base discussions and other deliberations of the Imaginative Curriculum Network that were available in June 2005 on the Higher Education Academy website (www.heacademy.ac.uk/2841.htm). They include three main articles:

- Tom Balchin – 'Assessing students' creativity: lessons from research'
- Lewis Elton – 'Designing assessment for creativity: an imaginative curriculum guide'.
- Norman Jackson – 'Assessing students' creativity: synthesis of higher education teachers' views'.

I quote here the information and advice offered by these three authorities in the field, under the rhetorical questions that emerged for me in developing this chapter. In this form, I believe they convey a powerful argument, without commentary from me, in support of the plan for assessing students' creativity which I elaborate in the second half of this chapter.

Should creativity be assessed?

- 'Evaluation is critical to the very idea of creativity' (Jackson).
- 'The views of higher education teachers on whether creativity can be assessed fall into four camps. Some teachers believe that students' creativity is assessed through explicit assessment criteria. Others believe that, at best, evaluation and recognition is implicit. The third group believe that it is not possible or desirable to assess creativity. Teachers in the fourth group value creativity, but don't know how to assess it' (Jackson).

Are we sufficiently clear about what we want to be assessed?

- 'It is necessary to operationalise the abstract word "creativity" if it is to be linked to assessment. Hence the use of the phrase "creative work". For work to be considered creative, it has to be: within its context and, in the case of students, at a level appropriate for them: both new and significant. An important aspect of that context is the creator' (Elton).
- 'While not all criticality is allied to creativity, all creativity must be allied to criticality. Hence, in order to recognise and assess creative work, it is necessary to assess both the creativity and the criticality involved, within the appropriate context' (Elton).
- 'It should be possible to separate subjective judgements of creativity from judgements of technical goodness and from judgements of aesthetic appeal. It is important to demonstrate that it is at least possible to separate these dimensions' (Balchin).

Should we assess both process and product?

- 'It is the concept stage where the unique ideas are brought forth, and the product stage is the manifestation of these creative ideas' (Balchin).
- 'Current research has shown that any identification of a thought process as creative must finally depend upon the fruit of that process – a product or response' (Balchin).
- 'There is almost universal agreement that understanding a student's creativity depends to some extent on their ability to understand and explain it' (Jackson).
- 'The complex and multidimensional nature of creativity cannot be captured effectively and comprehensively by any single instrument or analytical procedure' (Balchin).
- '... (that the same grade can be obtained on the basis of quite different strengths and weaknesses and that it therefore hides details of a student's

performance.) . . . This, in turn, has led to the idea of a profile in which each part is separately classified if appropriate, and not if not, the final outcome then being reported in the form of a profile' (Elton).

Why should the learning outcomes of an experience that develops creativity be specified in advance?

- 'Clearly, it is, in general, neither possible nor desirable to assess a piece of creative work against predetermined criteria – the criteria have to be interpreted in the light of the work' (Elton).
- 'Outcomes-based learning (OBL) is predicated on the teachers' notions of what will be valued at the end of the process. OBL also tends to focus on results rather than the process of acquiring the results – where creativity in action lies' (Jackson).
- 'Outcomes-based assessment systems that assume that all learning can be predicted are antithetic to learning that emerges in unpredictable ways' (Jackson).
- 'There is a dichotomy between the individuality and originality we say we are trying to promote and the way we place boundaries on creativity when we come to assess through the criteria we use' (Jackson).

Can the teachers, or other external judges, be relied on to assess creativity?

- 'Perhaps seeing possibilities in students' manifestations of creativity is an example of how teachers themselves must be creative when they are assessing students' creativity' (Jackson).
- 'Criterion referencing on the part of examiners implies what Eisner (1985) has called connoisseurship; the educated ability of experts in a particular field to assess work in it' (Elton).

If creative ability is often honed and developed in the experiences of failure, how can we recognise this in our assessment practices?

- 'Taking risks by moving into the unknown is part and parcel of trying to be creative. The risk of failure (dropping the ball) by not accomplishing goals that have been set is higher. Teachers have to be willing to let students *fail* (not achieve all they wanted to achieve) and value failure if this is the result of creative endeavour' (Jackson).

Will learning and development not both be enhanced by involvement of the learner in self-assessment, which will also further the process of assessment itself?

- 'Perhaps the primary role of the teacher is to help students recognise and understand their own creativity and help them express it and make claims against the evidence they feel is appropriate' (Jackson).

- 'Perhaps real empowerment of students only comes when they can catch their own creativity' (Jackson).
- 'There exists another useful way to measure creativity; to simply "ask the subject". The subject himself [sic] should have a good idea of his creative ability in a wide variety of areas, and especially the moment of inspiration that caused him/her to take creative action' (Balchin).
- 'If creativity is socially constructed then it is obligatory that the creative actors/artists (the students) are themselves involved in decisions about their own creativity' (Jackson).

Should we assess all practice, or best practice, in this context?

- 'In principle, a student's portfolio contains all that the student wishes to be assessed on and it starts with the idea of assessing what the student claims to be good at' (Elton).

Upon whose criteria should the assessment of creativity be based?

- 'Perhaps the most important feature (of a consensual definition of creativity) is its reliance on subjective criteria but, ultimately, the choice of these characteristics seems to be personal to the evaluator' (Balchin).
- 'Creativity assessment might be regarded as an attempt to recognise or identify creative characteristics or abilities among people, or to understand their creative strengths and potentials' (Balchin).
- 'This raises the issue of students' involvement in negotiating the criteria against which they will make claims and by which they will be judged' (Jackson).

And, as a worrying prompt for the closing remarks at the end of this chapter

- 'A serious obstacle can arise in trying to fit unorthodox forms of assessment into regulations not designed for them' (Elton).

Appendix 12.2

Sources of descriptions and evaluations of the practices that underlie the plan for assessing students' creativity

Cowan (1980b)	This paper describes a first year course 'without a syllabus' which received an award from the Royal Society of Arts, under the Education for Capability Scheme. In it, first-year students of civil engineering determined their syllabus as a totally open choice, but only undertook formative self-assessment.

Boyd *et al.* (1984); Cowan (1984, 1988)	In these writings, three of my students and I separately described an innovatory course in which the students decided what to study, and to what standards – and self-assessed themselves, after peer interaction, in a process that yielded marks which contributed to the award of their degree. This was in a discipline (civil engineering) where it was important to retain the approval of the Joint Board of Moderators. I assisted one of my students (Boyd and Cowan, 1986) to identify the way this setting influenced the students' learning.
Cowan *et al.* (1999); Weedon and Cowan (2002, 2003)	These papers relate to an undergraduate social science module in the UHI Millennium Institute programme, entitled 'Enquiry Skills'. This was developed iteratively, and in its final version (from 2002 until 2004) entailed allocating 50 per cent of the module marks to the evidenced claims for the development of enquiry skills defined by each learner, against criteria specified by each learner. The marks were to have been awarded according to the learner's audited judgement. In my own case, this was so. I am less sure in respect of all my colleagues. Old habits die hard.
Cowan (2002)	In this paper I detail in general terms a method of assessment formulated in qualitative terms against descriptions of 'Sound Standard', which is roughly midway between a bare Pass (40 per cent) and Distinction (usually 70 per cent). Since publishing and publicising this way of assessing without grades, I have had more positive feedback from academics who were previously unknown to me than for any other idea I have encouraged others to take up. It was used in the Enquiry Skills module I have mentioned above.
Cowan and Westwood (2006)	An account of the outcomes claimed by experienced university teachers who had voluntarily been engaging in reflective journalling with their own continuing professional development in mind. They claimed and assessed that development qualitatively at the conclusion of this small pilot.

13 Evaluating creativity through consensual assessment

Tom Balchin

Introduction

The aspect of creativity that poses the greatest challenge to higher education teachers is how to assess and evaluate it. This chapter considers some of the problems associated with the assessment of creativity in higher education students' learning, and describes a method for assessing creative performance that has been proven to work in school education and which could be adapted to higher education.

In synthesising the results of Imaginative Curriculum discussions on assessing creativity, Jackson (2005d) commented that, while many teachers believe that it is possible to help students use their creative abilities to better effect, far fewer think it is possible to assess these capabilities reliably – and even fewer are prepared to try to do it. higher education teachers hold diverse views on whether creativity can be assessed. A minority of teachers believe that students' creativity is evaluated in specific components of a programme through explicit assessment criteria. A majority of teachers believe that insufficient attention is given to recognising students' creativity and that, at best, evaluation and recognition is haphazard and implicit – a bi-product of assessing higher-order thinking skills. A third group of teachers value creativity but don't know how to assess it. A fourth group believe that it is just not possible to assess creativity or, if it was, it would be so subjective as to be meaningless or require too much effort. The final group believe that the very act of assessing creativity will cause it to disappear! But we should not be put off by such a contradictory and disparaging list of beliefs, as there is a sense that most higher education teachers would assess creativity in students' higher education learning if they were given appropriate support (mainly time to change), guidance and cultural encouragement to do so.

What is also clear is that many teachers believe that some forms of summative assessment are major inhibitors of creativity. Higher education in the UK is now based on an outcomes model of learning in which teachers attempt to predict the outcomes from a process that they orchestrate. However, learning emerges from creative processes in unpredictable ways – and, unless the learning outcomes, assessment criteria and assessment methods accommodate this way of thinking, it is unlikely that a student's creativity can be encouraged, demonstrated and evaluated through the assessment process. A further problem with the common forms of summative assessment in higher education is that they generally do not permit failure (a distinct likelihood in high-risk situations where students are attempting to do radical things for the first time). Summative assessment generally encourages students to play safe, and to seek to achieve the outcomes intended by the teacher, rather than the outcomes the student may like to achieve given more flexibility.

Manifestations of creativity in students' learning

Creativity is manifested in the engagements of learners in creative processes and in the products that result from their creative endeavours. In higher education, products might include such things as: essays and many other forms of writing, including reports, diaries and reflective logs, poems, the products of electronic discussions; posters, the results of problem working, design and synthesis – like independent projects, laboratory or field notebooks (Jackson, 2005d). They include visual and graphical representations – designs, sketches, drawings, paintings, photographs, videos, computer animations; physical and virtual models and constructions; performance – theatre, role play, simulation, dance, song and live or recorded presentations, and many other things.

Similarly, there are many possibilities for processes and contexts within which creative acts might occur and products be created. Processes may be individually constructed and self-directed or be constructed collaboratively with other people or involve elements of both. They may be developed within a pedagogy – like enquiry or problem-based learning, role play, design process or independent or team project, and a particular context like fieldwork or work placement. They may constitute rehearsals directed to creative performance, as in music or dance. Processes and creative journeys can be evaluated through direct observation of students, through video or audio records or through diaries and reflective personal accounts supported by evidence that authenticates the account.

Assessing creativity is difficult

Much effort has been devoted (from the end of 1950 onwards) to the identification of the special characteristics that lead to creativity, and to the ways that creative people perform their creative acts. This effort has led to the development of numerous instruments that are used in the identification of creative talent. Kaltsounis and Honeywell (1980), for example, have published an exhaustive list of 'creativity tests' and Torrance and Goff (1990) have identified 255 such instruments.

It must be emphasised that different researchers have studied different aspects of creativity and that often these cross-purposes have been reflected in the measuring processes. There is not one *accepted* method for the measurement of creativity in individuals or groups working collectively and by using different techniques (tests of cognition, attitudes, interests, personality, biography, etc.) to assess creativity, researchers are actually studying different phenomena! Another facet of such tests (like the Torrance tests of creative thinking) is that, although they have been shown to have a high validity rating, their relevance to university settings, where teachers need to recognise and reward students' creativity in the specific contexts in which they are learning, is questionable.

Assessing students' creativity is not a simple matter, so there has to be a good set of reasons to persuade teachers to do so. Here are some reasons for assessing creativity:

- It helps to demystify and operationalise the idea.
- It helps to develop a language for communication among professionals about the nature of creative abilities, skills and potential in their disciplinary contexts.
- It helps teachers to engage students and helps students to evaluate and recognise their own strengths and talents, enabling them to understand themselves better. By focusing students' attention on learning through assessment, they are more likely to believe that their creative enterprise is valued and the intrinsic motivations that are associated with creativity are more likely to be harnessed.
- By involving students in the assessment process, they are developing the skills of self-evaluation and self-judgement that are crucial to further learning and the improvement of their own performance and creative potential (Cowan, this volume, Chapter 12).
- It can encourage students to take risks in order to learn. Tolerating the non-accomplishment of desired goals will encourage students to engage in riskier endeavours.
- It provides feedback to teachers to enable them to discover unrecognised or untapped potential/talent.
- It provides information to help teachers evaluate the effectiveness of their strategies for promoting students' learning, and enables them to construct a picture of students' understandings of their own creativity.

In the following section I describe the idea of consensual assessment and propose that the approach offers a useful and relevant route to evaluating students' creative efforts. Furthermore, the process of developing consensual assessment within peer groups of teachers and students can be a powerful source of personal or professional development.

Consensual assessment

This concerns the idea that a product or response is creative to the extent that appropriate observers consensually agree it is creative. Appropriate observers are those familiar with the domain in which the product was created or the response articulated. This is not a particularly profound proposition, but the technique can be shown to be more reliable than many other tests, probably because it involves the views of experts from the domain the creative work under examination resides in. Teachers, who can be considered as experts in a subject domain, can recognise how a contribution from a student may vary from established works, constructs or the thinking or performances of other students. The most important criterion for creativity assessment procedures is that any ratings produced should be found to be as *reliable* as possible (Balchin, 2005). The discursive process used is not a weakness in the approach; inter-judge reliabilities reported in this area of research have been found to be moderately high.

To discover the reliability of this technique in relation to others, I examined more than 100 examples of creativity measurements from many diverse fields, from Jackson and Messik's (1965) tests of creative potential, to the Amabile (1995) KEYS (assessing the climate for creativity) Inventory and found that a few of these approaches require small groups of people (i.e. supervisors, peers, teachers) to make judgements about products, ideas or other people after discussion.

Factors to be considered

The first factor to consider is who the judges should be and what the judges should be looking for. In schools, it is the teachers, perhaps with the help of field-based professionals, who are the judges. The experiment in using consensual assessment described below was predicated on the basis of teachers being the judges of students' creativity. But in higher education, the situation is more complex. Teachers or small teaching teams are responsible for students' learning and the outcomes of their learning experiences, but the students themselves are also responsible for engaging with learning processes in ways that optimise their learning and achievements. There is a level of learner autonomy and expectation of independence in higher education that is not expected in schools. In the absence of a universal discourse on creativity, the issue for higher education is how to help students to recognise and make claims for their own creativity (Cowan, this volume, Chapter 12). Helping students to evaluate their own creativity must go hand-in-hand with helping them to make claims. Teachers and students should form an appropriate community of learners within which understandings and meanings of creativity can be socially constructed and evaluated in the precise situations and contexts for learning. Consensual assessment in higher education might therefore involve both the teacher and the learners.

An important question for those evaluating creativity is whether evaluators are able to distinguish creativity from other constructs such as intelligence, achievement, competence, etc. A non-systematic review of some appropriate studies indicates otherwise. Holland (1959) reports an interesting study in which school teachers, heads and guidance counsellors rate students on 12 traits, including originality. The results are revealing; originality correlated 0.72 with speaking skills and 0.84 with writing skills. The other nine correlations that involved originality ranged from 0.50 to 0.65. This indicates that there is a general difficulty in discriminating creativity from other attributes. Alternatively, perhaps these attributes are integral to an individual's creativity and are bound up in any judgement.

People who participate in the process of consensual assessment also have to be wary of establishing opinion-sets from (or before) the outset, which influence *all* of their judgements. Hocevar and Bachelor (1989) suggest that this may be termed the 'halo effect'. It is a dangerous feature of small groups that could result in a failure to discriminate creativity. Interestingly, Surowiecki (2005) found the same phenomenon in research that indicates groups (supplied with knowledge about a situation or product with a similar few pieces of knowledge in common) tend to discuss only the information in common that they view as most important. Rossman and Gollob knew about this effect in 1975, and stated that groups make better judgements regarding creativity and intelligence when the judgements are based on diverse information.

Törrönen (2001) indicates that small groups can polarise views, leading to the more extreme views of group being put forward as solutions. Group polarisation is still a phenomenon that is not well understood. It has been found to be the result of people doing their best to figure out what the right answer is and, in doing so, inadvertently makes people more likely to advocate extreme positions: which sociologists have termed the 'risky shift'. This seems to argue for larger groups and communities of interest rather than small, introverted groups. But solid as the evidence for polarisation is, so too is the evidence demonstrating that groups can become, as it were, depolarised, and that small groups make better decisions and come up with better answers than most of their members, and, surprisingly often, the group outperforms even its best member (Sunstein, 2003).

So, despite the amount of literature on the measurement of creativity, it seems that engaging in the process of understanding and evaluating creative achievement and activities through processes of consensus building to reach agreement is likely to yield real benefits to the professional understandings of teachers and, if students are involved, to students' understanding of their own creative abilities.

An example of consensual assessment

A research study to design creativity assessment tools for the field of design and technology education (hereafter d&t) was undertaken in 2004 with 14 London secondary school Heads of Department. The aim was to gather d&t expert teachers in their very practical field to see if they could use a creativity feedback tool (product sheet) using consensual assessment. The detailed results of the research can be found in Balchin (2005); what is important here are the lessons and general principles that were derived from the exercise.

The building of a *creativity feedback package* (CFP) was initiated by finding out the extent to which existing models of creative behaviour interact in the appropriate diagnoses of creative performance. It was found that it was possible to transfer a contextual organiser for creativity known as the '4 Ps' – people, process, product, and press (climate) – directly to the field of d&t. Rhodes (1961) first coined this phrase, but I have found Murdock and Puccio's (1993) thesis concerning its meaning to be more relevant to creativity assessment. Their finding was that *it is not preferable or even possible to incorporate all four facets during assessments*. In other words, it is not essential to know everything about the creation and situation; but, by gathering data about a combination of necessary elements (normally three out of the four Ps), a reasonably efficient evaluation or prediction of creative activity can be produced.

The *creative product* feedback sheet (one of three feedback sheets within the CFP) was designed as a score card to guide the teacher in judging and marking a product for creativity. The sheet has nine criteria for products to be scored against. However, numbers were not critical to this exercise, because the judge will have his/her unique scale of judgement and frames of reference to the product. The scores therefore have no real meaning as numbers, they only help the scorer get to grips with the criteria and force judgements (Balchin, 2005).

Four criteria describe the creative *concept*, or idea, and three criteria describe the *quality of build*, which evaluate how well the creative thoughts have been shown in the product. The emphasis in this evaluation sheet was that creativity is seen in *both* the concept *and* the standard of build that the product showed. But it is the *concept* stage where the unique ideas are brought forth, and the product sheet is the manifestation of those creative ideas. The latter cannot occur without the former; I propose that the *quality of build* is a 'vehicle' for the creative thought. The scorer therefore is given a 12-point Likert scale to use, intended to mirror the A, B, C and D of traditional mark schemes, with the corresponding pluses and minuses.

These criteria are: *uniqueness, associations of ideas, risk-taking, potential, operability, well-craftedness* and *attractiveness*. Concise definitions were attached to these criteria, which were themselves subsumed from an exhaustive list of qualities of creative products. The criteria were trialled in schools for nine months in order to see if they were able to describe creativity simply and without the danger of overlapping of criteria, yet retaining the complexity of the phenomenon.

The pilot study involved 14 heads of department (one panel of five, and three panels of three) as expert judges. The judges were each asked to use the criteria on the CFP product page to produce an *individual*, then a *consensual*, score of ten different products. The judges were all given the individual product sheet, asked to choose any of the ten products they liked, and given 30 minutes to assess them according to the criteria on the product sheet. The one rule was that if more than one judge was working on the same product, no collaboration would be allowed. It is important to bear in mind that no accompanying portfolio/ coursework was present. The judgements were made from the products alone, to see if agreement over the criteria could occur even when teachers did not know anything about the task or making process.

After this individual scoring time, the judges were asked to split into three groups and review three out of the ten products. They were split into three groups and given 40 minutes to rotate around the products, debating and reaching consensus before scoring each criteria (1–12). Serious debate was seen to take place inter-group. However it was observed that the judges were able to agree about criteria, without having to compromise their initial thoughts too much. In this way, individual scores were produced for ten products and consensual scores from three groups were produced for three products.

The results are reproduced below (using those produced by evaluating one of the products as an example) for the seven criteria used, with the degree of spread between the scores given in each criteria marked with circles. The horizontal line that many are on indicates the lateral degree of spread of each of the scores between '1' (furthest left) and '12' (furthest right). The spread of scores are indicated in the column of numbers to the right. The significance of the thin vertical line will become clear when this spread of scores are compared to those that resulted when products were scored consensually.

The chart shows the result (spread of scores) from the individual consensual assessing. Only one of the seven criteria, *association of ideas*, fell outside a spread of four marks. This was a difficult definition to present to teachers, but interestingly, two out of three scored it in exactly the same way. The other was working from her own particular *frame of reference*, which is a clue to the value of consensual assessing, which has the power to take all frames of reference into account.

Taken as a whole, the judges (scoring individually) showed a high degree of consensus over each score. This indicated that (most of) the criteria and definitions worked, and that there was enough 'clear space' between each definition for each to make sense. It also showed that the judges were pretty good at recognising the inherent creativity of a product without any discussion, simply by reference to other similar products that they are aware of. Moreover, individuals can arrive at similar conclusions without viewing any of the designing and making of the product.

Did consensual scoring tend to diminish personal bias or dislike, to give a fairer impression of creativity occurring? This was difficult to prove. However, when scoring consensually, it can be seen that the mean spread of scores per criteria diminished significantly when the judges were allowed to sharpen and hone their professional judgements about the product through debate aimed at reaching agreement.

The thin vertical lines on both Figures 13.1 and 13.2 show a *mid-line* between the scores. It brings to the attention the way that the consensual scoring groups tended to score the product more positively in terms of creativity; a feature seen on each consensual assessment when compared to individuals assessing the same product.

Comparing scores for individual and consensual assessment

The first four criteria are views about the product's *concept*. All four were scored very close to each other. For example, when it came to scoring *association of ideas*, each consensual group of four to six judges scored it *exactly the same* (without conferring between groups, as per instructions for the whole exercise). This was a significant and positive finding, because the product was unfinished. Nevertheless, the judges were able to see through the unfinished state and glimpse the creative thoughts that caused the construction to be the way it was.

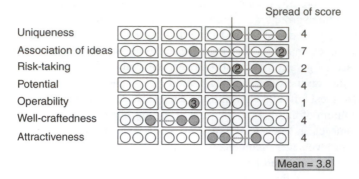

Figure 13.1 Spread of scores from individual scorers of one of the products.

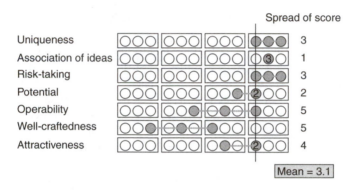

Figure 13.2 Spread of scores from consensual scorers of the product.

The unanimous agreement about this particular criteria (produced by three groups of judges, each scoring consensually) held fast with the other two products under group assessment. The *association of ideas* is a most important criteria at the heart of creativity, and it was important that each group of consensual assessors were able (with a one-line definition) to understand the notion well.

The last three criteria concerned the product's *quality of make*. In general, if the condition of the item is poor, creativity is harder to see and score. This is why *operability*, *well-craftedness* and *attractiveness* are important markers in creativity judgements, because they relate to the feeling of rightness of a product and the sense that ideas have been pulled together into a coherent whole. It can be seen that the three individual judges, and the three consensual judging groups especially, dispersed their scores for the product's *quality of make* around the scoring box, from 3–10. This was in contrast to the dispersal of scores for the product's *concept*, where the scores ranged from 8–12 (except for one score given to *association of ideas* by one group). When the judges were asked about this disparity, the answer was that the product was difficult to judge in terms of operability because there were different opinions over the intentions of the students who made it. This was an unforeseen factor, but it did highlight some of the problems of group assessing without knowing what the students' tasks were all about.

The judges were also given aspects of creativity to think about in relation to the product in front of them. Free-response boxes were provided with *prompts* to help them to reach their individual scores.

- What kind of unity can you see in it?
- What sense of rightness do you get from this product?
- To what extent does it give an understated or economical solution?
- Is it a coherent whole?
- What kind of aesthetic sense of organisation can you see in it?
- How far does it go to resolving a discord?

The result – a compilation of judges' views – was found to be useful because it demonstrated how different judges can make parallel judgements as they scored products in terms of creativity. The judges seemed to be able to converge on scores to give to the concepts, even though their ideas about the standard of build that should be achieved for creativity adequately to be shown differed. This was an indicator that creativity can be *reliably* recognised in a product, even if it was badly made and 'didn't work'.

This was a small sample of judges and products, but it illustrates a process for developing and refining judgements about creativity that seems to work. The judges agreed that the creativity resides in the concepts or idea. They could see that a product which may score badly in terms of *well-craftedness, operability* and *attractiveness*, many still score very highly in terms of *uniqueness, association of ideas, risk-taking* and especially, *potential*. They believed that it could encourage more creative thought during designing stages, and begin to give some sort of feedback/recognition to creative 'failure'.

Adapting this approach to higher education

One of the benefits of consensual assessment is that it engages teachers in purposeful professional discussion: in this case, discussion about creativity in relation to the products that their students produce within the learning processes and activities that they create. Through such conversations, teachers develop new and deeper understandings about the nature of creativity in the particular contexts in which it is being developed and displayed. Ultimately it is a means of developing better understanding of creativity within the disciplinary field.

The criteria to work around are the key to this process as they provide a starting point for the development of mutual understandings about creativity. They might be developed through the discursive process involving only teachers, or they might be part of a process of discussion and negotiation involving teachers and students.

The kind of consensual assessment sheet outlined above can be adapted not only to situations that require products to be produced by students, but also to situations where outcomes other than products are sought. For instance, in the solution of problems in quantum physics or a performance in dance, appropriate criteria may substitute for the *quality of build* criteria. The prompters for discussion are easily adaptable to productions in all disciplinary fields. The sheet itself is simple enough to be completed by a group of judges in approximately ten minutes.

In the author's view, *summative assessment* of creativity may not be necessary (or practical) in many higher education learning contexts. However, engaging students in assessing their own creativity in ways that lead to informed recognition of their creative effort, in order to produce useful *formative* feedback for the learner and the teacher, should be an essential feature of an assessment system to promote students' creativity and the development of self-awareness of their own creativity. This view mirrors that developed independently by John Cowan in Chapter 12 of this book. The process of students getting together to discuss their productions or creative processes, and co-creating criteria within a framework of prompts to guide conversation, would not only allow them to reflect on their own creative effort, but would enable them to construct new understandings of what creativity means in the particular contexts in which it was utilised. It would also enable them to represent their own creativity and, ultimately, to harness their own creativity to a higher degree. Consensual assessment involving teachers and students could be integrated into the sort of assessment process described by John Cowan.

14 Developing higher education teachers to teach creatively

James Wisdom

Introduction

A number of chapters in this book have emphasised the need for cultural change in higher education to one that is more accepting of the value of creativity. In this chapter I argue that an important step in accomplishing such cultural change is to help higher education teachers understand and value their own creativity and to recognise this as an integral part of their professionalism.

The need for creativity has never been greater as the role of a higher education teacher becomes more complex in its demands and challenges, and notions of professionalism in higher education become far more extensive. I note the progress that has been made in some areas, in particular in the preparation of new staff, but we still face two major challenges. We must further develop the concepts and practice of professionalism to enable all those who support students' learning to engage competently and with enthusiasm to improve the quality of the student experience. And we must become so skilled in this work that our programmes and our teaching become suffused with the values of creativity. The chapter ends with some reflections on the role of educational developers in leading and supporting this profound change to Higher Education cultures and work practices.

The conflicting roles of a modern academic

If one of the central functions of higher education is to challenge widely held assumptions, then perhaps we should especially celebrate its success in subverting our expectations of what it means to be a university teacher. As in so many other professions, the model of induction into a community through apprenticeship and imitative practice has been stretched beyond breaking point by internal growth and change, and by external demands.

One of the most significant areas of change has been in the preparation for the teaching element of a lecturer's role. Many institutions took a significant step from 1993 onwards when they offered programmes accredited by the Staff and Educational Development Association (SEDA), later by the Institute of Learning and Teaching in HE (1999–2004) and now by the Higher Education Academy and SEDA (Beaty, 2005).

The new lecturer today faces a daunting series of challenges. She or he may accept a post in a Department that is living in a culture of fierce competitiveness. With the PhD as the de facto entrance qualification and the cultural dominance of the Research Assessment Exercises (RAE), it is hardly surprising that new lecturers are in no doubt their reputations will be secured more by research than by any other aspect of their professional lives.

At the same time they may be expected to teach subjects new to them, to manage the paperwork of the quality-assurance elements of their teaching, to design courses using explicit learning outcomes, to develop resources, to teach diverse student groups and confidently to handle assessment practices. Meanwhile they will be inducted into their Department, be expected to maintain their research profile, and perhaps be moving or establishing a new home. They may also be taking a course that prepares them for their teaching role.

For many of these staff, their first real exercise of professional creativity is in balancing these conflicting demands. Course leaders and external examiners of the accredited courses in Teaching and Learning are sometimes in the privileged position of reading in portfolios the evidence which shows how stressful the initial steps into a new career can be, and how creative these colleagues have to be to survive and prosper in their new environment. From the perspective of this chapter, however, these are exactly the sort of conditions that require people to utilise all their resources and creativity in order to cope with and master the situation.

Development of higher education teachers

Becoming a professional higher education teacher

The movement to develop a professionalism of higher education teaching has grown in parallel to, and is interlinked with, the rapid changes to the overall provision of higher education, both in the UK and overseas. These changes have exposed some of the weaknesses of previous models of teacher preparation that are still deeply rooted in contemporary educational culture. Notions of apprenticeship and induction into a disciplinary culture are powerful ideas, reinforced by the subject-based structure of institutions and the reliance on the PhD.

The foundations of the development of professional higher education teaching can be seen in the model of accreditation devised and applied by SEDA. An account of the themes behind current practice is given by Sharpe (2004). From the interplay between reflective practice and the experiential learning cycle, and set in the context of declared values, a number of approaches have emerged, of which a key is the recognition of the experience and autonomy of the individual. The pedagogy of constructivism has also become very influential. At the same time, the development of professional knowledge and competence is seen to emerge within a social and communal context and by such processes as making tacit knowledge explicit and developing knowledge and understanding through use.

Although the foundations may exist, as Sharpe (2004) says, 'there is not yet an accepted model for the professional development of teachers in higher education', and she locates this situation within the dynamic processes of development. Two aspects of these processes are particularly relevant to the issue of preparing teachers to teach creatively. The first is the weakening of the notions of novice and expert, and therefore of initial training leading to continuing professional development. The other is the significance of situated learning, not just for its influence on the individual, but on the importance of building communities of practice that may run in parallel or counter to the existing structures of higher education. One implication is that it may be more important to be able to engage with any colleague who is seeking to develop their approaches to creativity, rather than trying to achieve long-term change simply by capturing the attention of each cohort of inductees. Another is that colleagues may be developing their professional understandings of creativity within many domains of knowledge in use, and that educational developers must be alive to the opportunities that this might present and help their disciplinary teaching colleagues connect to relevant conversations within their communities (see, for example, the Working Papers based on discussions of what creativity means in different disciplines (Jackson 2005a, 2005b, 2005c; Jackson and Burgess, 2005).

Support for professional development

In recent years, a number of significant elements have been put in place in the UK to support the academic who wishes to develop as a dual professional – committed both to their discipline community as a researcher and to their students as a professional teacher. There is now an extensive literature reporting on a wide range of educational practice. Investment has been made at national and institutional level in educational reform projects to meet immediate and longer-term needs. The Teaching Quality Enhancement Fund (Higher Education Funding Council England – Hefce) has supported projects in almost every discipline area through the Fund for the Development of Teaching and Learning (FDTL). Funding for local strategic pedagogic priorities has also been guided by institutional Learning and Teaching Strategies that all English and Welsh institutions are required to produce.

The Higher Education Academy Subject Centre networks for pedagogic practice through the disciplines are now well established. There is a growing community of higher educational researchers. Specialised communities have formed around pedagogic themes (for example, the Centre for Recording Achievement with its focus on personal development planning and the Imaginative Curriculum network with its focus on pedagogies for creativity). Promotion criteria more frequently include explicit commitment to teaching, and slowly real promotion routes are emerging. Many institutions have made learning and teaching appointments such as Fellows, Coordinators, Readers and Professors. Programmes for the continuing professional development of the many categories of staff who support student learning have been accredited, and support networks are in place to sustain and improve their quality.

It is fortunate indeed that these elements are now in place, because the practice of teaching has become more complex and challenging. Whatever the speed, the direction of travel is towards mass higher education – both in the raising of the school-leaving age and in increasing opportunities for life-long learning for all our citizens. Whoever pays and whenever they might pay, there is no doubt about the long-term direction of expenditure per head. Easy certainties are hard to find. Where long-established practice embodied long-held values, efforts merely to preserve the former no longer guarantee the protection of the latter.

New staff need to be familiar with the language and concepts of their institution's quality regime, which may embody a number of significant developments in underlying pedagogic practice. Many lecturers now use intended learning outcomes to plan programmes of study, and may need to be able to deploy a wide range of assessment processes aligned to those outcomes. They have to be able to design, deliver and assess the units within those programmes, and to evaluate them for further improvement. They have to develop their understanding of standards in relation to national, institutional and disciplinary expectations, and to be able to handle workload and credit issues equitably.

Their institution may well have invested heavily in modern equipment and a virtual learning environment, and have expectations about their impact on course delivery and workloads. Student groups might be large and complex in terms of their educational backgrounds, capacities to learn, motivations and life goals, and there may be institutional priorities in both widening participation and retention. In many institutions there is a growing expectation that teachers will engage in the scholarship of teaching and learning.

Educational developers are often charged to ensure that new lecturers can operate effectively in their institutions. While programmes for lecturer development may have started as induction sessions of 'emergency' teaching advice, full of hints and tips such as how to stimulate good discussion in seminars, they have now grown into full preparation for participants who will be both members of their disciplinary community and the profession of higher education teacher. For many new staff, a major exercise in creativity is learning how best to deploy their new professional skills for the simple enjoyment of knowing they are teaching well and inspiring and helping their students to learn.

Creativity, teaching and student learning

If the practice of teaching has not become simpler or easier, part of the challenge is to create working understandings of what it actually means to teach. Both new and established staff may be described as lecturers, yet they find many staff who are familiar with critiques of the lecture as a process; they may be employed as teachers, yet their main engagement might be around the facilitation of learning; they may join a Department to teach a subject, yet have to concentrate on general skills and the development of attributes and qualities; they may have invested years in developing an academic specialisation, yet learn from feedback and evaluation that the quality of the students' learning experience is powerfully determined by many other colleagues, perhaps who are administrative or support staff with little knowledge of the discipline.

There are a number of working papers supporting the Imaginative Curriculum project in which teachers describe their attitudes and practices to creativity. Three papers edited by Jackson (2005a, 2005b, 2005c) from disciplinary-centred discussions in History, Engineering and Earth and Environmental Sciences can be read beside Jackson's (2004b) *How Can Creativity Be Taught? Personal Accounts of Teaching to Promote Students' Creativity*, along with Martin Oliver's (2002) *Creativity and the Curriculum Design Process: a Case Study*. Within these accounts, there are four dimensions of becoming and being a teacher – the teacher as performer, as facilitator of learning, as a navigator through an institution's regulations and culture, and as a professional practitioner. Here we most need to concern ourselves with the first two dimensions.

> We did not attempt to 'teach' creativity but rather set in place conditions to help it happen.
>
> (Lisa Pybus, Nottingham Trent University,
> in *Personal Accounts*)

> I had to withhold my temptation to explain everything, so that creative opportunities existed for the students.
>
> (Adrian Page, London Metropolitan University,
> in *Personal Accounts*)

The performer–facilitator tension has run through conceptions of university teaching in recent years, as the practice of research and evaluation has grown to both challenge the existing orthodoxies and to provide a foundation for future higher education development. It is clear from the accounts of creative practice given in the three disciplinary working papers that they are primarily based on activity in which the students are working and learning for themselves. The teacher has shaped the course, planned the outcomes, set up learning activities and designed the assessment or validated the students' assessment. The teacher's role in these interactions is far from what Prosser and Trigwell (1999) have described as the Information Transmission/Teacher Focussed position derived from their Approaches to Teaching Inventory.

The implication of many of these accounts is that an active learning approach is at least a pre-condition for fostering creativity and, in many cases, is the element of creativity that lifts the students' experiences. The connection therefore between a teacher's own creativity and students' creativity lies in the creation of challenging learning environments that promote active and engaged learning, and encourage students to utilise their creativity along with their other abilities. While there is now an extensive literature documenting the practical application of such approaches in higher education, there are also some important analytical approaches that help us to understand the contexts and pre-conditions which are used by the teacher as designer and facilitator. The Course Experience Questionnaire (Wilson *et al.*, 1997; Ramsden, 2003) has been able to identify the significant interactions that affect the quality of the students' experience. The various Approaches to Study Inventories (see note 2) have illuminated the relationship between the teacher's actions in planning and delivering programmes and the students' approaches to their own learning. Biggs' (2003) taxonomy of the Structure of Observed Learning Outcomes has shown – perhaps more usefully than Bloom's (1956) Taxonomy of Educational Objectives – how the teacher creates the conditions for challenge and growth, which have combined with his emphasis on constructivism to illuminate more clearly what students actually do in their learning. Finally, Gibbs' (1992) work on the factors that improve the quality of students' learning has confirmed the opportunities for creativity which follow from changing the focus of teaching from a knowledge-driven personal performance to an explicit care for the student's growth of understanding.

Creativity within the professional development of teachers

Conditions for fostering creativity through teaching

There is some consensus among professional teachers and teacher educators that the setting of appropriate learning outcomes for modules and programmes is one of the most influential factors in creating conditions for fostering creativity. Teacher preparation programmes already place very great stress on the design of learning outcomes, and their adoption in quality assurance processes have ensured there is at least a common language for incorporation and integration of creativity.

It is important that preparing lecturers to teach creatively is not seen as an obligatory but marginal activity. Previous experiences with whole-institution initiatives that focused on learning outcomes (such as education for enterprise, or for capability) have taught developers a great deal about how best to achieve deep-seated change. Much has been done by discussion, education, persuasion and targeted funding. From practice and from research, educational development is familiar with the focus on constructive alignment (Biggs, 2002, 2003), with its emphasis on the relationship between the intended outcomes and the role of assessment. It follows that, for creativity to be widely accepted as a theme within the preparation and development of lecturers, a focus on 'assessment for creativity' will be essential (Cowan, this volume, Chapter 12). Perhaps the most sensitive aspect of any work to encourage creativity will be the balance between education and assessment for learning, rather than assessment for judging performance.

Seeing creativity as part of a set of abilities

Sternberg and Lubart (1996) offer a model of creativity for students' development, but it applies equally to the professional teaching context. The model suggests that a creative person uses three sets of abilities together (the synthetic, the analytic and the practical) and that each can be developed. Sternberg and Williams (1996) have devised a guide for teachers who wish to develop these abilities within their students and many of these abilities apply equally to the professional role of the teacher.

Sternberg and Williams focus on the teacher's role in developing students' self-efficacy, and particularly value the development of autonomy through reflective practice. They explore in detail the value of questioning within the educational process, and how best to create an environment that is open to new ideas, particularly in having the time to think. While they recognise the importance of an assessment and reward process that values creativity, they are insistent on the need to allow for risk and mistakes. Finally, while they are excited by the notion that true creativity is likely always to challenge the accepted norms, they recognise the value and skill of working creatively within any given environment.

There are some interesting parallels here with the experience of many teacher-preparation programmes, especially the emphasis on the value of reflection and the importance of self-assessment in professional learning. So many of these courses use the portfolio both as a vehicle for reflection on practice and as a method of formative self-assessment and, eventually, summative assessment that we may be witnessing a general growth in familiarity with an educational process that, up to now, has been specific to only a few disciplines. If we are looking for learning methods that can support creativity, then the portfolio's ability to embrace risk, reflection and assessment is very valuable.

Helping teachers understand their own creativity

One starting point in a professional development process is for the practitioner to examine their own understandings and experience of the area for development. The construction of personal meanings of creativity in the environment in which it is applied (in our case, notions of what being a creative teacher means) is central to such development.

Arising from the Imaginative Curriculum project, Jackson and Sinclair (2005) are developing and evaluating a 'generic tool' to help Higher Education teachers think about creativity in their own teaching and learning contexts (now being called a puzzler to help teachers solve their own creativity puzzles). The first version posed 15 major questions and three inventories to the reader, with examples and choices drawn from personal accounts to focus the responses. After considering what might be the characteristics of creativity within their discipline or programme, readers are then encouraged to explore their teaching practice in detail by testing it against some of their beliefs and the characteristics of creative teaching that have emerged during the project.

On courses for new staff, it is important for the educational developers to know what the participants regard as their own models of good teaching. They may have been influenced by gifted and creative teachers. They may have enjoyed studying and being taught in certain ways. They may have devised ways of learning in their particular discipline. They will have been successful in their work – to the extent that they themselves are now preparing to teach their subjects. These familiar, appropriate practices may well be dominant in their new Departments.

For many lecturers the aims of higher education are changing, as are the types of students and the resources and staffing for teaching. In order to be able to respond, lecturers need a wide repertoire of forms of course design, teaching methods and assessment activities. One of the functions of the new staff courses is to introduce participants to this wider range of ways of teaching, and in some Departments they are able immediately to deploy them in their normal work.

Difficulties can arise, however, in Departments where there is only a narrow range of teaching and assessment practices. The experience of working in Departments that are unable to respond to new challenges (such as taking more students, employing fewer staff or wishing to develop a more creative curriculum) is often that the staff within them continue to reproduce traditional approaches but at a more intensive level, damaging what is left of the work/life balance.

It can be hard to deploy teaching approaches that require cooperation or regulatory shifts when one is new to a well-established Department, especially if it has recorded high achievements in external measurement of teaching and research quality. Educational developers themselves must have a range of approaches that they can tailor to their colleagues' requirements. For some participants, their most productive work might well be to challenge established practice or to widen its range. At the same time others might use generic tools (such as the Sinclair and Jackson puzzler) to reflect on their current Departmental practice and deepen their understanding of the potential for creativity within the existing frameworks.

The role of educational developers in improving the environment to support creative teachers

Educational developers occupy a significant place in HE institutions (Land, 2003). They are no longer (if they ever were) simply dispensing hints and tips to harassed colleagues. When colleagues identify the range of obstacles to implementing creativity, the educational developer may be in a significant position to influence the process of change. From the Course Leader discussions and from those at Imaginative Curriculum conferences, there are four significant obstacles which have a relationship to institutional development. We need to consider these conditions in detail.

- Quality-assurance mechanisms that burden and do not support, and that do little to foster critical debate about pedagogic practice.
- Having to work with the restrictive requirements of professional bodies.
- Relying on the enthusiasm and energy of a few individuals rather than embedding creativity within the Departmental culture.
- Excessive focus on summative assessment and poor experiences of feedback to promote learning.

Quality assurance

The perception that quality-assurance mechanisms, particularly over assessment reform, are burdensome and therefore a potential inhibitor of teachers' creativity, is widespread. Even where colleagues know that change is possible, they are often defeated by their perception of how long it will take. Sometimes these mechanisms are the real obstacles they are thought to be, but often the perception is more powerful than the reality, as most academic regulatory frameworks are similar in their impact on course design, whatever institution has developed them. In the last 20 years, developments in such mechanisms have required consider-able documentation. Each HEI has now created an Academic Quality Assurance Handbook, the guidance for staff involved in course design and in leading course delivery. The development of modularised degree programmes has required a considerable amount of work to establish equivalence within institutional and national frameworks. Handbooks usually have full accounts of requirements, specifications, academic levels, workloads and prerequisites. As they are now becoming familiar processes, they are being used in some institutions with flexi-bility and confidence – it is like the significant step in learning an instrument, where the novice no longer needs to look at their hands but can concentrate more on the interpretation of the music.

The educational developer often has a pivotal role in the institutional conver-sation between staff when they are involved in academic regulation. It is a major staff development task to work with colleagues to understand and use the exter-nal quality and internal academic frameworks well. Their technical–rational purpose has been more to eliminate weakness than to stimulate creativity, and it sometimes requires all the skills and experience of an educational developer to show how they can be used at least to support creativity in student learning, if not actively to promote it.

Professional bodies

A similar discussion revolves around the relationship between academic depart-ments and accrediting professional bodies, some of which are perceived to be inhibiting reform (especially assessment reform) and creativity. There is some-times the same gulf between the actual contents of the documents, the declared values and the public pronouncement of the professional body on the one hand, and the perception of these features within a teaching department on the other.

In many professional bodies, there is a tension between protection of stand-ards and the encouragement of innovation. For example, the Bar Vocational Council's Course Specification Requirements and Guidance[1] declares:

> It considered that the freedom permitted to institutions by validation would enhance commitment among course teams and encourage greater creativity and diversity between courses

The Engineering Council UK's Standard for Professional Engineering Compe-tence[2] describes Chartered Engineers as:

> characterized by their ability to develop appropriate solutions to engineering problems, using new or existing technologies, through innovation, creativity and change.

Both the quality assurance and the professional body frameworks were partly created in the hope that they would provide the arena for debate and challenge, in the creation of the distinctive character of a Department and its courses. That distinctiveness must be established on the strongest possible grounds – valid and reliable pedagogy, sophisticated and effective learning practice, a strong evaluative and developmental tradition, ingenious course design aligning learning outcomes, teaching and learning activities and assessment, and effective team work, deploying the strengths of the many professionals who create the full student experience. Building those grounds within Departments is partly an educational development task. Where this is done, staff can then make a well-founded, robust and distinctive contribution to the development of their discipline.

Departmental culture

When it comes to issues such as changing the assessment regime or ensuring that skills development is handled on a programme-wide basis, then the limitations of the individual enthusiast are exposed. Improvements to student learning which focus on creativity will best be achieved by the group of staff who are designing, delivering, managing and servicing that programme working together. The clearest example of this is in the design of learning outcomes, which has to be done – at least in the first instance – as a communal activity in defining the characteristics of the programme. A significant part of the work of the educational developer is in supporting the course team both in the definition work at programme and module level, and also in the practical work of designing learning activities and assessment practices that ensure the spirit of the programme is shared by the students.

Assessment and feedback

The amount and character of much current summative assessment, and the weaknesses in much formative assessment practice, are two major educational issues that currently affect students' capacity to develop their creativity. In their survey of research into the relationship between assessment and the quality of student learning, Gibbs and Simpson (2004–5) confirmed the dominant part assessment plays in student learning, the importance of the coursework assignment in improving the quality of student learning, and both the significance of formative feedback and the decline in the quality of practice around it. Gibbs and Simpson note also the scale of the obstacles that educational developers and course teams might encounter when contemplating change to assessment practice:

> The most reliable, rigorous and cheat-proof assessment systems are often accompanied by dull and lifeless learning that has short lasting outcomes – indeed they often directly lead to such learning.

Aspects of assessment have figured prominently in the discussions with teachers and developers in the Imaginative Curriculum project, both because of the importance of the constructive alignment approach to the implementation of learning outcomes, and because of the effect rigid assessment practice has on both the capacity and the enthusiasm for change amongst teachers.

Educational developers can work to disseminate projects such as the FDTL *Formative Assessment in Science Teaching*,[3] in which the Gibbs and Simpson study can be found. Also, Institutional Learning, Teaching and Assessment Strategies have become one of the key ways in which educational developers can focus the institution on strategy, policy, resources and Departmental practice, rather than just on changing the activity of individual lecturers. For an example of this, see Eastwood (2004) on *Implementing an Institutional Assessment Strategy*. The use of such strategies will give lecturers the opportunities to design creativity into their modules and programmes with the expectation of it lasting beyond their short-term initiative.

The creativity challenge to educational development

Participants at the Imaginative Curriculum 2004 Conference were invited to consider how they might establish conditions that foster students' creativity. The key condition – namely the setting of appropriate learning outcomes – has been discussed earlier. The others were thought to be:

- Having sufficient time and space in the curriculum to allow students to develop their creativity.
- Having sufficiently varied and diverse working situations to enable all students to be creative.
- Allowing students the freedom to work in new and interesting ways.
- Challenging students with real, demanding and exciting work.
- Designing assessment that allows for outcomes which are not narrowly predetermined.
- Fostering a departmental climate that encourages reflection and personal development for both staff and students.
- Continuing academic debate within the discipline, and dialogue with the various stakeholders, about the nature of the subject and the role of creativity within it.

Although these conditions were generated for guidance to lecturers designing courses, many of them are also likely to be relevant to an institutional setting that encourages and promotes teachers' creativity. These principled statements are also relevant to educational developers working with colleagues on preparatory courses for staff who are new to teaching and across their institutions more widely, and in the final section of this chapter I will try to show how they represent challenges to the educational development community.

Time and space

We know that engaging with colleagues is likely to require time and space, if only because education is a personal, values-driven activity, and for pedagogic development and change to be worthwhile it has to be developed and valued by individuals and teams. The very quality of independence of mind which we espouse for our students makes the strategy of instruction-led educational change curiously ineffective. The challenge is to secure and protect good time and space so that the changes and developments can be deeply rooted. This applies in all areas – acting as an expert who simply fixes a problem, be it personal or institutional, may reduce others' capacity to learn and grow. One implication for educational developers is that teacher preparation through traditional PG Certificate course delivery may be insufficiently flexible to match up to the real needs of the participants, and it does little to mirror the subsequent demands that these new staff will be making on their own students. Indeed this may be the very first opportunity for such colleagues to experience the sorts of curriculum strategies that are now being promoted vigorously in HE, not least within this book.

Variety, diversity, challenge and assessment

If we consider it is important to recognise that students develop their creativity in a myriad of ways, then our course planning should create educational situations that are as varied and diverse as possible. If creativity is supported by challenging students with real, demanding and exciting work, and if students need to have the freedom to work in new and interesting ways, then the same models should apply to the interactions between educational developers and the staff of their institution.

Post Graduate Certificate courses appear to have gone some way to meeting these models in that many of them are created around the practice of work-based learning, and assessment outcomes are not narrowly predetermined. Participants are often able to tailor the generic content and course outcomes to their Departmental requirements, using experienced departmental mentors to help them, especially in the design of learning contracts that formalise this process. Similarly, the use of a portfolio as a device to report diverse experience, to reflect upon it in the context of the course outcomes and values, and to enable claims for awards to be made, allows the freedom to work in new and interesting ways.

Despite such developments, there is much work still to be done in relation to the more central task of developing skills and professionalism amongst *all* staff who teach and support student learning in HE. It must be a basic entitlement that all higher education staff can look forward to a working lifetime of active and enjoyable professional engagement and development. Being able to be creative is an important part of professional fulfilment and if we create situations that inhibit an individual's creativity we reduce the level of satisfaction they can get from their work (see the work of Csikszentmihalyi, 1997, on what makes people happy).

There are now three significant questions. The first is how to ensure that a modest early course for new lecturers can serve as the foundation for a lifetime's development as a teacher, in contrast to preparation for discipline research, normally over several years of supervised research-intensive study. The second is how to develop for established lecturers the same quality of support for their different priorities and personal career paths. For a third and crucially important group of staff – namely new and established staff who support the students' learning experience but who are not employed as lecturers – the question now must be how to engage in useful, appropriate and enjoyable professional development that connects the current emphasis on students' learning experiences to their existing professional loyalties. Focusing on creativity is more likely to guarantee positive answers to these three questions than much of the current rhetoric that treats investment in the 'human resource' as an element for business success.

One response to these questions may be through the Professional Development Framework developed by the SEDA[4] for the development and accreditation of a number of awards covering many of the areas which both lecturing and support staff currently need (SEDA-PDF). What is interesting about the model is its congruence with many of the conditions that foster creativity, as it has a set of values at its core, a set of generic development outcomes for all awards, and a set of specific development outcomes for each award. It is a good example of the educational development community modelling creativity within their practice.

Reflection, dialogue and debate

The final two conditions that foster creativity are the creation of an institutional climate which encourages and values critical reflection and personal development for both staff and students, and continuing academic debate and dialogue between the various stakeholders about the nature of professional teaching in higher education, and the role of creativity within it. As this chapter shows, there is now a solid body of experience in reflection and personal development with new staff certificate courses. There is a growing body of similar experience amongst the many thousands of established staff who applied to be registered as members of the ILTHE and through the development of initiatives such as SEDA's Professional Development Framework. And, as noted earlier, there are opportunities for QA processes to be used to foster critical debate about teaching and learning. Furthermore, the Progress File initiative is now encouraging students to be more reflective on their experiences too. We must hope that this chapter, and the book of which it is part, contributes to the dialogue about the nature of professional teaching within HE and the role of creativity within it.

Notes

1 Bar Vocational Council's Course Specification Requirements and Guidance. Online. Available at: www.legaleducation.org.uk/downloads/bvcspec04.doc.
2 Engineering Council UK's Standard for Professional Engineering Competence describes Chartered Engineers. Online, available at: www.ukspec.org.uk/files/ CE_IE.pdf.
3 Formative Assessment in Science Teaching. Online, available at: www.open.ac. uk/science/fdtl.
4 The Staff and Educational Development Association (SEDA) is at: www.seda.ac.uk.

15 Making sense of creativity in higher education

Norman Jackson

Conversations about creativity in higher education

> Few resources have been invested in the study of creativity relative to its importance both to the fields of psychology and to the world.
>
> (Sternberg and Lubart, 1999: 12)

Driven by the moral purpose of making a difference to students' lives by enriching their experiences and helping them develop their creative talents, as well as their intellectual abilities, the mission of the Imaginative Curriculum project is to promote conversations about creativity and encourage teachers, institutional and disciplinary communities and leaders, to think more deeply about its place in higher education. In the opening chapter I suggested that the 'problem' of creativity in higher education is best represented as an opportunity for improving a situation – the challenge of changing the prevailing culture so that greater value is placed on creativity in higher education, rather than seeing it as an issue in need of urgent attention.

> Culture is the *result* of all the daily conversations and negotiations between the members of an organisation. They are continually agreeing (sometimes explicitly, usually tacitly) about the 'proper' way to do things and how to make meanings about the events of the world around them. If you want to change a culture you have to change all these conversations – or at least the majority of them.
>
> (Seel, 2005: 1)

To change the prevailing culture, we have to change the paradigm within which that culture is propagated. 'A paradigm is a constellation of concepts, values, perceptions and practices shared by a community, which forms a particular vision of reality that is the basis of the way a community organizes itself' (Capra, 1997: 6). We might illustrate the current paradigm we work in by reference to the way we penalise mistakes rather than see 'mistakes' as important lessons for learning. By perceiving 'mistakes' as opportunities for, and proof of, learning instead of failure, we begin to change the paradigm to one that is more enabling and valuing of creative effort.

If changing the paradigm within which the higher education experience is created is our fundamental challenge, then we need to create the conditions that favour *emergence* of a new paradigm. Emergence is 'the process by which patterns or global-level structures arise from interactive local-level processes' (Mihata, 1997: 31). As Paul Tosey (this volume, Chapter 4) reminds us, the emergence of new ways of thinking, being and doing come about through the interaction of people and their participation in *conversation*. This belief that we can only begin to change a culture by promoting conversation has framed the way in which we have sought to engage higher education communities. Our first and most important step in this process of encouraging emergence has been directed to understanding what creativity means to people working and studying in higher education, and how the idea is operationalised in different teaching and learning settings. But the concept of conversation seems too small to embody what we are trying to do, and I am attracted to Stephen Covey's idea of 'voice' as a more powerful representation of the significant self from which conversation and creativity emerge.

> Voice lies at the nexus of talent (your natural gifts and strengths – *including creative talents*); passion (those things that naturally energize, excite, motivate you); need (including what the world needs enough to pay you for *and the needs you identify and feel a need to fulfil*); and conscience (that still, small voice within that assures you of what is right and that prompts you to actually do it).
>
> (Adapted from Covey, 2004: 5; my additions in italics)

Academics' voices

The 'voice' of academics draws on their rich and varied experiences and perceptions of creativity, and their understandings of how generic concepts are operationalised in disciplinary practices (like being a historian, engineer or social worker), and in teaching, curriculum design and students' learning. Giving attention to these perceptions has revealed something of the 'complexity and contested nature of creativity'. Based on the findings of our research (Chapters 6 to 9), we have to conclude that creativity is not a concept that can be reduced to a few simple ideas that are easily operationalised. Nevertheless, many higher education teachers create their own meanings and operationalise their ideas in their teaching and curriculum designs. The most common ideas academics associate with creativity are presented in this section.

Originality

This involves a quality of 'new-ness' (Edwards *et al.*, this volume, Chapter 6); and making a contribution that adds to what already exists. It is connected to the ideas of: *doing/producing new things* (inventing, innovation and adaptation or re-creation). A sense of significance/utility or usefulness is implicit in this quality of newness. In the disciplinary context, *originality* can be represented as *creating something new and useful to the discipline*; in other words, *changing the domain*. It is different to personal invention, adaptation and innovation, which are still creative but are new to the individual rather than the discipline.

Being imaginative

This involves using imagination to think in certain ways that move us beyond the known into the unknown, that see the world in different ways or from different perspectives, that utilise analogical reasoning and metaphors to transfer concepts from one domain to another, that generate possibilities and produce novel interpretations and solutions. *Imagination* seems to be central to the mental agility that is necessary for being an effective practitioner in a discipline (see Jackson and Shaw, this volume, Chapter 8). People working in a disciplinary setting imagine things that only they can imagine when their knowledge, understanding and skills are engaged and stimulated by particular situations and the things that matter to them in the disciplinary world they inhabit. Imagination provides inspiration, sustains motivation, generates ideas and possibilities, and facilitates hypothesis-making and the interpretation of situations that cannot be understood by facts alone; including the many situations where data are incomplete.

Exploring or 'adventuring' for the purpose of discovery

This is often directed towards discovering possible solutions to complex problems or turning ideas into unique performances. It involves drawing on imagination to generate ideas, being open to new ideas and experiences, finding and examining possibilities, producing novel combinations out of familiar ideas/things through generating and testing possibilities, experimenting and taking risks.

Synthesising and making sense of complexity

Because working with complex problems often involves working with multiple and incomplete data, the capacity to synthesise, make connections and see new patterns and relationships seems to be particularly important in sense-making (interpreting, hypothesising, solution finding) and working towards better understandings and meanings.

Communicating meaning

The products of creativity: ideas, theories, insights, explanations, often through story-telling – each discipline has its own forms of story telling.

Students' voices

The second, but more limited, conversations have sought to give voice to higher education students. A number of research studies have shown (Saljo, 1979; Prosser *et al.*, 1994; Ramsden, 2003) that students' approaches to learning may be related to their conceptions of learning. Their perceptions of the learning environment and what is expected of them, and their conceptions of learning and their approaches to learning, appear to be related. We might speculate that students' perceptions of creativity in the academic learning environment, the extent to which they perceive the environment as encouraging or inhibiting their creativity, and how personal creativity influences their approaches to learning, are part and parcel of this milieu.

> The most sophisticated conceptions of learning, and the 'best' approaches to learning, then, may enable students to demonstrate creativity through their learning outcomes. The reverse could also be true: students with limiting conceptions and approaches may not be able to 'be' creative or 'demonstrate' creativity within a specific learning domain.
>
> (Reid and Petocz, 2004: 48)

Oliver *et al.* (this volume, Chapter 5) indicate that these relationships are likely to be complex. Students found it hard to explain what they thought creativity was, drawing on a number of different discourses and often presenting contrasting or even inconsistent positions at different points in a conversation. But in a complex perceptual world perhaps that is not so different to teachers! Perhaps the most significant finding from these initial explorations of the students' voice suggests that creativity lies at the heart of a student's own identity (Dineen, this volume, Chapter 9 and Oliver *et al.*, this volume, Chapter 5):

> even where creativity was not taught, not considered teachable and not valued in assessment, it was still relevant in defining how the students saw themselves. The use of creativity as a discourse – currently so confused and inconsistent – becomes vital in this respect, since claims to an emergent creative identity can only be warranted if they can be articulated. In this sense, it may be possible that even a small change – helping students to learn how to talk about creativity, particularly in the context of their study – would have an important effect, enabling students to lay claim to creativity in a way that currently eludes them within academic contexts.
>
> (Oliver *et al.*, this volume, Chapter 5)

This helps us to anchor our claim to moral purpose and provides a wonderful insight into the important role for higher education – to help students develop their own understandings and awareness of their own creativities as part of their own identity-building.

Higher education and creativity

Creativity and teaching

The creativity of the higher education teacher has something to do with connecting in imaginative and useful ways the knowledge, application and process skills, and ways of seeing the world from a disciplinary perspective to the needs and interests of students so that they might learn and be inspired to engage in learning in the subject: 'I don't teach, what I do is help people see' (Dineen, this volume, Chapter 9). It requires a depth of knowledge and understanding acquired through diligent and disciplined study in the field, combined with the transdisciplinary knowledge and understanding acquired through the study and practice of teaching and experience how students learn (and even how particular students learn). It is the cognitive and practical challenge that this knowledge and insight-rich world provides that energises the innate curiosity and creativity of the committed higher education teacher and we should celebrate and recognise this uniqueness. That we have a systemic culture that is, at best, ambivalent to this unique expression of human creativity never ceases to amaze me, and it is this attitude that we must alter if we are to bring about the sorts of changes to students' learning and experiences of learning that we are promoting. But perhaps this change is not so difficult to accomplish. The voices of the academics who contributed to our studies reveal that many believe that they are creative in their teaching and have provided many examples of their own creativity. The survey of National Teaching Fellows conducted by Marilyn Fryer (see this volume, Chapter 7) is particularly noteworthy and provides us with a useful lever for attitudinal change. Only three out of 94 expert teachers believed that they were not creative, and 70 per cent believed that they were quite creative. Chapters 6, 8 and 9 reveal that this belief extends well beyond the NTF community.

Social–cultural influences

Teaching and learning systems, while site- and context-specific, do not stand in isolation from the wider social–cultural environment. Mihaly Csikszentmihalyi reminds us that, while creativity originates in the minds, actions and interactions of individuals, it is fundamentally a social–cultural concept:

> Starting from a strictly individual perspective on creativity, I was forced by the facts to adopt a view that encompasses the environment in which the individual operates. This environment has two salient aspects: a cultural, or symbolic, aspect which here is called the *domain*; and a social aspect called the *field*. Creativity is a process that can be observed only at the intersection where individuals, domains and fields interact.
>
> (Csikszentmihalyi, 1999: 314)

This way of thinking led Csikszentmihalyi to develop the idea that creativity is the result of the interactions that occur in a system whose components and relationships could be defined:

> Creativity can be observed only in the interrelations of a system made up of three main parts. The first of these is the *domain,* which consists of a set of symbolic rules and procedures. ... Domains are in turn nested in what we usually call culture, or the symbolic knowledge shared by a particular society, or by humanity as a whole. The second component of creativity is

the *field,* which includes all the individuals who act as gatekeepers to the domain. It is their job to decide whether a new idea or product should be included in the domain . . . the third component of the creative system is the individual *person.*

(Csikszentmihalyi 1997: 27–28)

We might animate this social–cultural view of creativity with Amabile's (1983) characterisation of creativity as the confluence of intrinsic motivation, domain-relevant knowledge and abilities, and creativity-relevant skills which include: a cognitive style that involves coping with complexity and breaking and re-forming one's mental models of the world; knowledge of heuristics for generating novel ideas – such as trying a counterintuitive approach or forming associations and connections with improbable ideas; a work style characterised by concentrated effort, high energy and curiosity that drives self-motivation.

Figure 15.1 provides a visual representation of the system within which creativity originates, is applied, recognised and results in newness that is utilised by the field and change in the cultural domain. In adapting Csikszentmihalyi's model for our purposes, I have used Stephen Covey's concept of voice to represent the potentially creative individual whose imaginations have been fired, who is motivated to think and behave in particular ways (e.g. the characteristics described by Amabile, 1983), who uses their talents in a purposeful way to achieve their goals and whose decisions are made within a personal ethical framework.

For creativity to occur, the individual must interact with the domain. In higher education, the academic disciplines and inter-disciplinary fields of study are the fundamental cultural domains (Becher, 1989) and the main sites for interaction are related to problem finding and problem working (including the production of new

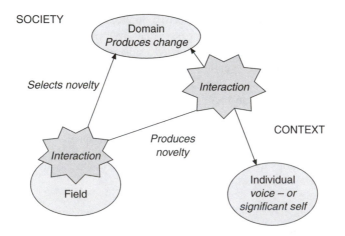

Figure 15.1 Representation of a creativity system adapted from Csikszentmihalyi (1999, Figure 16.1: 315) and incorporating Covey's (2004) representation of voice as the significant self from which creativity flows.

knowledge). Problems are envisaged to be of two basic types – issues that need to be resolved and opportunities for something different. In other words, the primary catalyst and context for creativity occurs at the point of intersection between individuals working on the problems they need to resolve within a domain. These problems may be generated by the individual, by peers in the field, by clients or society.

Individuals' responses to problem working situations in a domain may result in novelty, or a variation in knowledge and/or practice within the domain. In many cases the novelty will only directly affect a small number of people and specific situations and contexts. While an individual's creativity would be acknowledged by other members of the field, it is either not diffused to other members of the field or it is so site- or situation-specific as to have no wider utility. But in some circumstances a second set of interactions occur between the creative person or their ideas and products and members of the field. The effects of novelty are recognised by other members of the field and the field selects this novelty and incorporates it into disciplinary thinking and practice in the domain. In doing so, the domain is changed.

Only the second of the two scenarios described above would fit Csikszentmihalyi's definition of a creative person: 'someone whose thoughts or actions change a domain, or establish a new one' (Csikszentmihalyi, 1997: 27–8). But if we accept that there are levels of creativity, and that some forms are only useful and appropriate at a local level (e.g. to solve a specific problem in a specific situation), then the more site-specific forms of creativity must also be valid. If we accept this as a proposition then we have a rationale for the development of students' creative potential.

The investment theory of creativity (Sternberg and Lubart, 1996) might be utilised to explain the second set of interactions in a creativity system. According to this theory:

> creative people are ones who are willing and able to buy low and sell high in the realm of ideas. Buying low means pursuing ideas that are unknown or out of favour but that have growth potential. Often when these ideas are first presented they encounter resistance. The creative individual persists in the face of resistance and eventually sells high, moving on to the next new unpopular idea.
>
> (Sternberg and Lubart, 1996: 10)

Application to higher education teaching and learning

We can adapt Mihaly Csikszentmihalyi's systems views of creativity to the systems that higher education teachers create to promote and develop students' creativity (Figure 15.2). In the teaching and learning system, the teacher is the representative of the field e.g. history. The teacher acts as a process organiser, task creator, facilitator and monitor to ensure that the best conditions and support that can be given are provided (Jackson and Sinclair, this volume, Chapter 10). The teacher also acts as a representative of the field to judge the worth of products,

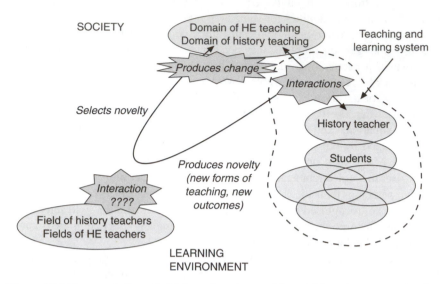

SOCIETY

Domain of HE teaching
Domain of history teaching

Teaching and
learning system

Produces change

Interactions

Selects novelty

History teacher

Students

*Produces novelty
(new forms of
teaching, new
outcomes)*

*Interaction
????*

Field of history teachers
Fields of HE teachers

LEARNING
ENVIRONMENT

Figure 15.2 Representation of a higher education teaching and learning system that has been established to promote students' creativity (adapted from Csikszentmihalyi, 1999, Figure 16.1: 315). All the components of the system are connected.

performances or other outcomes of learning. This judging process may, however, be a collaborative affair, as in the model proposed by Cowan (this volume, Chapter 12) and endorsed by Balchin (this volume, Chapter 13).

Learners are the people in the system whose creativities are being stimulated and developed by the teacher's pedagogic strategies. Each learner brings a unique set of experiences and subjectivities to draw upon: their personal psychology, imagination, knowledge, talents and attitudes. Given this diversity, within any student group there is likely to be a diverse range of attitudes and responses to the teacher's interventions.

The subject discipline is the domain in which the interaction takes place. It provides a rich knowledge base and endless sources of stimulation, while the teacher and the curriculum experiences provide the learning and assessment scenarios, problems and problem working contexts within which students' creativity can be energised and acted upon. The outcomes are the individual, or collective, thinking and actions of the students.

Implicit in this way of thinking about a system to promote students creativity, is the idea that the individual history teacher is connected to the field of history teachers and a wider field of teachers of other subjects who may also influence the discipline-based teacher. We may also recognise in the cultural domain not just the culture of the history discipline, but also the culture of higher education teaching and learning and the organisational/departmental cultures within which learning takes place. The latter may be more, or less, supportive of a creative ethos.

In the illustrative example, the history teacher creates conditions to encourage and enable students to be creative (for example, a challenging problem). The teaching and learning process becomes the vehicle for interaction between the history teacher, students as engaged active learners and the disciplinary field of study. Students respond in different ways to the challenges provided, and they gain experience of being creative. The teacher's role is to help students to experience and understand their creativity. Conversations, through which personal and collective meanings can be constructed, and reflection to aid meaning making, are crucial, and John Cowan outlines in Chapter 12 of this book a process for facilitating such conversation and capturing the social construction of meanings in the contexts in which they are grown.

It should be noted that personal creativities (teachers and students) are contained within the teaching and learning system. The changes that take place are the changes in participants' understandings. But there may be occasions where the products of this system (for example, new forms of pedagogy such as that elaborated by Caroline Baillie and John Cowan in Chapters 11 and 12 of this book) would be diffused through, and recognised more widely by, the field of history teachers or higher education teachers more generally. In this way, novelty in teaching changes the domain of higher education teaching.

This way of looking at creativity in higher education highlights the importance of the disciplinary or subject domains. Conversations with academics reveal that while creativity may be recognised in their discipline, it is not really valued beyond the rhetorical level. Similarly, the analysis of QAA benchmarking statements (Jackson and Shaw, Chapter 8) reveals that few subjects explicitly recognise creativity as a component of students' higher education learning. Articulating what creativity means in a disciplinary domain or field of professional practice, by fostering conversation, would seem to be an important first step in the process of cultural change.

Principles for constructing teaching and learning environments to promote students' creativity

I hope that you believe, as I do, that the contributors to this book have demonstrated strong and positive connections between higher education teaching, disciplinary study and practice, and creativity. In this section I will try to draw on what we have learnt through the Imaginative Curriculum project to develop some general principles for creating higher education teaching and learning environments that are more likely to promote students' creativity.

Align creativity with discipline culture and needs

Many higher education teachers will only invest time, energy and intellectual effort in developing teaching and learning systems that are consistent with the norms, values and forms of intellectual engagement, problem working and other practices in their subject (Edwards *et al.*, this volume, Chapter 6). As a general principle, we might expect that teaching and learning environments aimed at promoting students' creativity will need to be consistent with these things and grown within conceptions of what it is to be creative in the discipline(s) being studied. Exploring and growing understandings of what it means to be creative as a historian, chemist or any other disciplinary practitioner is a necessary prerequisite for the sorts of cultural change that will facilitate the systematic development of learning environments which support and encourage students' creativity in higher education. The outcomes of these conversations need to inform QAA Subject Benchmark Statements which, in the UK, constitute the formal expression of what is valued in students' undergraduate learning in a subject, and provide a reference point for curriculum design and curriculum review.

Align creativity to the interests, creative identities and needs of students

> *Students' voices* – being creative made things more interesting and more satisfying, suggesting a positive link between experiences and creativity.
>
> (Oliver *et al.*, this volume, Chapter 5)

There appears to be good alignment between academics' perceptions that they have to engage students' interests (Edwards *et al.*, this volume, Chapter 6) and students' perceptions that there is a positive relationship between being creative and interesting, satisfying and fulfilling experiences. Equally importantly is the idea that creativity is integral to students' self-identity – to being who they are in the many different contexts in which they study, work and play. 'Where creativity was not taught, not considered teachable and not valued in assessment, it was still relevant in defining how the students saw themselves' (Oliver *et al.*, this volume, Chapter 5).

Barnett and Coate (2005) have criticised the higher education curriculum for a lack of engagement in promoting students' identities, and have highlighted the need to change this situation if we are to properly prepare students for an uncertain and unknowable world.

> We resort unashamedly to a language that is barely heard in higher education. It is a language of 'self' and 'being' and 'becoming'.... It is a language that speaks to a student's developing inner self; a self that has to be developed if students are going to acquire durable capacities for flourishing in a world that is, to a significant degree, unknowable.
>
> (Barnett and Coate, 2005: 63)

A concern for creativity would help higher education to engage with the issues of self-identity, being and becoming; that goes for teachers, as well as *all* students! I stress *all* because creativity is inclusive in a way that few other outcomes of higher education can be. Late in the evolution of this chapter I was ashamed to realise that I had not thought enough about students and their different needs. In particular, I tried to imagine what creativity meant to someone who had a disability, perhaps someone who could not see the world as I did, but who had to see it through their imaginations and their other senses. I felt humbled and the insight I gained was that people who have a disability must be far more creative than I in order to cope and prosper in a world that is designed for people who do not have a disability. A concern for creativity that is grown from the perceptions and insights of each student, rather than the minds of their teachers, would be inclusive and would embrace the needs, interests and unique identities of all students.

Be clear about the purposes of teaching for creativity

Purposes might be visualised in a number of ways. First, as a way of enriching students' overall experiences of higher education and engaging them in interesting, challenging and motivating activities. Second, as a way of improving students' capacity to learn, solve challenging problems and perform within a disciplinary and/or programme-learning context (as outlined above). Third, to help students to develop as more rounded and complete individuals and to help them to develop their creative capacities, self-identity and self-efficacy. Improving students' metacognition – their self-awareness and capacity for self-critical evaluation of their own creativity and its effects – would be an important educational goal in such learning environments. Jackson and Sinclair (this volume, Chapter 10) provide some conceptual models to illustrate the enhanced effects on the development of students by enabling them to develop their creative potential.

Act as a role model to show students what it means to be creative

One of the best ways for students to learn about creativity is to show them what it means to you as a teacher. The process of higher education teaching, with its endless opportunities for exploring ideas and concepts, seeing the world from different perspectives, connecting, combining and synthesising, developing new knowledge, and the most creative act of all – changing the way people see the world and helping people construct new meaning – offers no better medium for demonstrating personal creativity. All we have to do is to observe ourselves, reflect deeply and critically analyse our own working practices to illuminate what creativity means to us in our teaching and scholarship. And what better way to convey our values and our ethics to our students?

Use the learning process to involve students in the social construction of knowledge

Creativity in a disciplinary context is a wonderful topic to show students the power of the social construction of knowledge. By facilitating good conversation and using strategies for knowledge capture and harnessing the electronic medium (e.g. web logs), students can see how their individual perceptions and understandings grown from experiences can be connected to make powerful stories, and that many powerful stories from within the group can change the way they think and their very belief systems. John Cowan (this volume, Chapter 12) provides us with an exhilarating insight into the dynamics of such a system.

Be clear about the learning outcomes you are intending to promote

I am going to raise two very different perspectives here. The first acknowledges that higher education involves developing students so that they can work with and come to understand complexity. So there are ample opportunities for developing the extended abstract (EA) outcomes of learning (Biggs, 2003) like hypothesising, reflecting, generating ideas, applying the known to 'far' domains and working with problems that do not have unique solutions.

> EA outcomes are not just indicators of fluency or the products of brainstorming for any old outcomes, the whackier the better ... they show the Torrance feature of flexibility, i.e. the categories have been shifted. The outcome adds value to the information given. At the highest academic levels creativity would be manifested by moving beyond the framework given, a paradigm shift, and that is where originality comes in.
>
> (John Biggs, email contribution to Imaginative Curriculum network discussion, July 2002)

Design learning outcomes that can accommodate creativity

We live in a paradoxical world and higher education is full of paradox that seeks to both define and constrain what we do, while simultaneously encouraging people to adventure beyond the known. As teachers we want students to comply and conform to our designs and intentions to learn the sorts of things that we believe are essential, yet where creativity is concerned we need them to behave in original ways to produce novelty. Part of the problem we have with creativity in higher education is the threat it poses to the status quo as we teach students to unlearn the compliant habits they have acquired through years of formal education. Securing compliance is deeply engrained in the culture of instruction and I sense that the instructional mindset so apparent in the discourses of USA educators has simply been camouflaged in the UK through the medium of predictive learning outcomes – at the end of this module, a student will be able to do x, y and z!

How often have we heard in the academics' voice, that students' creativity is being stifled by learning outcomes that assume that all learning can be prescribed and anticipated in advance? We have to learn how to construct these outcomes in ways that are not too specific, that encourage the recognition of unanticipated outcomes and enable students to make claims for outcomes that they recognise. We have to learn to accommodate negotiation and the students' voice in the design of our learning outcomes. We have to treat the crafting of an outcome, the formulation of standards and the evaluation of those standards as a dynamic and evolving process, not a static act of design. We can learn much from the way learners develop their own learning outcomes in negotiated work-based programmes and John Cowan (this volume, Chapter 12) points the way in more orthodox higher education settings.

Show how creative outcomes will be evaluated and assessed

In a teaching and learning system, outcomes are closely related to purposes. We have seen in both the academics' and students' voices the widespread beliefs that the way we have systematised assessment in higher education works against the promotion of students' creativity. But many teachers have clear views about the characteristics of creativity in particular situations and contexts, the types of thinking and behaviours they want to promote and the sorts of products and performances they anticipate emerging from the processes they create. However, these things can be combined in complex and individualistic ways and they are not so easy to quantify and grade in the way that some other learning outcomes are.

higher education teachers associate students' creativity with certain ways of thinking (Jackson, 2005a–d, and this volume, Chapters 6–9), e.g. imaginatively, conceptually, independently, originally, divergently (associatively), laterally, critically and reflectively, deconstructing and reconstructing, synthesising, connecting and combining ideas in fresh and useful ways. Learning activities have to be designed to encourage these forms of thinking and to reveal them in the outcomes of learning – products, performances or other tangible manifestations of thinking.

We are in the territory of complex learning and it is not easy for students or teachers to capture or recognise these forms of learning. John Cowan provides a framework that combines the personal and social construction of meanings of creativity by learners in their particular study contexts with the co-creation of standards and self-evaluation of performance. Tom Balchin's model of consensual assessment (this volume, Chapter 12) can also be integrated into the framework.

Being creative often involves taking risks, some of which might not be successful. When we are concerned with creativity, we have to create learning outcomes that recognise that taking risks and not succeeding is integral to learning – and that learning from 'mistakes' is one of the most valuable forms of learning we can acquire.

Be clear about levels and expectations of creativity

'Students' creative work may be underestimated or dismissed within a domain because of lecturers' unrealistic expectations of developing creativity' (Edwards *et al.*, this volume, Chapter 6). Creativity operates on a continuum from the inventions and interventions that change the world, through those that change a domain, to those that have local and personal significance: 'a sort of *personal effectiveness* in coping well with unknown territory and in recognising and making choices ... life-wide creativity' (Craft, 2002; see this volume, Chapter 3). In higher education, as in school education, we are primarily concerned with the latter, but we must aspire to prepare people to take on challenges at the level of creative change in the domain. In addressing the issue of level in Chapter 10 of this book, Jackson and Sinclair cite the framework developed by Taylor

(1959), who elaborated the idea of five levels of creative engagement – the second and third levels – academic and technical and inventive – being particularly relevant to Higher Education. But more importantly, perhaps, we are laying the foundations for our students to develop the capacities and habits for thinking that will enable them to operate at the highest levels of creativity in their chosen careers. We are also laying the foundations for becoming experts in a domain and perhaps promoting students' creativity also has something to offer here (see Dreyfus and Dreyfus, 1986; Dufresne *et al.*, 1995).

Adopt and invent facilitative teaching methods

Teaching and learning systems that are effective in promoting students' creativity tend to be flexible and adaptable, involve active partnership and the emotional energies of participants, and draw on a range of facilitative teaching approaches. An analysis of nearly 40 accounts of teaching that was intended to encourage students to be creative in a range of disciplinary contexts (Jackson, 2005a–d) revealed the things that higher education teachers do to promote students' creativity. Teachers have to prepare students for this way of learning and create conditions that are conducive to their creativity by: giving students permission to be creative; providing time for students to be creative; and providing safe curricular spaces where students can try out new things. Their role is to help students to gain the confidence and skills to be creative by: equipping them with appropriate thinking and process-creation skills; building their confidence to take risks and designing assessments that do not penalise them if they are not successful; developing their self-confidence to work in unpredictable situations; and promoting the development of self-awareness and reflective learning.

Negative views that take the stance that creativity cannot be taught are based on transmission models of teaching where teachers attempt to transfer their own knowledge and sense-making to students through lecture-dominated teaching; where students' engagements in learning are predominantly based on information transfer, and are heavily prescribed and controlled by the teacher; and where summative assessment drives the learning process. Teaching to facilitate students' creativity requires teachers to be equipped with an appropriate repertoire of facilitation skills, belief, confidence and self-awareness to be able to engage a group of students in processes whose outcomes can only be partially imagined (Jackson, 2005a–d; see also this volume, Chapters 10, 11 and 12).

Utilise problem-focused learning and adventures in learning

Working with complex fuzzy indeterminate problems that do not have unique solutions connects higher education learning with the disciplinary worlds that lie outside higher education. Academics and non-academic disciplinary practitioners, like clinicians, social workers and engineers, believe that creativity is something used in working with problems that are challenging, new, unpredictable and/or emergent (Jackson and Shaw, this volume, Chapter 8). It seems self-evident that nurturing students' creativity in higher education is best achieved through a process- or activity-based curriculum that engages students in challenging, novel and unpredictable ways of working and learning (Jackson, 2003).

There are many sites and opportunities for creativity in disciplinary thinking and practice, and these can be connected within frameworks of problem working. While the nature of the problems and the way they are visualised and addressed varies from discipline to discipline, finding, formulating, exploring, interpreting and finding solutions to complex concrete or abstract problems is the key focus for creative thinking and action in all disciplinary contexts.

Andriopoulos and Lowe (2000) use the term 'adventuring' to describe the process through which individuals explore and come to understand uncertainty. They recognise three categories of adventuring, all of which are relevant to the academic creative enterprise, namely, introspecting, scenario-making and experimenting. Introspecting is when people explore uncertainty from what is already known. Those that wish to adventure within a field need to have the basic knowledge of their specific field. At the highest levels, if you want to change a domain you need to know what already exists in the domain. Scenario making refers to the development of possible routes to tackle a particular situation. Hypothesising, as a way of visualising possible courses of action and their consequences, is a core process. Experimenting refers to processes through which possibilities or scenarios are tested and evaluated. Through this process, observations and other sorts of information are synthesised and evaluated. Adventuring involves risk-taking and mistake-making. Learning cultures that are averse to risk-taking and penalise mistakes inhibit adventuring and therefore the potential for creativity. As part of our cultural transformation, we need therefore to redefine what we mean by mistakes in the context of complex learning.

A visual representation of problem working as a process of adventuring is given in Figure 15.3. The problem working situation is called *'How do I teach this topic or help students develop these skills and attitudes?'* The same framework might be adapted to problem working in any disciplinary context.

Utilise an appropriate pedagogic model

In Chapter 10 of this book, Jackson and Sinclair provide a pedagogic model for a teaching and learning system that would support the development of students' creativity, underpinned by the sorts of reasoning that is articulated above. Figure 15.3 shows how this model might be used to represent the process of exploration that is associated with higher education teaching. A synthesis of the idealised practices, procedures, conditions and cultures that might characterise the broader institutional environment within which such a pedagogic model might be supported is provided in Figure 15.4.

Imagining a different future

I will conclude this chapter in the way I started the book, by envisioning the future but this time in terms of the small incremental and practical steps that will

Knowledge and understanding for the future
The taken for granted stock of problem working knowledge that can be drawn upon in future, Jackson (2004). A source of ideas and inspiration for future creative enterprise.

Exploring or 'adventuring'
• How do I teach this topic to these students or how do I enable these students to develop these skills and attitudes?
• How can I interest/engage my students?
• What do I need to know?
• How can I find out? Who can help me?
• Development of knowledge resources for teaching and learning.
• Synthesising, interpreting, sense making.
• Experimenting – taking risks, trying out new strategies, making mistakes.
• Monitoring and responding to students' responses and needs.
• Evaluating results and learning from the experience of trying.

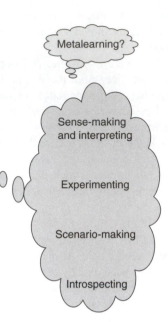

Figure 15.3 Representation of creativity in the problem working process that relates to teaching (adapted from Jackson and Shaw, Chapter 8, this volume Figure 8.1, and incorporating the idea of adventuring – exploring uncertainty – Andriopoulos and Lowe, 2000).

help us move towards the sort of cultural change that has been advocated throughout the latter half of this book.

In one sense we have already created a different future because this book, and all the thinking and ideas contained within it, now exists, and the people who thought these things are different as a result of the thinking they have done. Our idealistic hope is that the ideas within this book will have an effect on the thinking and actions of others, and that in this way ideas and change will be diffused around the higher education system. But we are also pragmatists and it is the network of interest that we are growing through the Imaginative Curriculum project that will sustain the enterprise. The way ahead lies in engaging more and more academics and students in conversations that enable meanings and understandings to be explored in disciplinary and interdisciplinary fields of study, and in programme- and module-specific contexts. This is something that can only be achieved through local agents or activists – people who care enough to want to bring about cultural change to become active participants in bringing about the change. We have to work with the idea of emergence (Tosey, this volume, Chapter 4) and believe that small changes made by individuals and small groups of committed teachers can eventually influence and change the patterns of the system as a whole. We also have to look more widely at how creativity is utilised in the workplace and professional practice settings so that academics and students can see the relevance of creativity and work towards creating a

Organisational cultures that value the creativity of staff and recognise that development of students' creative potential is an important part of their higher-education (Tosey, this volume, Chapter 4).

QA bureaucracies and systems that can accommodate these forms of emergent learning that do not require fine specification of creative outcomes. That encourage the emergence of new forms of teaching and learning, permit active experimentation and recognise that it is sometimes necessary to make mistakes in order to learn (Tosey, this volume, Chapter 4).

Local teaching cultures that recognise and value creativity and teaching groups willing to examine their own understandings of creativity in the particular contexts of the programmes and employment roles that they support.

Disciplinary cultures that recognise and value creativity, that foster conversation about creativity and make these values explicit in QAA Subject Benchmarking Statements (Jackson and Shaw, this volume, Chapter 8).

A curriculum – that provides safe spaces for students to experiment and learn from mistakes as well as successes. Process- or activity-based curricula that engage students in challenging, novel and unpredictable problem working and learning (Jackson, 2003).

Process standards that define the nature of teacher-student encounters, relationships and learning activities, that foster conversation and encourage co-creation of the experience (Knight, 2002).

Designs that are general rather than detailed specifications of knowledge, skills, attitudes, values, behaviours against which students will be able to make and defend claims (Knight, 2002).

Assessment that is consistent/authentic with learning intentions and does not assume that all learning can be predicted in advance. Assessment that is a formative, negotiated and iterative process of self-critical evaluation that recognises students' own meaning making (Cowan, this volume, Chapter 12).

Teaching that is facilitative, questioning and non-judgemental rather than didactic. The idea of a creativity coach might be more appropriate (Jackson and Sinclair, this volume, Chapter 9).

Teachers whose engagements are informed by reflection and action research, who are equipped with a repertoire of teaching and learning strategies and facilitation skills, who are willing to act as role models for the types of creativity they are seeking to foster (Jackson and Sinclair, this volume, Chapter 9; Baillie, this volume, Chapter 10; Cowan, this volume, Chapter 12 and Wisdom, this volume, Chapter 13).

Students who participate as willing and active partners in the learning enterprise. Who are prepared for this way of learning and who are willing to share and develop their understandings with other students.

Figure 15.4 A constellation of interconnected practices, cultures and conditions that are more likely to promote creativity in the higher education environment. Above all, the environment has to value and encourage active conversation and the co-creation of understandings of what creativity means in the context in which it is being used.

more creative society (Richard Smith-Bingham, this volume, Chapter 2). It is the process of conversation, the diffusion of knowledge and progressive deepening of individual and collective understanding that will eventually bring about the sorts of cultural change we are seeking.

We also need to connect our emergent understandings of creativity in higher education learning and employment settings to pedagogic knowledge of the teaching and learning strategies and environments that really do stimulate students into creative thinking and action. Higher education does not have a monopoly on creative pedagogies. We must learn from the efforts of our colleagues in schools and be open to the techniques used by consultants and trainers in the world of organisational development and personal coaching. We need to learn how to make safe spaces within a crowded curriculum. We need to develop teachers so that they are knowledgeable, skilled and confident facilitators. We need to develop our administrative and bureaucratic systems so that they permit rather than suppress new experiential designs. And most importantly, we have to develop our capacity to recognise, evaluate and reward the complex achievements that are associated with creative enterprise. It is perhaps in the area of assessment that we do need a revolution – or at least fundamental and far-reaching debate about the way the current paradigm supports or inhibits students' creativity. Perhaps John Cowan has lit a spark.

And so we return to our deep moral purpose, without which all our efforts are futile. If we are to make a difference to students' lives by helping them develop their creative talents as well as their intellectual abilities, then students must believe this. They have to be active partners in co-creating this new world in which creativity is more valued than at present. We have to see the world through their eyes and work with them to expand their horizons. The belief that creativity lies at the heart of every person's identity, and that we are denying students their identity if we do not recognise and value this, should be all the encouragement we need to sustain our vision of a different world.

A sort of closure

Beginning and ending a book are often the hardest things to do. I think this story provided by Fred Buining provides a fitting end to our initial adventure.

> On the shores of another sea, an old potter retires. His eyes cloud over, his hands tremble, the hour to say goodbye has arrived. Then the ceremony of initiation begins: the old potter offers the young potter his best piece. As tradition dictates among the Indians of northwest America, the outgoing artist gives his greatest work to the incoming one. And the young potter doesn't keep that perfect vase to contemplate or admire: he smashes it on the ground, breaks into a thousand pieces, picks up the pieces, and incorporates them into his own clay.

As teachers, we both lead and stay behind. This is not a process embedded in a three- or four-year programme, but should be an attitude we live each day. For we pass on masterpieces everyday and it is for the young artists to select among those pieces, the ones they want to smash and incorporate into their own work and identity. And from the moment we as teachers and higher education institutes can accept young artists to smash our masterpieces, knowing they do not smash us, neither our quest nor the outcome, but see and honour their smashing as the expression of the authentic human drive to create and re-create, as we have smashed and created in our own lives. From that moment we will be free as educators/teachers and universities to start our real teaching (Fred Buining, pers. comm., April 2005).

References

Allott, S. (2005) 'People, not ideas', *Prospect*, April.

Amabile, T.M. (1983) *The Social Psychology of Creativity,* New York: Springer-Verlag.

Amabile, T.M. (1988) 'A model of creativity and innovation in organizations', in B.M. Staw and L.L. Cunnings (eds) *Research in Organizational Behavior,* Greenwich, CT: JAI.

Amabile, T.M. (1995) *KEYS: Assessing the Climate for Creativity,* Greensborough, N.C.: Centre for Creative Leadership (assessment package).

Amabile, T.M. (1996) *Creativity in Context*, Bolder, CO: Westview.

Amabile, T.M. (1997) 'Motivating creativity in organisations: on doing what you love and loving what you do', *California Management Review,* 40(1). Online, available at: www.open.ac.uk/science/fdtl/documents/lit-review.pdf (accessed August 2005).

Andriopoulos, C. and Lowe, A. (2000) 'Enhancing organizational creativity: the process of perpetual challenging', *Management Decision*, 38(10): 734–42.

Baillie, C. (ed.) (2003) *The Travelling Case: Creativity in Art, Science and Engineering. How to Foster Creative Thinking in Higher Education,* UK Centre for Materials Education. Online, available at: www.heacademy.ac.uk/3271.htm (accessed August 2005).

Balchin, T. (2005) 'A creativity feedback package for teachers and students of design and technology in the UK', *International Journal of Design and Technology Education*, 10(2): 31–43.

Balchin, T. (2005) *Assessing Students' Creativity: Lessons from Research*. Online, available at: www.heacademy.ac.uk/2841.htm (accessed August 2005).

Balke, E. (1997) 'Play and the arts: the importance of the 'unimportant'', *Childhood Education,* 73(6): 353–60.

Barabási, A. (2002) *Linked: the New Science of Networks*, Cambridge, MA: Perseus Publishing.

Barnett, R. (2000) 'Supercomplexity and the curriculum', in M. Tight (ed.) *Curriculum in Higher Education*, Buckingham: SRHE and Open University Press, 254–66.

Barnett, R. and Coate, K. (2005) *Engaging the Curriculum in Higher Education,* Buckingham: SRHE and Open University Press.

Bateson, G. (1972) *Steps to an Ecology of Mind*, London: Paladin, Granada.

Bateson, G. and Bateson, M.C. (1988) *Angels Fear*, London: Rider Books.

Battram, A. (1998) *Navigating Complexity,* Dover, NH, The Industrial Society.

Beaty, L. (2005) 'Towards professional teaching in Higher Education: the role of accreditation', in P. Ashwin, (ed.) *Changing Higher Education: the Development of Learning and Teaching,* London: RoutledgeFalmer.

Becher, T. (1989) *Academic Tribes and Territories: Intellectual Enquiry and the Cultures of Disciplines*, Buckingham: SRHE and Open University Press.

Beetlestone, F. (1998) *Creative Children, Imaginative Teaching,* Buckingham: Open University Press.

Biggs, J. (2002) *Aligning Teaching and Assessment to Curriculum Objectives. Imaginative Curriculum Guide.* Online, available at: www.heacademy.ac.uk/resources.asp?process= full_record&section=generic&id=154 (accessed August 2005).

Biggs, J. (2003) *Teaching for Quality Learning at University,* Buckingham: SRHE and Open University Press, second edn.

Bjerstedt, A. (1976) 'Explorations in creativity', *Didakometry & Sociometry,* 8(1): 3–19.

Blinder, A. and Morgan, J. (2000) *Are Two Heads Better than One? Monetary Policy by Committee,* U.S. National Bureau of Economic Review Working Paper 7909.

Bloom, B. (1956) *Taxonomy of Educational Objectives,* New York: Longmans, Green.

Blythe, T. (1999) 'Approaching poetry: entry points to understanding', in L. Hetland, and S. Veenema, (eds) *The Project Zero Classroom: Views on Understanding,* Cambridge, MA: Project Zero, Harvard University Graduate School of Education.

Blythe, T. and the teachers and researchers of the Teaching for Understanding Project (1998) *The Teaching for Understanding Guide,* San Franscisco, CA: Jossey-Bass.

Bohm, D. and Peat, P.D. (1989) *Science, Order and Creativity,* London: Routledge.

Boud, D.J. (ed.) (1995) *Enhancing Learning Through Self Assessment,* London: Kogan Page.

Boud, D.J., Cohen, R. and Sampson, J. (eds) (2001) *Peer Learning in Higher Education: Learning from and with Each Other,* London: RoutledgeFarmer.

Bourdieu, P. and Passeron, J.-C. (1977) *Reproduction in Education, Society and Culture,* London: Sage.

Boyd, H.R., Adeyemi-Bero, A. and Blackhall, R.F. (1984) *Acquiring Professional Competence Through Learner-Directed Learning,* in Occasional Paper No. 7. London: Royal Society of Arts.

Boyd, H.R. and Cowan, J. (1986) 'A case for self-assessment based on recent studies of student learning', *Assessment and Evaluation in Higher Education,* 10(3): 225–35.

Brohn, D.M. and Cowan, J. (1977) 'Teaching towards an understanding of structural behaviour', *The Structural Engineer,* 55(I): 9–18.

CACE (Central Advisory Council for Education in England) (1967) *Children and their Primary Schools, Report of the Central Advisory Council for Education in England (The Plowden Report),* London: HMSO.

Capra, F. (1997) *The Web of Life: a New Synthesis of Mind and Matter,* London: Flamingo.

Carter, S., Mason, C. and Tagg, S. (2004) *Lifting the Barriers to Growth in UK Small Businesses: The FSB Biennial Membership Survey, Report to the Federation of Small Businesses,* London: Federation of Small Businesses.

Checkland, P. (1999) *Systems Thinking, Systems Practice,* London: Wiley.

Claxton, G. (1997) *Hare Brain, Tortoise Mind,* London: Fourth Estate.

Claxton, G. (2005) *Wising Up: Can We Accelerate the Growth of Wisdom?* Keynote lecture given at ESRC Seminar 'Creativity: Using it Wisely?' University of Cambridge, April 2005.

Collings, J.A. (1978) *A Psychological Study of Female Science Specialists in the Sixth Form,* unpublished PhD Thesis, University of Bradford.

Collings, J.A. and Smithers, A. (1984) 'Person orientation and science choice', *European Journal of Science Education,* 6(1): 55–65.

Collins, A., Brown, J.S. and Holum, A. (1991) 'Cognitive apprenticeship: making thinking visible', *American Educator.* Online, available at: www.org/arch/artcles/brown_seely.htm (accessed August 2005).

Cooper, H., Braye, S. and Geyer, R. (2004) 'Complexity and interprofessional education', *Learning in Health and Social Care*, 3(4): 179–89.

Council on Competitiveness (2004) *Innovate America*. Online, available at:
www.compete.org/ (accessed August 2005).

Covey, S. (2004) *The 8th Habit: from Effectiveness to Greatness*, London and New York:
Simon and Schuster.

Cowan, J. (1977) 'Individual approaches to problem-solving', *Aspects of Educational
Technology, Vol. X.* London: Kogan Page.

Cowan, J. (1980a) 'Improving the recorded protocol', *Programmed Learning and Educational Technology,* 17(3): 160–3.

Cowan, J. (1980b) 'Freedom in the selection of course content – a case study of a course
without a syllabus', *Studies in Higher Education,* 3(2): 139–48.

Cowan, J. (1981) 'Design education based on an expressed statement of the design
process', *Proceedings of the Institution of Civil Engineers,* Part 1, 70: 743–53.

Cowan, J. (1984) *Acquiring Professional Competence Through Learner-Directed Learning,* in Occasional Paper No. 7. London: Royal Society of Arts.

Cowan, J. (1986) *Education for Capability in Engineering Education, DEng thesis,*
Heriot-Watt University.

Cowan, J. (1988) 'Struggling with self-assessment', in D.J. Boud (ed.) *Student Autonomy
in Learning*, London: Kogan Page.

Cowan, J. (1998) *On Becoming an Innovative University Teacher*, Buckingham: SRHE
and Open University Press.

Cowan, J. (2002) Plus/Minus Marking: a Method of Assessment Worth Considering?
Online, available at: www/heacademy.ac.uk/resources.asp?process=full_record&
section=generic&id=425 (accessed June 2005).

Cowan, J. (2004a) 'Beyond reflection – where next for curricula which concentrate on
abilities?' in C. Baillie, and I. Moore, (eds) *Effective Learning & Teaching in Engineering,* London and New York: RoutledgeFalmer.

Cowan, J. (2004b) 'Education for higher level abilities: beyond alignment, to integration?' in V.M.S. Gil, *et al.* (eds) *Challenges in Teaching & Learning in Higher Education,* University of Aveiro: Aveiro, Portugal.

Cowan, J., Joyce, J., McPherson, D. and Weedon, E.M. (1999) 'Self-assessment of reflective journalling – and its effect on the learning outcomes', 4th Northumbria Assessment Conference.

Cowan, J, and Westwood, J. (2006) Collaborative and reflective professional development – a pilot'. *Active Learning in Higher Education*, 7(1): 61–9.

Craft, A. (1997) 'Identity and creativity: education for post-modernism?', *Teacher
Development: International Journal of Teachers' Professional Development,* 1(1):
83–96.

Craft, A. (2000) *Creativity Across the Primary Curriculum: Framing and Developing
Practice,* London: Routledge.

Craft, A. (2001) 'Little c Creativity', in A. Craft, B. Jeffrey and M. Leibling, (eds) *Creativity in Education*, London: Continuum, 45–61.

Craft, A. (2002) *Creativity and Early Years Education: a Lifewide Foundation,* London:
Continuum.

Craft, A. (2003) 'The limits to creativity in education, *British Journal of Educational
Studies,* 51(2).

Craft, A. (2005) *Creativity in Schools: Tensions and Dilemmas,* London: Routledge-
Falmer.

Craft, A., Miell, D., Joubert, M., Littleton, K., Murphy, P., Vass, E. and Whitelock, D. (2004) 'Final Report for the NESTA's Fellowship Young People Project', *Ignite*, September 2004.

Creative Partnerships Online, available at: www.creative-partnerships.com/news/ pressreleases/28584 (accessed August 2005).

Creative Partnerships (2005) Online, available at: www.creative-partnerships.com/ (accessed August 2005).

Cropley, A.J. (1967) *Creativity*, London: Longman.

Cropley, A.J. (2001) *Creativity in Education and Learning*, London: Kogan Page.

Csikszentmihalyi, M. (1997) *Creativity: Flow and the Psychology of Discovery and Invention*, New York: HarperCollins.

Csikszentmihalyi, M. (1999) 'Implications of a systems perspective for the study of creativity', in R.J Sternberg and T.L. Lubart (eds.) *Handbook of Creativity*, Cambridge, Cambridge University Press, 313–35.

Cultural Commission in Scotland (2005) *Final Report to Scottish Ministers*, Scottish Executive. Online, available at: www.scotland.gov.uk/Publications/ 2005/06/ 22145256/52593

Danvers, J. (2003) 'Towards a radical pedagogy: provisional notes on learning and teaching in art and design', *JADE*, 22(1): 47–58.

DCMS (Department for Culture, Media and Sport) (2001a) *Creative Industries Mapping Document*. Online, available at: www.culture.gov.uk/global/publications/ archive_2001/ ci_mapping_doc_2001.htm (accessed August 2005).

DCMS (Department for Culture, Media and Sport) (2001b) *Culture and Creativity: the Next Ten Years*. Online, available at: www.culture.gov.uk/NR/rdonlyres /E3C16C65-D10B-4CF6-BB78-BA449D0AEC04/0/Culture_creative_next10.pdf (accessed August 2005).

De Corte, E. (2000) 'Marrying theory building and the improvement of school practice', *Learning and Instruction*, 10: 249–66.

Dellas, M. and Gaier, E.L. (1970) 'Identification of creativity in the individual', *Psychological Bulletin*, 73: 55–73.

Department for Education and Employment (1999) *All Our Futures: Creativity, Culture & Education*, National Advisory Committee on Creative and Cultural Education, Sudbury: Department for Education and Employment.

Department for Education and Employment (2000) *Curriculum Guidance for the Foundation Stage,* London: Qualifications and Curriculum Authority.

Department for Education and Employment, Qualifications and Curriculum Authority (DFEE/QCA) (1999a) *The National Curriculum Handbook for Teachers in Key Stages 1 and 2,* London: Qualifications and Curriculum Authority.

Department for Education and Employment, Qualifications and Curriculum Authority (DFEE/QCA) (1999b) *The National Curriculum Handbook for Teachers in Key Stages 3 and 4,* London: Qualifications and Curriculum Authority.

Department for Education and Skills (2003) *Excellence and Enjoyment*, London: HMSO.

Department for Education and Skills (2004a) *Personalised Learning for Every Child, Personalised Contact for Every Teacher*, Press Notice 2004/0050.

Department for Education and Skills (2004b) *Personalised Learning Around Each Child*, DfES website, January 2004. Online, available at: www.standards. dfes.gov.uk/ personalisedlearning/about/ (accessed December 2004).

Department for Education and Skills (2004c) *A National Conversation about Personalised Learning,* Nottingham, DfES Publications.

Department for Education and Skills (2005a) Online, available at: www.standards.dfee.gov.uk/excellence (accessed August 2005).

Department for Education and Skills (2005b) Online, available at: www.teachernet.gov.uk/ professionaldevelopment/resourcesandresearch/bprs/search/ (accessed August 2005).

Department for Trade and Industry (DTI) (2003) *Competing in the Global Economy: the Innovation Challenge*. Online, available at: www.dti.gov.uk/innovationreport/ (accessed August 2005).

Department of Trade and Industry (DTI) (2005) Online, available at: www.dti.gov.uk/bestpractice/innovation/innovation-creativity.htm (accessed August 2005).

Dewulf, S. and Baillie, C. (1999) *CASE: Creativity in Art, Science and Engineering: How to foster creativity*, Sudbury: Department for Education and Employment.

Dictionary of Philosophy of Mind (n.d.) Online, available at: www.artsci. wustl.edu/~philos/MindDict/imagination.html (accessed August 2005).

Dreyfus, H. and Dreyfus, S. (1986) *Mind over Machine: the Power of Human Intuition and Expertise in the Era of the Computer,* New York: Free Press.

Dufresne, R.J. Leonard, W.J. and Gerace, W.J. (1995) *Our Model of Knowledge, Cognition and Learning*. Online: available at umperg.physics.umass.edu/perspective/ model/ and umperg.physics.umass.edu/perspective/researchFindings/document_view (accessed August 2005).

Eastwood, P. (2004) *Implementing an Institutional Assessment Strategy*. LTSN Generic Centre Assessment Series, No 15. Online: available www.heacademy. ac.uk/ embed-ded_object.asp?id=20389&prompt=yes&filename=ASS094 (accessed August 2005).

Edwards, C.P. and Springate, K.W. (1995) 'ERIC clearing house on elementary and early childhood education. Department for Education and Skills' (2003) *Excellence and Enjoyment*, London: HMSO.

Eisner, E.W. (1985) *The Art of Educational Evaluation*, London: Falmer Press.

Elton, L. (2005) *Guide to Assessing Creativity*. Online, available at: www.heacademy.ac.uk/ 2841.htm (accessed August 2005).

Eriksson, A. (1970) *Pedagogisk-psykologiska problem-lararenkater om kreativitet I skolan*, Malmö: Malmö University Press.

EU Presidency Conference (2004) Report of discussions from conference on Adaptability and Adjustment to Change in the Workplace, 26 and 27 February 2004.

Eve, R.A., Horsfall, S. and Lee, M.E. (eds) *Chaos, Complexity & Sociology: Myths, Models & Theories,* Thousand Oaks, CA: Sage.

Feist, G.J. (1999) 'The influence of personality on artistic and scientific creativity', in R.J. Sternberg, (ed.) *Handbook of Creativity*, Cambridge: Cambridge University Press.

Fenwick, T. (2003) 'Reclaiming and re-embodying experiential learning through com-plexity science', *Studies in the Education of Adults* 35(2): 123–41.

Filmore, P. and Thomond, P. (2003) 'The medicine wheel' in C. Baillie (ed.) *The Travel-ling Case: Creativity in Art, Science and Engineering. How to Foster Creative Think-ing in Higher Education*, UK Centre for Materials Education. Online, available at: www.heacademy.ac.uk/3271.htm (accessed August 2005).

Florida, R. (2002) *The Rise of the Creative Class: and How it's Transforming Work, Leisure, Community and Everyday Life*, Basic Books.

Floyd, A. (1976) 'Cognitive styles', *Personality and Learning, Block 5*, Buckingham: Open University Press.

Frayling, C. (2005) *'The Only Trustworthy Book...': Art and Public Value*. Talk to the Royal Society of Arts, February 5. Arts Council of England. Online, available at: www.artscouncil.org.uk/documents/news/artsandpublicvaluesdoc_ phpugtHdM.doc. (accessed August 2005).

Fryer, M. (1989) *Teachers' Views on Creativity*, PhD Thesis, Leeds Metropolitan University.

Fryer, M. (1994a) 'Management style and views about creativity', in H. Geschka, S. Moger and T. Rickards (eds) *Creativity and Innovation: the Power of Synergy,* Darmstadt, Germany: Geschka and Partner Unternehmensberatung.

Fryer, M. (1994b) *An Anglo-Portuguese Comparative Study of Effective & Creative Teaching in Higher Education*. Report to the British Council in Lisbon.

Fryer, M. (1996) *Creative Teaching and Learning*, London: Paul Chapman Publishing.

Fryer, M. (2000) 'Assessing creativity in schools', in V. Nolan (ed.) *Creative Education: Educating a Nation of Innovators,* Stoke Mandeville, Bucks: Synectics Education Initiative.

Fryer, M. (2003) *Creativity Across the Curriculum – a review and analysis of programmes designed to develop creativity*, Qualifications and Curriculum Authority. Online, available at: www.ncaction.org.uk/creativity/index.htm (accessed August 2005).

Fryer, M. (2004) *Creativity & Cultural Diversity*, Leeds: CCET Press.

Fryer, M. (2006) 'Making a difference: a tribute to E. Paul Torrance from the United Kingdom', *Creativity Research Journal*, 18(1): 121–8.

Fryer, M. and Collings, J.A. (1991) 'Teachers' views about creativity', *British Journal of Educational Psychology*, 61: 207–19.

Fullan, M. (1999) *Change Forces: the Sequel,* London: Falmer Press.

Fullan, M. (2003) *Change Forces With a Vengeance*, London: RoutledgeFalmer.

Gardner, H. (2005a) *The Ethical Responsibilities of Professionals,* Keynote lecture given at ESRC Seminar, 'Creativity: Using it Wisely?', University of Cambridge, April.

Gardner, H. (2005b) *Can There Be Societal Trustees in America Today?* Keynote lecture given at ESRC Seminar, 'Creativity: Using it Wisely?', University of Cambridge, April.

Gelb, M.J. (1996) *Putting Your Creative Genius to Work: How to Sharpen and Intensify your Mind Power*, Illinois: Nightingale Conant.

Getzels, W. (1982) 'The problem of the problem', in R.M. Hogarth (ed.) *Question Framing and Response Consistency,* San Francisco, CA, Jossey-Bass.

Gibbs, G. (1992) 'Improving the quality of student learning through course design', in R. Barnett, (ed.) *Learning To Effect*, Buckingham: SRHE and Open University Press.

Gibbs, G. and Simpson, C. (2004–5) 'Does your assessment support your students' learning?', *Learning and Teaching in Higher Education*, 1(1): 3–31.

Gleick, J. (1987) *Chaos,* London: Sphere Books.

Goldstein, J. (1999) 'Emergence as a construct: history and issues', *Emergence*, 1(1): 49–72.

Griffiths, M. and Woolf, F. (2004) *Report on Creative Partnerships Nottingham Action Research*, Nottingham: Nottingham Trent University.

Grinder, J. and Delozier, J. (1986) *Turtles All The Way Down,* Portland, OR: Metamorphous Press.

Haggis, T. (2004) 'Theories of dynamic systems and emergence: new possibilities for an epistemology of the "close up"?', paper presented at SCUTREA 34th Annual Conference, University of Sheffield, UK, 6th–8th July.

Halliwell, S. (1993) 'Teacher creativity and teacher education', in D. Bridges, and T. Kerry, (eds.) *Developing Teachers Professionally*, London: Routledge.

Hannan, A. and Silver, H. (2002) *Guide to Innovation in Teaching and Learning.* Online, available at: www.heacademy.ac.uk/resources.asp?process=full_record&section=generic&id=192 (accessed August 2005).

Harvey, L. (1997) *Graduates' Work: Organizational Change and Students' Attributes*, Birmingham, UK: Centre for Research into Quality, University of Central England.

Hender, J., Dean, D., Rodgers, T. and Nunamake, Jr. J. (2001) 'Improving group creativity: brainstorming versus non brainstorming techniques in a GSS Environment', Proceedings of 34th Hawaii International Conference on System Sciences.

Heron, J. (1974) *The Peer Learning Community,* Surrey: Human Potential Research Project, University of Surrey.

Hey, A. and Walters, P. (2003) *The New Quantum Universe,* Cambridge: Cambridge University Press.

Hocevar, D. and Bachelor, P. (1989) 'A taxonomy and critique of measurements used in the study of creativity', in J.A. Glover, R.R. Ronning and C.R. Reynolds (eds) *Handbook of Creativity*, New York: Plenum Press, 53–75.

Holden, J. (2004) *Capturing Cultural Value: How Culture has Become a Tool, of Government Policy*, Demos. Online, available at: www.demos.co.uk/catalogue/ culturalvalue (accessed August 2005).

Holland, J.L. (1959) 'Some limitations of teacher ratings as predictors of creativity', *Journal of Educational Psychology*, 50: 219–23.

Holmes, L. (2002) 'Emergent identity, education and distributed assessment: an ethnomethodological exploration', Paper presented at 'Ethnomethodology: a Critical Celebration' conference, University of Essex, March. Online, available at: www.re-skill.org.uk/papers/assessment.html (accessed August 2005).

Homer-Dixon, T. (2000) *The Ingenuity Gap: Can We Solve the Problems of the Future?* Canada: Vintage.

Honey, P. and Mumford, A. (1986) *Using Your Learning Styles,* Peter Honey Publications.

Houchin, K. and MacLean, D. (2005) 'Complexity theory and strategic change: an empirically informed critique', *British Journal of Management*, 16: 149–66.

Hubbard, R.S. (1996) *A Workshop of the Possible: Nurturing Children's Creative Development*, York, Maine: Stenhouse Publishers.

Humphreys, M. and Hyland, T. (2002) 'Theory, practice and performance in teaching: professionalism, intuition and jazz', *Educational Studies,* 28: 5–15.

IBM (2005) *Global Innovation Outlook.* Online, available at: t1d.www-306. cacheibm.com/e-business/ondemand/us/pdf/IBM_GIO_2004.pdf (accessed August 2005).

Imison, T. (2001) 'Creative leadership: innovative practices in a secondary school', in A. Craft, B. Jeffrey, M. Leibling, (2001) (eds) *Creativity in Education*, London: Continuum.

Jackson, N.J. (2002) *Designing for Creativity: a Curriculum Guide.* Online, available at: www.heacademy.ac.uk/3018.htm (accessed August 2005).

Jackson, N.J. (2003) 'Nurturing creativity through an imaginative curriculum', *Educational Developments*, 4(2): 8–12. Online updated version, 'Creativity in Higher Education', available at: heacademy.ac.uk/creativity.htm (accessed August 2005).

Jackson, N.J. (2004a) 'Developing the concept of metalearning', in J.H.F. Meyer and L.S. Norton (eds) *Metalearning in Higher Education*, special issue of *Innovations in Education and Training International,* 41(4): 391–403.

Jackson, N.J. (ed.) (2004b) *How Can Creativity Be Taught? Personal Accounts of Teaching to Promote Students' Creativity.* Online, available at: www.heacademy.ac.uk/ 3016.htm (accessed August 2005).

Jackson, N.J. (2005a) *Creativity in Earth and Environmental Sciences and Education Earth and Environmental Science Education*, Imaginative Curriculum Working Paper. Online, available at: www.heacademy.ac.uk/2762.htm (accessed August 2005).

Jackson, N.J. (2005b) *Creativity in Engineering and Engineering Education*, Imaginative Curriculum Working Paper. Online, available at: www.heacademy.ac.uk/ 2762.htm (accessed August 2005).

Jackson, N.J. (2005c) *Creativity in History and History Education*, Imaginative Curriculum Working Paper. Online, available at: www.heacademy.ac.uk/ 2762.htm (accessed August 2005).

Jackson, N.J. (2005d) *Assessing Students' Creativity: Synthesis of Higher Education Teachers' Views*. Online, available at: www.heacademy.ac.uk/2841.htm (accessed August 2005).

Jackson, N.J. and Burgess, H. (2005) *Creativity in Social Work and Social Work Education*. Imaginative Curriculum Working Paper. Online, available at: www. heacademy.ac.uk /2762.htm (accessed August 2005).

Jackson, N.J and Sinclair, C. (2005) *Creative Puzzler*. Online, available at: www.heacademy.ac.uk/3016.htm (accessed August 2005).

Jackson, N.J., Gough, D., Dunne, E. and Shaw, M. (2004) 'Developing an infrastructure to support an evidence informed approach to Personal Development Planning', Paper presented at Higher Education Academy, Third Mike Daniel Symposium on Institutional Research, 'What does evidence based practice mean in higher education?' Manchester, July. Online, available www.heacademy. ac.uk/1673.htm (accessed August 2005).

Jackson, P.W. and Messick, S. (1965) 'The person, the product and the response: conceptual problems in the assessment of creativity', *Journal of Personality*, 33: 309–29.

Jeffrey, B. (2001a) 'Challenging prescription ideology and practice: the case of Sunny first school', in J. Collins, K. Insley and J. Soler, (eds) *Developing Pedagogy: Researching Practice*, London: Paul Chapman.

Jeffrey, B. (2001b) 'Primary pupil's perspectives and creative learning', *Encyclopaideia*, 9.

Jeffrey, B. (2003a) 'Countering Student instrumentalism: a creative response', *British Educational Research Journal*, 29, 4.

Jeffrey, B. (2003b) *Creative Learning and Student Perspectives*. Online, available at: opencreativity.open.ac.uk (accessed August 2005).

Jeffrey, B. (2004) *End of Award Report: Creative Learning and Student Perspectives (CLASP) Project,* submitted to ESRC, November.

Jeffrey, B. and Craft, A. (2001) 'The universalization of creativity in education', in A. Craft, B. Jeffrey and M. Leibling, (eds) *Creativity in Education,* London: Continuum.

Jeffrey, B. and Craft, A. (2004) 'Teaching creatively and teaching for creativity: distinctions and relationships', *Educational Studies,* 30(1).

Jeffrey, B. and Woods, P. (2003) *The Creative School: a Framework for Success, Quality and Effectiveness*, London: RoutledgeFalmer.

Johnson, S. (2001) *Emergence: the Connected Lives of Ants, Brains, Cities and Software,* London: The Penguin Press.

John-Steiner, V. (2000) *Creative Collaboration,* New York: Oxford.

Josephs, A.P. and Smithers, A.G. (1975) 'Personality characteristics of syllabus-bound and syllabus-free sixth-formers', *British Journal of Educational Psychology*, 45: 29–38.

Jowell, T. (Secretary of State for Culture, Media and Sport) (2004) *Government and the Value of Culture*, DCMS. Online, available at: www.culture.gov.uk/NR/ rdonlyres/DE2ECA49–7F3D-46BF-9D11-A3AD80BF54D6/0/valueofculture.pdf (accessed August 2005).

Jupp, R., Ciara, F. and Bentley, T. (2001) *What Learning Needs: the Challenge for a*

Creative Nation, Demos/Design Council. Online, available at: www.demos.co.uk/ catalogue/learningneeds (accessed August 2005).

Kagan, J. (1966) 'Reflection – impulsivity. The generality and dynamics of conceptual tempo', *Journal of Abnormal Psychology*, 71: 17–24.

Kaltsounis, B. and Honeywell, L. (1980) 'Instruments useful in studying creative behaviour and creative talent', *Journal of Creative Behaviour*, 14: 56–67.

Karoly, L.A. and Panis, C.W.A. (2004) *The 21st Century at Work: Forces Shaping the Future Workforce and Workplace in the United States*, Rand Corporation. Online, available at: www.rand.org/pubs/monographs/2004/RAND_MG164.pdf (accessed August 2005).

Kauffman, S. (1996) *At Home in the Universe: the Search for Laws of Complexity*, Harmondsworth: Penguin.

Kessler, R. (2000) *The Soul of Education: Helping Students Find Connection, Compassion and Character at School*, USA: Association of Supervision and Curriculum.

Knight, P. (2001) 'Complexity and curriculum: a process approach to curriculum-making', *Teaching in Higher Education*, 6(3): 371–83.

Knight, P. (2002) *Notes on a Creative Curriculum*. Online, available at: www.heacademy.ac.uk/3016.htm (accessed August 2005).

Knight, P. and Yorke, M. (2003) *Learning, Curriculum and Employability in Higher Education*, London: RoutledgeFalmer.

Knowles, M.S. (1986) *Using Learning Contracts*, San Francisco, CA: Jossey-Bass.

Kok, W. (2003) *Jobs, Jobs, Jobs: Creating More Employment in Europe*, Report of the Employment Taskforce to the European Heads of State. Online, available at: europa.eu.int/comm/employment_social/employment_strategy/pdf/etf_en.pdf (accessed August 2005).

Lambert, R. (2003) *Lambert Review of Business-University Collaboration*, Her Majesty's Treasury. Online, available at: www.hm-treasury.gov.uk/media/ EA556/lambert_review_ final_450.pdf (accessed August 2005).

Land, R. (2003) 'Orientations to academic development', in H. Eggins and R. Macdonald (eds) *The Scholarship of Academic Development*, Buckingham: SRHE and Open University Press.

Lao Tzu (1963) *Tao Te Ching* (trans. D.C. Lau) Harmondsworth, Middlesex: Penguin.

Laurillard, D. (1993) *Rethinking University Teaching*, London: Routledge.

Lave, J. and Wenger, E. (1991) *Situated Learning: Legitimate Peripheral Participation*, Cambridge: Cambridge University Press.

Law, R. (2005) *Improve Your Life Through Explorativity*, Unpublished book manuscript.

Leach, J. (2001) 'A hundred possibilities: creativity, community and ICT', in A. Craft, B. Jeffrey and M. Leibling, (eds) *Creativity in Education*, London: Continuum.

Lengrand, L. et Associés, PREST (University of Manchester) and ANRT – France (2002) *Innovation Tomorrow*, European Commission. Online, available at: ftp://ftp.cordis.lu/pub/innovation-policy/studies/studies_innovation_tomorow.pdf (accessed August 2005).

Lewin, R. (1993) *Complexity: Life on the Edge of Chaos*, London: Phoenix.

Lissack, M. (1999) 'Complexity: the science, its vocabulary, and its relation to organizations', *Emergence; a Journal of Complexity Issues in Organizations and Management* 1(1): 110–26.

Losada, M. and Heaphy, E. (2004) 'The role of positivity and connectivity in the performance of business teams: a nonlinear dynamics model', *American Behavioral Scientist*, 47: 740–65.

McGoldrick, C. and Edwards, M. (2002) *Creativity and Curriculum Design: What Do*

...ned Imaginative Curriculum Research Study. LTSN June. Online, available at: ...heacademy.ac.uk/1644.htm (accessed August 2005).

...J. (1993) *Applied Imagination: Principles and Procedures of Creative Problem-ing*, Buffalo: Creative Education Foundation.

...ne, T. (2003) 'Against "creativity": a philistine rant', *Economy and Society*, 32(4): ...–525.

..., G. and Scott, B.C.E. (1972) 'Learning strategies and individual competence', *Inter-ational Journal of Man–Machine Studies*, 4: 217–53.

...itt, K. (1984) 'Sectoral patterns of technological change: towards a taxonomy and a ...heory', *Research Policy*, 13: 343–74.

...vitt, K. (2001) 'Public policies to support basic research: what can the rest of the world learn from US theory and practice? (and what they should not learn)', *Industrial and Corporate Change*, 10(3): 761–79.

Pedagogy for Employability Group (2004) *Pedagogy for Employability*. Higher Education Academy. Online, available at: www.heacademy.ac.uk/1433.htm (accessed August 2005).

Perkins, D. (1999) 'From idea to action', in L. Hetland and S. Veenema, (eds) *The Project Zero Classroom: Views on Understanding*, Cambridge, MA: Project Zero, Harvard University Graduate School of Education.

Perkins, D.N. (1981) *The Mind's Best Work*, Cambridge, M.A: Harvard University Press.

Perutz, M.F. (2003) *I Wish I'd Made You Angry Earlier: Essays – Science, Scientists, and Humanity*, Cold Spring Harbor Laboratory Press. Online, available at: www.entemp.ie/publications/employment/2004/adaptabilityconference.doc (accessed August 2005).

Poincaré, H. (1970) 'Mathematical creation', in P.E. Vernon (ed.) *Creativity*, Harmondsworth: Penguin Books, 77–88.

Polanyi, M. (1966) *The Tacit Dimension*, London: Routledge and Kegan Paul.

Popescu-Nevianu, P. and Cretsu, T. (1986) 'Study of teachers' creative abilities', *Revue Roumaine des Sciences Sociales*, 30(2): 129–34.

Price, I. and Shaw, R. (1998) *Shifting the Patterns*, Chalford, Gloucestershire: Management Books 2000 Ltd.

Prigogine, I. and Stengers, I. (1984) *Order Out of Chaos*, New York: Bantam Books.

Prosser, M. and Trigwell, K. (1999) *Understanding Learning and Teaching: the Experience in Higher Education*, Buckingham: SRHE and Open University Press.

Prosser, M., Trigwell, K. and Taylor, P. (1994) 'A phenomenographic study of academics' conceptions of science learning and teaching', *Learning and Instruction*, 4: 217–32.

Puccio, J.G. (1994) 'An overview of creativity assessment', in S.G. Isaksen (ed.) *The Assessment of Creativity*, Buffalo, NY: Center for Studies in Creativity.

Qualifications and Curriculum Authority (QCA) (2004) Online, available at: www.ncaction.org.uk/creativity/about.htm.

Qualifications and Curriculum Authority (QCA) (2005a) *Creativity: Find It, Promote It – Promoting Pupils' Creative Thinking and Behaviour Across the Curriculum at Key Stages 1, 2 and 3 – Practical Materials for Schools*, London: Qualifications and Curriculum Authority

Qualifications and Curriculum Authority (QCA) (2005b) Online, available at: www.ncaction.org.uk/creativity/about.htm (accessed August, 2005).

Raina, M.K. (2004) '"I shall be many": the garland making perspective on creativity and cultural diversity', in M. Fryer (ed.) *Creativity and Cultural Diversity*, Leeds: CCET Press.

Ramsden, P. (2003 edition) *Learning to Teach in Higher Education*, London: Routledge, second edn.

Academics Think? Commissioned Imaginativ
LTSN Generic Centre. Online, available a
(accessed August 2005).

May, R. (Lord May of Oxford) (2002) *President's* .
Society. Online, available at: www.royalsoc.ac.uk/p
August 2005).

Miell, D. and Littleton, K. (2004) *Collaborative Creativ*
Books.

Mihata, K. (1997) 'The persistence of "Emergence"', in R.A.
Lee (eds) *Chaos, Complexity & Sociology: Myths, Models*
Oaks, CA: Sage: 30–38.

Millar, G.W. (1995) *E. Paul Torrance: the Creativity Man,* Norwoo.

Millar, G.W. (2004) *The Making of a Beyonder,* Bensenville, IL: Sch.

Mitroff, I.I. (1974) *The Subjective Side of Science,* San Francisco, CA: .

Murdock, M.C. and Puccio, G.J. (1993) 'A contextual organiser for con.
research', in S.G. Isaksen *et al.* (eds) *Understanding and Recognising*
Emergence of a Discipline, Norwood, NJ: Ablex, 249–80.

Murphy, P., McCormick, B., Lunn, S., Davidson, M. and Jones, H. (2004) 'E.
schools', *Final Evaluation Report, Executive Summary,* London and Milton .

NACCCE (National Advisory Committee on Creative and Cultural Education,
ment for Education and Employment) (1999) *All our Futures: Creativity, Cultu*.
Education, London. Online, available at: www.dfes.gov.uk/naccce/ index1..
(accessed August 2005).

National College for School Leadership (NCSL) (2005) Online, available .
www.ncsl.org.uk/index.cfm?pageid=randd-activities-creativity (accessed August
2005).

Newton, D., Newton, L. and Oberski, I. (1998) 'Learning and conceptions of understanding in history and science: lecturers and new graduates compared', *Studies in Higher*
Education, 23(1): 43–57.

Ng, A.K. (2003) 'A cultural model of creative and conforming behaviour', *Creativity*
Research Journal, 15(2 & 3): 223–33.

Nickerson, R.S. (1999) 'Enhancing creativity', in R.J. Sternberg (ed.) *Handbook of Cre-*
ativity, Cambridge: University of Cambridge, 392–430.

Nicol, D. and MacFarlane-Dick, D. (in press) 'Formative assessment and self-regulated
learning: a model and seven principles of good feedback practice', *Studies in Higher*
Education.

Nisbettt, R.E. (2003) *The Geography of Thought,* New York: The Free Press.

Noland, R.G., English, D.W. and Von Eschenbach, J.F. (1984) 'Perceptions of gifted students and their education', *Roeper Review,* 7(1): 27–30.

Northedge, A. (2003) 'Enabling participation in academic discourse', *Teaching in Higher*
Education, 8(2): 169–80.

Office for Standards in Education (OFSTED) (2003a) *Expecting the Unexpected: Devel-*
oping Creativity in Primary and Secondary Schools, HMI Report 1612, E-publication.

Office for Standards in Education (OFSTED) (2003b) *Improving City Schools: How the*
Arts Can Help, HMI Report 1709, E-publication.

OFSTED (2004) *Excellence in Cities Primary Extension: Real Stories,* Document Reference HMI2394. Online, available at: www.ofsted.gov.uk (accessed August 2005).

Ohuche, N.M. (1986) 'The ideal pupil as perceived by Nigerian (Igbo) teachers and Torrance's creative personality', *International Review of Education,* 32(8): 191–6.

Oliver, M. (2002) *Creativity and the Curriculum Design Process: a Case Study,* Com-

Reason, P. and Goodwin, B. (1999) 'Toward a science of qualities in organizations: lessons from complexity theory and postmodern biology', *Concepts and Transformations,* 4(3): 281–317.

Reid, A. and Petocz, P. (2004) 'Learning domains and the process of creativity', *The Australian Educational Researcher*, 31(2): 45–62.

Rhodes, M. (1961) 'An analysis of creativity', *Phi Delta Kappan*, 42: 305–10.

Ritchart, R. (2002) *Intellectual Character: What It Is, Why It Matters and How to Get It,* San Francisco, CA: Jossey-Bass.

Robinson, K. (2001) *Out of Our Minds: Learning to be Creative,* Oxford: Capstone.

Rogers, C. (1952) *On Becoming a Person,* London: Constable.

Rossman, B.B., and Gollob, H.F. (1975) 'Comparison of social judgments of creativity and intelligence', *Journal of Personality and Social Psychology*, 31: 271–81.

Ryhammar, L. and Brolin, C. (1999) 'Creativity research: historical considerations and main lines of development'. *Scandinavian Journal of Educational Research,* 43(3).

Ryle, G. (1949) *The Concept of Mind,* London: Hutchinson.

Safter, H.T. (1993) *Exiting from Within: the World of Highly Creative and Gifted Children*, Buffalo, NY: Bearly.

Salter, A., D'Este, P., Martin, B., Geuna, A., Scott, A., Pavitt, K., Patel, P. and Nightingale, P. (2000) *Talent, Not Technology: Publicly Funded Research and Innovation in the UK*, SPRU. Online, available at: www.sussex.ac.uk/sprutest/ documents/saltertalentshort.pdf (accessed August 2005).

Saljo, R. (1979) 'Learning about learning', *Higher Education*, 8: 443–51.

Saunders, L. (2004) 'Evidence-led professional creativity: a perspective from the General Teaching Council for England', *Educational Action Research,* 12(1): 163–67.

Schaefer, C. (1973) 'An exploratory study of teachers' descriptions of the ideal pupil', *Psychology in Schools*, 10(4): 444–7.

Schön, D. (1983) *The Reflective Practitioner*, San Francisco, CA: Jossey-Bass.

Schunk, D.H. and Zimmerman, B.J. (1994) *Self-Regulation of Learning and Performance: Issues and Educational Applications*, Hillside, NJ: Lawrence Erlbaum Associates.

Schunk, D.H. and Zimmerman, B.J. (1997) 'Social origins of self-regulated competence', *Educational Psychologist,* 32, 195–208.

Schunk, D.H. and Zimmerman, B.J. (1998) *Self-Regulated Learning: From Teaching to Self-Reflective Practice,* New York: Guilford Press.

SCONUL Advisory Committee on Information Literacy (1999) *Information Skills in Higher Education*. Online, available at: www.sconul.ac.uk/activities/inf_lit/ papers/Seven_pillars2.pdf (accessed August 2005).

Scott-Morgan, P. (1994) *The Unwritten Rules of the Game*, London: McGraw-Hill.

Seel, R. (2002) *Emergence in Organisations*. Online, available at: www.new-paradigm.co.uk/emergence-human.htm (accessed August 2005).

Seel, R. (2004) *Culture and Complexity: New Insights on Organisational Change*. Online, available at: www.new-paradigm.co.uk/culture-complex.htm (accessed August 2005).

Seel, R. (2005) *Creativity in Organisations: An Emergent Perspective*. Online, available at: www.new-paradigm.co.uk/creativity-emergent.htm (accessed August 2005).

Seltzer, K. and Bentley, T. (1999) *The Creative Age: Knowledge and Skills for the New Economy,* London: Demos.

Shallcross, D.J. (1981) *Teaching Creative Behaviour: How to Teach Creativity to Children of All Ages*, Englewood Cliffs, NJ: Prentice Hall.

Shallcross, D.J. (1985) *Teaching Creative Behavior*. Buffalo, NY: Bearly.

Sharma Sen, R. and Sharma, N. (2004) 'Teachers' conception of creativity and its nurture in children: an Indian perspective', in M. Fryer (ed.) *Creativity and Cultural Diversity,* Leeds: CCET Press.

Sharpe, R. (2004) 'How do professionals learn and develop? Implications for staff and educational developers', in D. Baume and P. Kahn, (eds) *Enhancing Staff and Educational Development,* London: RoutledgeFalmer.

Shaw, M. (2005) *Indicators of Creativity in QAA Subject Benchmarking Statements*. Online, available at: www.heacademy.ac.uk/2762.htm (accessed August 2005).

Shaw, P. (2002) *Changing Conversations in Organizations: A Complexity Approach to Change*, London: Taylor & Francis.

Sitra, (2005) *Making Finland a Leading Country in Innovation: Final Report of the Competitive Innovation Environment Development Programme*, Sitra. Online, Available at: www.sitra.fi/ Julkaisut/ohjelmat/inno1engl.pdf (accessed August 2005).

Sonnenburg, S. (2004) 'Creativity in communication: a theoretical framework for collaborative product creation', *Creativity and Innovation Management,* 13(4): 254–62.

Stacey, R.D. (1999) *Strategic Management & Organisational Dynamics: The Challenge of Complexity*, New York: Financial Times Prentice Hall, third edn.

Stacey, R.D. (2000) *Strategic Management and Organizational Dynamics: the Challenge of Complexity,* London: Routledge.

Stacey, R.D. (2001) *Complex Responsive Processes in Organizations: Learning and Knowledge Creation*, London: Routledge.

Stacey, R.D., Griffin, D. and Shaw, P. (2000) *Complexity and Management: Fad or Radical Challenge to Systems Thinking?* London: Routledge

Stein, M.I. (1974) *Stimulating Creativity, Volume 1: Individual Procedures,* New York: Academic Press.

Stein, M.I. (1975) *Stimulating Creativity, Volume 2: Group Procedures,* New York: Academic Press.

Stein, M.I. (1984) *Making the Point*, Amagansett: The Mews Press.

Stein, M.I. (1986) *Gifted, Talented, and Creative Young People: a Guide to Theory, Teaching and Research*, New York: Garland Publishing Inc.

Sternberg, R.J. and Lubart, T.I. (1995) *Defying the Crowd: Cultivating Creativity in a Culture of Conformity,* New York: Free Press.

Sternberg, R.J. and Lubart, T.I. (1996) 'Investing in creativity', *American Psychologist,* 51 (7): 677–88.

Sternberg, R.J. and Lubart, T.I. (1999) 'The concept of creativity: prospects and paradigms', in R.J. Sternberg (ed.) *Handbook of Creativity*, Cambridge: Cambridge University Press.

Sternberg, R.J. and Williams, W.M. (1996) *How to Develop Student Creativity*, Alexandria, VA: Association for Supervision and Curriculum Development.

Strategy Unit (Prime Minister's) (2005) *Strategic Audit: Progress and Challenges for the UK*. Online, available at: www.strategy.gov.uk/downloads/work_areas/strategic_audit/strategic_audit2.pdf (accessed August 2005)

Sunstein, C. (2003) *Why Societies Need Dissent*, Cambridge, MA: Harvard University Press.

Surowiecki, J. (2005) *The Wisdom of Crowds: Why the Many are Smarter than the Few*, London. Abacus.

Swede, G. (1993) *Creativity: a New Psychology*, Wall and Emerson.

Synectics Education Initiative, Esmee Fairbairn Foundation, Department for Education and Skills and The Open University (2004) *Excite! Excellence, Creativity and Innovation in Teacher Education,* London: SEI.

Tait, J. (2002) *What Conditions and Environment Could Support Teachers in Finding Space for 'Creativity' in their Work with Curriculum?* Commissioned Imaginative Curriculum Research Study. LTSN June. Online, available at: www.heacademy.ac.uk/1644.htm (accessed August 2005).

Taylor, A. (1959) 'The nature of creative process', in P. Smith (ed.) *Creativity*, New York: Hastings House.

Taylor, D.W. (1960) 'Thinking and creativity', *Annals of the New York Academy of Sciences*, 91: 108–27.

Thomas, N.J.T. (1999) 'Are theories of imagery theories of imagination? an active perception approach to conscious mental content', *Cognitive Science,* 23(2): 207–45.

Thrift, N. (2000) 'Performing cultures in the new economy', *Annals of the Association of American Geographers*, 90(4): 674–92.

Torrance, E.P. (1962*)* *Guiding Creative Talent*, Englewood Cliffs, NJ: Prentice-Hall.

Torrance, E.P. (1965) *Rewarding Creative Behavior*, Englewood Cliffs, NJ: Prentice-Hall.

Torrance, E.P. (1975) *Preliminary Manual: Ideal Child Checklist*, Athens, GA: Georgia Studies of Creative Behavior.

Torrance, E.P. (1984) *Mentor Relationships: How They Aid Creative Achievement, Endure, Change and Die,* Buffalo, NY: Bearly.

Torrance, E.P. (1995) *Why Fly?,* Norwood, NJ: Ablex.

Torrance, E.P. (2002a) Personal communication.

Torrance, E.P. (2002b) *The Manifesto: a Guide to Developing a Creative Career,* Westport, CT: Ablex.

Torrance, E.P. and Goff, K. (1990) 'Fostering academic creativity in gifted Students', *The Educational Resources Information Centre* (ERIC) ED321489, ERIC Digest No. E484.

Torrance, E.P and Myers, R.E. (1970) *Creative Learning and Teaching*, New York: Harper and Row.

Törrönen, J. (2001) 'The concept of subject position in empirical social research', *Journal for the Theory of Social Behaviour*, 31(3): 313–29.

Tosey, P. (1993) 'Interfering with the interference', *Management Education and Development,* 24(3): 187–204.

Tosey, P. (2000) *Teaching on the Edge of Chaos: Complexity Theory, Learning Systems and Enhancement*, Learning & Teaching Support Network, Generic Centre. Online, available at: www.ltsn.ac.uk/application.asp?section=generic&app=resources.asp& process=full_record&id=55 (accessed August 2005).

Von Eschenbach, J.F. and Noland, R.G. (1981) 'Changes in student teachers' perceptions of the ideal pupil', *The Creative Child and Adult Quarterly*, 6(3): 169–77.

Waldrop, M. (1992) *Complexity: the Emerging Science at the Edge of Order and Chaos*, London: Penguin.

Watts, D.J. (2003) *Six Degrees: the Science of a Connected Age*, London: Heinemann.

Watzlawick, P., Weakland, J. and Fisch, R. (1974) *Change – Principles of Problem Formation and Problem Resolution,* New York: W.W. Norton.

Weedon, E.M. and Cowan, J. (2002) 'Commenting electronically on students' reflective learning journals', in C. Rust (ed.). *Improving Student Learning, Theory and Practice Using Learning Technology,* Oxford: Oxford Centre for Staff and Learning Development, 203–16.

Weedon, E.M. and Cowan, J. (2003) 'The Kolb Cycle, reflection and all that ... what is new?', In C. Rust (ed.) *Improving Student Learning, Theory and Practice – 10 years on*, Oxford: Oxford Centre for Staff & Learning Development, 97–108

Wegerif, R. (2004) 'Reason and creativity in classroom dialogues', unpublished paper based on seminar given at *The Open Creativity Centre Seminar Series,* Milton Keynes, UK, March 2003.

Wells, G. (1999) *Dialogic Inquiry*; Cambridge: Cambridge University Press.

Wheatley, M.J. (1999) *Leadership and the New Science: discovering order in a chaotic world,* San Francisco, CA: Berrett-Koehler, second edn.

Wilson, K., Lizzio, A. and Ramsden, P. (1997) 'The development, validation and application of the Course Experience Questionnaire', *Studies in Higher Education,* 22: 3–25.

Woods, P. (1990) *Teacher Skills and Strategies,* London: Falmer Press.

Woods, P. (1993) *Critical Events in Teaching and Learning*, Lewes: Falmer Press

Woods, P. (1995) *Creative Teachers in Primary Schools*, Buckingham: Open University Press.

Woods, P. (2002)' Teaching and learning in the new millennium', in C. Sugrue and D. Day, (eds) *Developing Teachers and Teaching Practice: International Research Perspectives,* London and New York: RoutledgeFalmer.

Woods, P. and Jeffrey, B. (1996) *Teachable Moments: the Art of Teaching in Primary Schools,* Buckingham: Open University Press.

Work Foundation (2005) *The Tipping Point: How Much is Broadcast Creativity at Risk?*, Online, available at: www.theworkfoundation.com/pdf/BBC_ Report_summary.pdf (accessed August 2005).

Yeomans, M. (1996) *Creativity in Art and Science: a Personal View*, National Society for Education in Art and Design (NSEAD).

Yorke, M. (2002) 'Subject benchmarking and the assessment of student learning', *Quality Assurance in Education*, 10(3): 155–71.

Zimmerman, B. (2000) 'Self-regulatory cycles of learning', in G.A. Straka, (ed.) *Conceptions of Self-Directed Learning, Theoretical and Conceptual Considerations,* New York: Waxman, 221–34.

Zimmerman, B. and Schunk, D.H. (2004) 'Self-regulating intellectual processes and outcomes: a social cognitive perspective', in D.Y. Dai and R.J. Steinberg (eds) *Motivation, Emotion and Cognition: Integrative Perspectives on Intellectual Functioning and Development,* Mahwah, NJ: Lawrence Erlbaum.

Index

8th Habit: From Effectiveness to Greatness 9

abilities: blending and utilising 123–5; creativity
  as part of 188–9
abstract representation 154
academia 54–5
academic achievement 45, 80
Academic Quality Assurance Handbook 191
academics: conflicting roles of 183–4; perceptions
  of creativity 90–1, 94–103; voices 198; *see also*
  teachers
accreditation models 184
accreditation professional bodies 191–2
action, constraints to 36–7
action planning 145, 147
active learning approach 187–8
adaptation, elimination of 158–9
adaptive systems 29, 31
adventuring 199, 211
agreement and certainty matrix 33–4
analogies 146
analysis, assessment of 157
analytic abilities 124, 188
anxiety, defence against 34
apprenticeship: creative learning as 23–4; *see also*
  cognitive apprenticeship; craft-based
  apprenticeship
art and design: assessment 114–17; methodology
  109–10; perspectives on creativity 110–12;
  teacher–student relationships 112–14
artistic disciplines 152
Arts Council 22
assessment 53–4, 66–7, 69, 77, 84–7, 92, 114–16,
  156–72, 192–3, 194–5; art and design courses
  114–17; process of 66–8, 174; scores for
  179–81; teachers' views of 173; through
  student work 84–6; *see also* consensual
  assessment; self-assessment
assessment of creativity: appendices 168–72;
  introduction 156–7; plan for assessing 161–8;
  by the process 157–8; by the product 158–9;
  relation of student-centred learning to
  self-assessment 159–61
attractiveness 78–81
authenticity of activity/task 23–4

autonomy 66, 68–9, 176, 189

Bar Vocational Council 191–2
benchmarking 91–5
brainstorming 50, 68, 82, 144, 146, 151–2

CACE *see* Plowden Report
CASE: Creativity in Art, Science and Engineering
  132, 143–4
Centre for Recording Achievement 185
Centres for Excellence in Teaching and Learning
  (CETLs) 3, 17, 39
change 29, 38
change agency, moral nature of 40
chaos theory 31
child-centred practices 20–1
class size 86–7
COCD box 147
cognitive abilities 157,
cognitive apprenticeship 126–7; relationship with
  self-regulated learning and creativity 127–8
collaborative assessment 116–17
collaborative creativity 30
collaborative learning 37, 113–14
collective work 24–5
command and control paradigm 41–2
communication 90–1, 95, 101–2, 199
complex adaptive systems 31–2, 38
complex learning 123–5
complex problems 97–8, 199
complex responsive processes 33–5
complexity: making sense of 91–4, 97–101;
  theory 31–3, 40–41
compliance 208
conflict 40
connectivity 32–3, 37–40
conscience 9
consensual assessment 175–7; adaptation to
  higher education 181–2; difficulty of
  assessment 174–5; example of 177–81;
  introduction 173–4; manifestations of creativity
  174
constructive alignment 63, 128, 192–3
contradiction matrix 151
convergent thinking 93

conversational model of learning 50
core knowledge 63, 65–6
counter-rational ideas 41–2
craft-based apprenticeships 127
creative activities 47–8
Creative Education Foundation 145
Creative Industries Minister 10
creative leadership 22
creative outcomes, evaluation/assessment of 209
Creative Partnerships 22
creative problem solving 143–5
Creative Problem Solving (CPS) techniques
    145–7
creative study 51–3
creative teaching *see* higher education teachers
creative thinking 49–51
creative-thinking techniques: approaches to
    creative thinking 145–52; creative problem-
    solving 143–5; Creative Universities project
    143; implications for facilitation of creative
    thinking 152–5; introduction 142; *see also*
    Torrance Tests
Creative Universities project 143
creativity: abilities 124; and academic disciplines
    54; academic values 51, 54, 57; academics'
    views on 59–73, 74–88, 90, 110–12; activities
    92–4; agenda for HE 17; agents for 31, 32, 38;
    apprenticeship in 23, 26, 126–7; argument for
    10–11, 102; aspects 78–80, 181; and
    assessment, 53, 84, 114–5, 116, 175, 177, 209;
    assessing process 157; assessing product 158;
    and other attributes 176; barriers to 7, 36, 39,
    84, 85, 86; challenge 193–5; and change xviii,
    12; characteristics of 60–2, 119, 121, 202;
    collective 24; conceptions 20, 23–4, 44–5,
    60–2; conditions for 153; constraints on 36, 39,
    70, 84–6; context for 6, 10, 29, 131;
    conversations about 197–200; criteria 85–6,
    178; and culture 16, 27, 89; culture change 73;
    curriculum designs for 62–6, 68, 69; curriculum
    objectives 3; definitions 8–9, 12–14, 110–11,
    162–3; descriptions of 44; developing students'
    80–2; development 25–8, 80–2, 109–17,
    118–41; disciplinary views on 89–108; and
    economy 11, 20; and employability 6, 12, 71;
    employer interests in 6; and emotion 49;
    enabling 40–2; enhancement 142–55; and
    enterprising society 12–13; entrepreneurialism
    13; environment 27; and ethics 28; everyday
    life 19, 23; expectations 209–10; expertise
    122–3; exploration 99; features of 60–2, 90–3,
    119–23, 198–9; and feedback in 24, 63, 66,
    115, 176, 182, 192; Government interests in
    12–13; and graduateness 56; and identity 55,
    111, 121; and imagination i, 1, 96, 104–5, 199;
    impact of higher education expansion 87;
    individual 24; information resources 138–40;
    inhibitors 70, 86; and innovation 10–12, 29,
    90–5, 104–5; through interaction 25; and IT 20;
    and knowledge-based economy 12; leadership
    of 4; in learning 51; and learning outcomes

173; lecturer views on 109; levels of 121–2,
    209–10; life-wide 19; measurement of 174,
    177; approaches to mind-body 150;
    mind–mapping 82; models of 45–6, 121; and
    motivation for 48, 113; need for 10–12, 29–31;
    official interest in 62; originality 75, 78, 90–5,
    104–5, 198; outside arts subjects 21; ownership
    of 45; and pedagogy 46, 112, 130–1;
    perceptions 43–4, 78–80; personal 118;
    perspectives 110–12; policy for, 10–17;
    principles for 205–11; problem-working, 97–9,
    105–6, 143, 144, 211; processes of, 22, 38–40,
    43; problem with, in higher education 2–5;
    qualities of 44; reasons for, xviii–xix, 11;
    researching into 43–58, 59–73, 74–88, 89–98,
    109–17; risk 16, 64; role of facilitation 152;
    role models of 46; self-assessment 159, 165;
    sense making 99; in schools 20; sites for 95;
    situated 23, 26; stimulating 25; strategy for
    development of 130; students' views on 43–58,
    110–11; in studying 51; systems view 202;
    teaching for 25, 64–5, 113, 210; and teaching
    112–13, 200–1; in teaching 7; teaching and
    learning 80, 128–9; and teaching quality 50;
    techniques to develop 143, 153; and uncertainty
    20
Creativity Find it! Promote It! 22
Creativity Action Research Awards 22
Creativity Centre 74, 86
creativity development courses 76–7
creativity feedback package (CFP) 177–8
creativity puzzles 189
creativity tests 174
critical thinking 64
cultural capital 72–3
cultural change 197–8, 211–14
Cultural Commission, Scotland 10
cultural context of creativity 23–4, 48
cultural domains 201–5; importance of 89–90
cultural influences 201–3
culturally specific creativity 27
curiosity 96–100
curricula, academic perspectives of: assessment
    process 66–8; conceptions of creativity 60–2;
    designing final-year courses 68–9; designing
    first-year courses 68–9; designs for creativity
    62–6; employability 71; higher education
curriculum 60; academics' conceptions 60;
    methodology 59–60; organisational
    environment 70
curriculum designs 62–6, 159; final-year courses
    68; first-year courses 68–9
curriculum review process 63
curriculum-based initiatives 21–3

Department for Education and Employment
    (DfEE) 21
Department for Education and Science (DfES) 22
Department of Trade and Industry (DTI) 22
departmental culture 192
design and technology 177–81

DfES/DfEE: Best Practice Research Scholarships 22; Creative Partnerships 22; Early Learning 21; Excellence in Cities 21; Innovations Unit 22; personalised learning 22; Synectics 22
discipline culture 205–6
disciplines 54–5, 79–80; creativity in 94–103; representations of creativity in 104–7
discovery 90–1, 99, 199
dissipative structure, theory of 31
divergent thinking 66, 93
diversity 31, 194
domains of creativity 121–3
dynamic interactions 11–12

e-learning 37
Early Learning Goals 21
Earth Science 95, 97, 98, 99, 100, 101–2
edge of chaos *see* agreement and certainty matrix
Education Action Zones 21
educational developers: assessment and feedback 192–3; departmental culture 192; professional bodies 191–2; quality assurance 190–1
educational development: reflection dialogue and debate 195; overview 193–4; time and space 194; variety and diversity 194–5
Einstein, Albert 28
emergence in human systems 29, 31–3, 198; conditions for 32–3
emergent paradigm 41–2
emotional dimension of learning 39
empathy 113
employability 71
employment, competences for 20
engagement, levels of 122
Engineering 96, 97–8, 99, 100, 101, 102
Engineering Council 191–2
enquiry-based learning (EBL) 39
environmental impacts on creativity 27–8
Environmental Science 95, 97, 98, 99, 100, 101–2
environments: encouraging 13–14; for study 52; *see also* learning environments
essays 53–4, 67
ethics 28, 61–2
ethnicity issues 79
ethos 83
European Union, knowledge-based economy 10–11
evaluation, problem-solving 147
examinations 53–4, 66–7, 72
Excellence and Improvement 22
Excellence in Cities 21
expectations 72, 209–10
Expecting the Unexpected 22
exploration 9, 98–9, 105, 199
explorativity 9
extended abstract (EA) outcomes of learning 208
extended abstract (EA) thinking skills 123
external orientation 64

facilitating learning 186–7
facilitation 152–3

facilitation of creativity: aims and objectives 77; background literature 74–7; methods 77; recommendations 87–8; results/discussion 78–87
facilitative teaching methods 210
factory-farming solutions 86, 87
failure, re-defining 115–16
final outcomes, focus on 116–17
first-order change 38, 40
first-wave thinking/developments 20–1
final-year courses 68–9
first-year students 116–17
flower technique 146
forethought 125–6
formal assessment 84–6, 114–17
Formative Assessment in Science Teaching, FDTL 193
framed expression 45
fun 65
functionality 151
Fund for the Development of Teaching and Learning (FDTL) 39–40, 185, 193

gender differences 79
global connectivity 37
good educational practice, transferability of 39
'graduateness' as identity 56–7, 91
group polarisation 177
group work 65

'halo effect' 177
'hidden' curriculum 66
higher education: aspects of provision 86; changing system of 6–7; consensual assessment 181–2; conversations about creativity 197–200; creative voices in 8–9; and creativity 200–5; creativity in 7–8; curriculum 60; different world of 1–2; impact of expansion 86–7; problems in 5–7; role of 16–17; systems views of creativity 201–3
Higher Education Academy (HEA) 37, 74, 90, 168, 183, 185
Higher Education Funding Council England (HEFCE) 39–40, 185
higher education institutions, as creative places 33–5
higher education teachers: conflicting roles of 183–4; creativity challenge to educational development 193–5; creativity within professional development 188–90; development of 184–6; role of educational developers 190–3; teaching and student learning 186–8
History 96, 98, 100, 101, 102, 107–8
holistic courses 67–8
human systems 30–1; analogous to evolving ecological systems 33–5; conditions for emergence 32–3; emergence in 31–3
hypothesising 211

Idea Factory 154
Ideal Pupil Checklist 74–5, 76

ideality 151
ideas, association of 178–81
Ideas, generation of 92–6; action planning, 147;
    analogies, 146; clustering, 147; COCD box
    analysis, 147; flower technique, 146; medicine
    wheel, 147; mind mapping 82; reversals, 146
ideas generation sessions 50
identities of students 55–7, 206–7
identity 55, 111, 121, 200
imagination 78, 90–7, 100–7, 199
Imaginative Curriculum network 156, 168, 185,
    190, 193, 212
Imaginative Curriculum project i, xi, 1, 3, 6, 9, 17,
    43, 59, 90, 119, 132, 173, 187, 189, 192–3,
    197, 205
imitation: departure from 72; elimination of
    158–9
*Implementing an Institutional Assessment
    Strategy* 193
incremental creativity 44
individual work 24–5
informal assessment 84–6, 116–17
'ingenuity gap' 142
innate creativity 45–6
Innovate America report 10–11
innovation 29, 90–5, 104–5
innovation agenda 10–12
Innovation Unit, DfES 22
Institute of Learning and Teaching in HE 183
institutional approval 84
intentionality 32
interactive feedback 24–5
'interference with the interference' 29, 33, 40–2
internal barriers 153
internal orientation 64
Internet 52
interpretation 99–101
intuition 122, 127
invention 95, 104
investment theory of creativity 203

KEYS Inventory 176
knowledge: assessment of 157; characteristics 123
knowledge transfer experiments 143–5
knowledge-based economies: needs of 12, 20;
    social construction of 207

lateral thinking 65, 82
learner autonomy 176
learner inclusive approach *see* teaching for
    creativity
learning 186–8: adventures in 210–11;
contracts for 36; impact of higher education
    expansion 86–7; manifestations of creativity in
    174; views on 80
Learning and Teaching Support Network (LTSN)
    143
learning environments, principles for constructing
    205–11
learning outcomes model 36, 173, 192–3, 208–9;
    design of 188

learning style theory 84
learning systems 128–32
Leeds Metropolitan University 76
levels of creativity 121–3
Lisbon agenda 10–11
literature, facilitation of creativity 74–7
'lived' curriculum 60
Liverpool John Moores University (LJMU) 59, 68
local connectivity 37
locus of control 24

managerialism 86, 87
marketised creativity 27–8
medicine wheel 147–50, 152
metacognition 45
mind and body techniques 150, 152
Mind Over Machine 122
modelling expertise and approaches 23
modular programmes 191
modules; length of 70
motivation for creativity 48–9, 113

National Advisory Committee on Creative and
    Cultural Education (NACCCE) 21
National College for School Leadership 22
National Curriculum 20–1
National Endowment for Science, Technology
    and the Arts *see* NESTA
National Teaching Fellows, views of 74–88
National Teaching Fellowships 17, 84
Nature of Creative Process, The 122
'nature or nurture' 45–6
needs 9; meeting 62–3
NESTA 10, 74; investment strategy 15–16
networks, prevalence of 37–8
'new-ness', quality of 60
non-hierarchical relationships 112
Nothing Special 150
Nowhere Foundation 147, 149
nurtured creativity 45–6
nurturing role 16–17

OFSTED 22, 26
operability 78–81
opinion-sets 177
organisational consulting 40–1
organisational environments 70
original creativity 44, 61
originality 93, 95–6, 104, 198–9
outcomes model of learning *see* learning
    outcomes model

paradigm 197
passion 9, 198
patents, study of 151
pedagogic models 211; appendices 133–41;
    characteristics of creativity 119–21; domains
    and levels of creativity 121–3; effective
    teaching and learning systems 128–32;
    implications for higher education 123–8;
    introduction 118–19

peer approval/criticism 54, 184
peer learning 37
performance 125, 126
personal creativity 13, 205
personal effectiveness 19
personal qualities 83
personal standards/targets 163
Personality Checklist 76
Plowden Report (CACE) 20
pluralistic view of creativity 15
polarised views 177
policy-makers, challenges for 12–14
policy, history of 20–5
portfolio 189, 194
Portugal, teaching styles 76
postgraduate certificate course delivery 194
potential creativity 45–6, 78–81
practical abilities 124, 188
practice, differences in 34–5
problem-focused learning 210–11
problems: definition of 5–6; finding/working with
    2–5, 67–8, 105, 107, 211; identification 19;
    solving 19, 97–9, 105–7, 123, 143–5
process, assessment by 157–8
product, assessment by 158–9
professional bodies 191
professional development 185–6; creativity within
    188–90
Professional Development Framework,
    (SEDA-PDF) 195
professionalism 184–9
Progress File initiative 195
Project 1000 74, 75–6, 79–80, 84
Project Zero, Harvard University 25

Qualifications and Curriculum Authority (QCA)
    21, 22, 24, 119
qualitative approaches to research 27
quality and standards 29
quality assurance 159–60, 188, 190–1
Quality Assurance Agency 34, 205; Subject
    Benchmark Statements 89–90, 206; Subject
    Review 39
question formulation 144, 145–6

radical creativity 44
Raising Achievement Through the Arts 22
random association methods 145
reality, escape from 45
recall, elimination of 158–9
recognition 61
reflection 189, 194–5
reflection, value of 189
reflective engagement 163–5
research and development (R&D) expenditure 13
Research Assessment Exercises (RAE) 184
research into creativity 26–7
resourcefulness 103
resources: for creativity 51–2; lack of 70
reversals technique 146
reward, creativity as 51

risk-taking 24, 91, 99, 178–81, 189; in
    investments 15–16
role models 46–7, 207
routine-dependency 71
rule-following/bending/breaking characteristics
    122
rules-based subjects 55

Santa Fe Institute, New Mexico 31–2
Scandinavian universities 168
scenario making 211
schools: conceptions of creativity 23–4; creativity
    in 19–28; developing creativity 25–8;
    first-wave thinking/developments 20–1;
    relationship between individual/collective work
    24–5; second-wave thinking/developments
    21–3; third-wave thinking/developments 23
schools-based creativity 28
second-order change 38, 40
second-wave thinking/developments 21–3
self-assessment: importance of 161–8; relation to
    student-centred learning 159–61
self-efficacy 189
self-identity 206–7
self-preservation 70
self-reflection 125, 126–7
self-regulated learning 125–6; cognitive
    apprenticeship to support 126–7; relationship
    with cognitive apprenticeship and creativity
    127–8
seminars 50
sense-making 63–4
situated learning 185
skills 93; levels of 122–3
SMART performance criteria 62, 72
Snowflake model 121
social construction of knowledge 207
social context of creativity 23–4, 48
social creativity 30
social environment, roles/relationships in 20
Social Work 96, 97, 99, 102, 103
socio-cultural influences 201–3
spaces, creation of 64, 65, 194
Staff and Educational Development Association
    (SEDA) 183, 184, 195
stasis 34–5
stereotypes 71–2
story-telling 90–1, 102–3
stress 150
student experiences of creativity: academia and
    the disciplines 54–5; assessment 53–4;
    conceptions of creativity 44–5; creative study
    51–3; creative teaching 49–51; creativity
    outside of study 47–8; methodology 43;
    motivation for creativity 48–9; nature or
    nurture 45–6; role models 46–7; student
    identities 55–7
student feedback 37, 63
student–teacher relationships 112–14
student-centred learning, relation to
    self-assessment 159–61

students: creative identities 206–7; interests 206–7; needs 205–7; perceptions of creativity 200; voices 199–200
study: creativity inside 51–3; creativity outside 47–8; habits 69
subject benchmarking statements 91–4
subject perspectives on creativity: academic perceptions of creativity 90–1, 94–103; appendix 107–8; importance of cultural domains 89–90; interpretations 103–4; representation of creativity in disciplines 104–7; subject bench-marking statements 91–4
success, re-defining 115–16
supportive factors 82–4
Sweden, teacher study 75
Synectics 22
synthesising 199, 101
synthetic abilities 188
systems thinking 5, 98
systems views of creativity 201–3; application to higher education teaching and learning 203–5

talent 9
teacher development *see* higher education teachers
teacher–student relationships 112–14
Teachernet 22
teachers: creativity of 189–90; as facilitators/performers 187; *see also* academics
teaching 186–8; conditions for fostering creativity 188; constraints on preferred ways of 84; and creativity 200–1; impact of higher education expansion 86–7; strategies 80–2; techniques 49–50; views on 80
teaching approaches: conventional forms of 50; repertoire of 65–6; student's views on 112–14
teaching environments, principles for constructing 205–11
teaching for creative thinking: conditions 153; facilitation 152–3; participants 153; problems 153–4; process 154
teaching for creativity 25–8, 113; purposes of 207
Teaching Quality Enhancement Fund 185

teaching systems 128–32
technical disciplines 152
technologies 142
Theory of Inventive Problem Solving *see* TRIZ
thinking outside the disciplinary box 100–1
thinking skills 90–4, 123,
third-wave thinking/developments 23
time 194
'token' creativity 51
'toolkit' approach to creative thinking 145–7
Torrance Tests of Creative Thinking (TTCTs) 74–5, 76, 86, 175
tradition, break with 61
traditional apprenticeships 127
traditional conception of innovation 11
transferability 39
transmission models of teaching 210
Travelling Case, The 143, 149
triggers for creativity 30–1, 34–5
TRIZ Theory of Inventive Problem Solving, 151–2, 154
tutorials 50

unconscious decision-making 122
understanding, assessment of 157
uniqueness 78–81
universalized creativity 13, 20
universities, as sites for creativity 16–17
university, transition to 73
University College London (UCL) 59
university spin-out companies 13

variety 194
vivas 67
voice 202; concept of 9, 198; academics 198; students 199–200

well-craftedness 78–81
whole-institution initiatives 188
work avoidance strategies 52–3
work placements 49–50
work-based learning 194